■ 2005 Annual Edition

# OUR DAILY BREAD ®

For Personal and Family Devotions                    Vol. 11

## CONTENTS

ACKNOWLEDGMENTS

FOREWORD

DISCOVERY SERIES

ENROLLMENT INFORMATION

OUR DAILY JOURNEY

DAILY DEVOTIONALS (JANUARY–JUNE)

WHY DID JESUS HAVE TO DIE?

DAILY DEVOTIONALS (JULY–DECEMBER)

WHERE TO FIND IT IN THE BIBLE

TOPIC INDEX

YOU WERE ON HIS MIND

Copyright © 2004 RBC Ministries                    ISSN: 0119-0520

**Mailing Address:** P.O. Box 288, Greenhills, 0410 Metro Manila

**Street Address:** 7 P. Guevarra St., Brgy. Sta. Lucia,
                    1500 San Juan, Metro Manila

**Phone:** (2) 722-2010 or (2) 726-6544 • **Fax:** (2) 725-5058
**E-mail:** philippines@rbc.org • **Internet:** www.rbcinternational.org

# ACKNOWLEDGMENTS

COVER PHOTO:

Army Bay, N. Z., © David Harvey

WRITERS:

Henry G. Bosch • J. David Branon • Anne M. Cetas
Dennis J. De Haan • M. R. De Haan, M.D. • Martin R. De Haan II
Richard W. De Haan • David C. Egner • Vernon C. Grounds
Albert Lee • Julie Ackerman Link • David C. McCasland
Haddon W. Robinson • David H. Roper • Herbert Vander Lugt
Joanie E. Yoder

POEMS:

Feb. 13 — Gerald E. Bonney, © Renewal 1950 Singspiration, Inc.
Mar. 17 — Avis B. Christiansen, © Renewal 1965 Singspiration, Inc.
Mar. 25 — Ira Stanphill, © Renewal 1974 Singspiration, Inc.
Jul. 1 — Esther Kerr Rusthoi, © 1941, 1969 Singspiration, Inc.
Jul. 11 — George Bennard, © 1913, 1941 The Rodeheaver Co.
Aug. 14 — Haldor Lillenas, © 1917, 1945 Hope Publishing Co.
Sep. 1 — Will H. Houghton, © 1936, 1964 Hope Publishing Co.
Sep. 2 — Oswald J. Smith, © 1937 The Rodeheaver Co.
Sep. 24 — John W. Peterson, © 1961 Singspiration, Inc.
Oct. 27 — Albert S. Reitz, © 1925, 1953 Broadman Press
Nov. 20 — Baynard Fox, © 1958, 1963 Fox Music Publications
Nov. 22 — John W. Peterson, © 1968 Singspiration, Inc.
Dec. 21 — John Mohr, © 1987 Jonathan Mark Music & Birdwing Music

BIBLE QUOTATIONS:

Scripture taken from the New King James Version. Copyright © 1982
by Thomas Nelson, Inc. Used by permission. All rights reserved.

# Foreword

Civil rebellions, kidnappings, bombings, and terrorist threats seem to make daily headlines in the Philippines and around the world. These unnerving events threaten our security and cause many to question the very meaning of life. While the Lord Jesus Christ walked on earth, He reminded His disciples that ". . . in this world you will have trouble" (John 16:33) and proclaimed that He came ". . . that they may have life, and have it to the full" (John 10:10). Life of that caliber can be experienced only as the result of a personal relationship with the living God through His Son, Jesus Christ. He alone can give security and a sense of purpose to life.

One of the greatest challenges facing believers in Christ is to take His message to our world. Without exception, each of us can participate in the Great Commission given to believers before Christ ascended into heaven (Matthew 28:18-20). RBC Ministries, in partnership with you, our readers, is involved in this ministry. It is our prayer that you will join us in sharing the message of Christ's offer of eternal life with more of our friends and neighbors in the Philippines this year.

One simple way to share the message is to purchase extra copies of *Our Daily Bread* to give to your friends, to leave in your office, or to give to your customers. Many *ODB* readers are already doing this, but there is still much more we can do to reach the Philippines for the Lord. As people come to know Christ personally, they too will experience the full impact of His promise that they would "have life, and have it to the full."

David T. Harvey
Philippine Director
RBC Ministries

# DISCOVERY SERIES

- **Bible-based teaching**
- **Practical application**
- **Timely topics**

Choose from over 100 booklets written with you in mind. Each 32-page booklet can strengthen your faith as you consider your salvation, your relationship with Christ, and your involvement in reaching others with the message of the gospel. All are available for your personal or group study, or as tools to help you help others. For a list of titles and information on how you can receive these booklets, write to RBC Ministries, P.O. Box 288, Greenhills, 0410 Metro Manila.

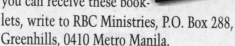

## THIS BOOK IS PROVIDED BY:

## TO RECEIVE FUTURE EDITIONS

If you received this booklet through your church, radio station, local bookstore, or from a friend, and you are not on the RBC mailing list, please write to RBC Ministries c/o the address at the bottom of the back cover of this book. We will send you information on how you can obtain your own copy of future editions. We will also add your name to the mailing list, and you will receive an alert when it is time to enroll each year.

## OUR DAILY JOURNEY

# *Our Daily Bread* for students and young adults

Campus Journal is now called Our Daily Journey

*Our Daily Journey* is the ideal devotional for the young people in your life. Written in a contemporary and upbeat style, *ODJ* tackles the tough issues they face and helps them find biblical answers. Daily articles provide the opportunity to personally apply and record each article's teaching and impact.

*Stop by your local Christian bookstore today to pick up a copy for every young person in your life!*

Also available direct from RBC Ministries for an enrollment fee of 30 pesos if you pick it up at the office at 7 P. Guevarra Street, Brgy. St. Lucia, San Juan, or 60 pesos if you want it mailed to you. Send order and fee to: RBC Ministries, P.O. Box 288, Greenhills 0410, Metro Manila.

## RBC Ministries
RADIO BIBLE CLASS – FOUNDED 1938

# RESTORING THE YEARS

READ:
Joel 2:12-27

---

I will restore to you the years that the swarming locust has eaten. —Joel 2:25

---

THE BIBLE IN ONE YEAR:
■ Genesis 1–3
■ Matthew 1

**H**ow many years have you lost to the locust? Have self-indulgence, sensuality, sinful motives, and personal ambition robbed you of joy, peace, and fruitfulness? Perhaps you feel discouraged when you think of all the time that seems to have been wasted, never to be reclaimed.

If so, consider the words of the Lord through the prophet Joel. God told the people of Israel that even though they had been disobedient to Him and had been disciplined through a plague of locusts, there was still hope. The Lord said that He is "gracious and merciful, slow to anger, and of great kindness" (Joel 2:13). Then He promised, "I will restore to you the years that the swarming locust has eaten" (v.25).

When we confess our sin to the Lord, He is quick to forgive our past and fill our future with hope. He can bring good out of our wasted years. He does that by teaching us humility through our failures, and by helping us to understand the weaknesses we have in common with others.

Although our previous years may have been blighted by sin, God is eager to restore us and give us much fruit from our labor. What we have learned from the past can now result in productive service for Him and heartfelt praise to Him. The year ahead is filled with hope! — David Roper

*Forgive me, O Lord, for all of my sin,*
*Please make my heart pure and cleanse me within;*
*To You I confess, my ways have been wrong;*
*Restore now my joy and fill me with song.* —Fitzhugh

---

**No matter how dark your past,**
**with Christ your future is bright.**

# NOBLE PLANS

**READ:**
Isaiah 32:1-8

---

A generous man devises generous things, and by generosity he shall stand. —Isaiah 32:8

---

THE BIBLE IN ONE YEAR:
- Genesis 4–6
- Matthew 2

There's a difference between saying, "I would like to visit England sometime" and saying, "I'm planning to visit England next week." One statement expresses a desire; the other indicates definite preparation.

So often we enter a new year with hopes, desires, and resolutions that can be the seeds of positive change. But the key to what actually happens in our lives is in making definite plans. That involves thought, purpose, and effort.

Isaiah wrote about a future time when "a king will reign in righteousness" (Isaiah 32:1). This prophetic passage tells us about the coming rule of Christ, but it also gives us a principle that we who bow before Jesus as King can apply today. Isaiah contrasted the schemer who "devises wicked plans" with the generous or noble person who "devises generous things" (vv.7-8). As Christ's followers, we are to be generous people.

What plans have we made for increased generosity during this new year? Are we only hoping to give more time and attention to others, or have we made some specific commitments? If we want to help a person or a cause financially, have we written the first check?

This is a great time to make noble plans that honor God with our vision and generosity. —David McCasland

*In Jesus' name our prayer we raise,*
*Whose guiding hand has blessed our days;*
*And may we, Lord, in godly fear*
*Serve You throughout this coming year.* —Anon.

---

**God's plans include you.**
**Do your plans include God?**

# "I SMILE"

**READ:**
Psalm 118:14-21

---

If anyone is in Christ,
he is a new creation;
old things have passed
away; behold, all things
have become new.
—2 Corinthians 5:17

---

THE BIBLE IN ONE YEAR:
■ Genesis 7–9
■ Matthew 3

A few years ago, singer Russ Lee came out with a song titled "I Smile." When you discover how his life was changed by Jesus Christ, you'll know why he sings a song that says, "I smile when I think about the way You turned my life around. I smile when I think about the happiness in You I've found."

When Russ was 17, his days were wasted on drugs, alcohol, boredom, and pain. His life was full of self-inflicted trouble and hopelessness. One day, while listening to an old rock song called "I Can't Get No Satisfaction," he realized that this described his life. Two days later, a friend invited him to church. There Russ heard that real satisfaction comes from knowing Jesus Christ, so he reached out in faith to Him.

So, what was the first thing Russ did after trusting Christ? According to the book *Touched By The Savior* by Mike Yorkey, Russ said, "I walked back out to my car. In the trunk was a garbage bag filled with drugs I had been selling. *I won't be needing these again,* I thought, and I was right. I threw the bag away. From that day forward, God transformed my life from the inside out. I became a new creation."

No wonder Russ Lee can sing with exuberance, "I smile." Can you?  — *Dave Branon*

*BECOMING A NEW CREATION*
*To find out how to have new life in Jesus, read the booklet* Why Does It Make Sense To Believe In Christ?
www.discoveryseries.org/q1104

---

**A song in the heart puts a smile on the face.**

# ALWAYS FOR US

**READ:**
**Ruth 1**

---

If God is for us, who can be against us?
—Romans 8:31

---

THE BIBLE IN ONE YEAR:
■ Genesis 10–12
■ Matthew 4

Naomi, her husband, and their two sons left Israel and moved to Moab because of a famine (Ruth 1:1-2). One son married Ruth, the other married Orpah. Eventually Naomi's husband and sons died (vv.3,5), so she decided to return to Israel. But she felt that her daughters-in-law would be better off staying in Moab (vv.6-13). She tried to dissuade them from going with her by saying, "No, my daughters; for it grieves me very much for your sakes that the hand of the LORD has gone out against me!" (v.13).

Was Naomi right in her thinking about God? Perhaps the family had displayed a lack of faith by moving to pagan Moab, but God certainly was not against her. He proved this by wonderfully providing for her and Ruth after they returned to Israel. (Read the rest of the book — it's short.)

You may be unemployed, terminally ill, have a disabled child, or care for a loved one with Alzheimer's. God hasn't promised to keep us from such problems. But He has proven that He is always "for us" as Christians by what He did through Jesus (Romans 5:8-9). Nothing, not even death, can separate us from His love (8:35-39).

The Lord is never "against us," not even when He chastens us (Hebrews 12:5-6). He is always for us!   —Herb Vander Lugt

*Our God is always there for us —*
*Receiving every prayer,*
*Delighting in our words of praise,*
*Responding with His care.*   —Sper

---

**The One who died to save you will never be against you.**

# GET INTO THE STEW

READ:
**Matthew 5:11-16**

You are the salt of
the earth.
—Matthew 5:13

THE BIBLE IN ONE YEAR:
■ Genesis 13–15
■ Matthew 5:1-26

It's common, cheap, and used around the world. It has stirred up wars, led to the establishment of trade routes, and paid the salaries of soldiers. Today it serves chiefly as a preservative and a flavoring. What is it? It's that crystalline substance we call salt.

Jesus, who was a master of using ordinary things to illustrate spiritual realities, talked about salt when He was teaching His disciples how they were to serve as agents of His kingdom. He said, "You are the salt of the earth" (Matthew 5:13).

If we think of salt as a preservative, we can assume Jesus wants us to prevent moral decay in our society. And if we think of salt's ability to enhance flavor, we can be sure He wants us to help people discover the joy of knowing and living for Him.

Salt stored away on a shelf is not fulfilling its function. In a similar way, unless we are actively at work sharing God's life-enhancing truth, we are not serving as spiritual salt. After all, the place for salt is in the "stew" of human activities. Instead of just criticizing the corruption of our culture as well as the flatness of the life so many people endure, let's get into the stew — for we are the salt of the earth. —Vernon Grounds

*Called to be salt and light in this world,*
*Called to preserve and to shine,*
*Called to reflect the glory of God —*
*Oh, what a calling is mine!* —Fitzhugh

**A salty Christian makes others thirsty for Jesus,
the Water of Life.**

# THE GREAT POTTER

**READ:**
Jeremiah 18:1-6

As the clay is in the potter's hand, so are you in My hand.
—Jeremiah 18:6

THE BIBLE IN ONE YEAR:
■ Genesis 16–17
■ Matthew 5:27-48

One definition of the word *attitude* is "the angle of approach" that an aircraft takes when landing. Author Chris Spicer writes: "Attitudes are to life as the angle of approach is to flying." He adds, "Attitude is the way we choose to think about things; attitudes will cause us to react and behave in a certain way." He also says that attitudes are not inborn or accidental. They are learned and absorbed reactions; therefore they can be changed.

During my thirties, the Lord began convicting me of my wrong thinking toward myself, others, and life — negative, self-pitying, and bitter thinking. With the help of God's Word, I recognized my need for change in three main areas: my attitudes, actions, and reactions. But I feared I couldn't change. One day I read in Jeremiah 18 how the potter refashioned some marred clay (which is what I felt like) into a different vessel, as it pleased the potter. What I couldn't do, my great Potter could! I only needed to be cooperative clay.

Today this vessel is far from finished. But as I put myself in the Potter's hands, He keeps working on me and shaping my attitudes and actions. I call them Christ-attitudes, Christ-actions, and Christ-reactions.

The great Potter can do the same for you. — Joanie Yoder

*Have Thine own way, Lord! Have Thine own way!*
*Thou art the Potter, I am the clay;*
*Mold me and make me after Thy will,*
*While I am waiting, yielded and still.* — Pollard

**A change in the heart brings a change in behavior.**

# JOY LIST

READ:
John 15:9-17

These things I have spoken to you, that My joy may remain in you, and that your joy may be full.
—John 15:11

THE BIBLE IN ONE YEAR:
■ Genesis 18–19
■ Matthew 6:1-18

Writer C. W. Metcalf was working as a hospice volunteer when he met 13-year-old Chuck, who was terminally ill. One day Chuck gave Metcalf half a dozen sheets of paper with writing on both sides and said, "I want you to give this to my mom and dad after I die. It's a list of all the fun we had, all the times we laughed." Metcalf was amazed that this teenager on the verge of death was thinking about the well-being of others.

Metcalf delivered the list. Years later he decided to make a list of his own. Surprisingly, he found it difficult at first to compile his "joy list." But as he began looking each day for the moments of laughter, satisfaction, and joy, his list began to grow.

Any joy list that we compile will no doubt include many references to the presence and power of Jesus Christ. No matter what our circumstances, joy is His gracious gift to all who trust Him. Even as Jesus faced the cross, He looked beyond its agony to the glad result of His sacrifice. He told His disciples, "These things I have spoken to you, that My joy may remain in you, and that your joy may be full" (John 15:11).

Why not begin your own joy list today. It can be a good reminder of the Lord's faithful love and the gladness of heart He brings. — David McCasland

*Because life's circumstances change,*
*Our happiness may not remain;*
*But if we're walking with the Lord,*
*Our inner joy He will sustain.* — Sper

---

**To multiply your joy, count your blessings.**

## OUR HOME IS AHEAD

READ:
**Hebrews 11:8-10**

---

By faith [Abraham] dwelt in the land of promise as in a foreign country.
—Hebrews 11:9

---

THE BIBLE IN ONE YEAR:
■ Genesis 20–22
■ Matthew 6:19-34

Now that I'm getting closer to the end of life's journey, I'm thinking more like a transient. I suppose it's natural. Abraham first described himself as "a foreigner and a visitor" when he was buying a burial plot for Sarah (Genesis 23:4). Time and death make you think about such things.

Most elderly believers say the same thing: There's no home for us this side of heaven. Like Pilgrim in Bunyan's *The Pilgrim's Progress,* once we've caught sight of the Celestial City we can never be content with anything less. Like Abraham, we look for a city whose builder is God (Hebrews 11:10).

In Tolkien's *Lord Of The Rings,* as Frodo and the other hobbits set out on their great adventure, they sing, "Home is behind, the world ahead." But for Christians, it's the other way around: The world is behind; our home is ahead.

There are no valleys of weeping there, for "God will wipe away every tear from [our] eyes; there shall be no more death, nor sorrow, nor crying. There shall be no more pain, for the former things have passed away" (Revelation 21:4). That promise makes the present journey easier to endure.

Put another way, it's the hope of going *home* that keeps me going. I can hardly wait to get there!   — David Roper

*I have a home in heaven above,*
*From sin and sorrow free,*
*A mansion which eternal love*
*Designed and formed for me.*   — Bennett

---

**The more you look forward to heaven,**
**the less you'll desire of earth.**

# WHO'S GUILTY?

READ:
Matthew 7:1-5

Hypocrite! First remove
the plank from your
own eye.
—Matthew 7:5

THE BIBLE IN ONE YEAR:
■ Genesis 23–24
■ Matthew 7

A North Carolina man accused his estranged wife of being married to two men. When the woman was arrested, she didn't deny the charge of bigamy. She not only admitted her guilt, but she also told authorities that she must have been crazy to get married twice without having gone through divorce or widowhood.

That was only half the story. What surprised her, she said, was that her husband would turn her in, because he was guilty of the same crime. When the countercharges were explored, the husband admitted that he too was illegally married to two women.

This husband is an example of what Jesus described in Matthew 7:1-5. While having a "plank" in his own eye, the man pointed critically to a "speck" in the eye of his wife. Both had broken the law by being married to two people at the same time. His sin, however, was the greater because he was arrogant to think that he could get away with judging another person for the same sin he was committing.

The message is clear. Christ shows mercy to us when we admit our sin, but He judges our hypocrisy and pride when we refuse to be humbled in His presence.

Let's deal with our own sin and not become experts in pointing out the sins of others. — Mart De Haan

> Don't be too harsh with the one who sins,
> Nor pelt him with word or stone,
> Unless you are sure, yes, doubly sure,
> That you have no sins of your own. — Anon.

---

**Most of us are far-sighted about sin—
we see the sins of others but not our own.**

# THE WORLD IS WATCHING

**READ:**
1 John 2:1-11

---

He who says he abides in [Jesus] ought himself also to walk just as He walked.
—1 John 2:6

---

THE BIBLE IN ONE YEAR:
■ Genesis 25–26
■ Matthew 8:1-17

If the people in your community were asked about the Christians who live there, what do you think they would say? Would they say they recognize Christians by their love, or because of something else?

Consider these two true situations: In one small town a restaurant decided to close on Sunday nights because the staff refused to work for the after-evening-church crowd. The people who came from church were rude, messy, and left small tips.

In another town, the manager of a store that sold concert tickets reported that some of the rudest people she had ever met were several who had bought tickets to hear a well-known Christian singing group.

Sometimes we don't realize it, but the non-Christian world is watching us. Our neighbors and acquaintances and others we encounter notice our behavior. They know that if we claim to be followers of Christ we are supposed to be kind and compassionate. They know that our lives should reflect love and Christlikeness (John 13:35; 1 John 2:6). They know that we shouldn't be so busy with our own interests that we don't love other people.

Let's make sure the people who are watching our lives will want to get to know our Savior. — Dave Branon

*I want my life to shine for Jesus*
*So that everywhere I go*
*The watching world will see He loves them*
*And His saving grace will know.* — Hess

---

**Nothing is so attractive as being like Christ.**

# HIM ONLY

**READ:**
Ezra 4:1-5

---

We alone will build to the LORD God of Israel, as King Cyrus the king of Persia has commanded us.
—Ezra 4:3

---

THE BIBLE IN ONE YEAR:
■ Genesis 27–28
■ Matthew 8:18-34

A Christian youth organization in Singapore learned that the local horse-racing club wanted to donate a significant sum of money to its work. The gift would be helpful, but the organization had taken a position against gambling. Now it had to decide whether accepting money from a racing club that derived its revenue from gambling would compromise its commitment to Christ.

Zerubbabel, Jeshua, and the heads of the families of Israel faced a similar dilemma. They were being offered help to rebuild the temple by Assyrian settlers in the land who had intermarried with remnants of the tribes of Israel. Later known as Samaritans, these people were adversaries of Israel (Ezra 4:1). Zerubbabel's response was decisive: "We alone will build to the LORD God." Why such exclusivity? In 2 Kings 17:33, we learn that those who offered help "feared the LORD, yet served their own gods."

We need to be reminded often of the first commandment: "You shall have no other gods before Me" (Exodus 20:3). Although the Lord can use even unbelievers to accomplish His purposes, we are never to compromise our loyalty to Him. By our words and our actions we must show that we worship Him and Him only. — Albert Lee

*The dearest idol I have known,*
*Whate'er that idol be,*
*Help me to tear it from Thy throne*
*And worship only Thee.* — Cowper

---

**There are many ways to worship God,
but only one God to worship.**

# EITHER COLD OR HOT

READ:
Revelation 3:14-22

I know your works, that you are neither cold nor hot. I could wish you were cold or hot.
—Revelation 3:15

THE BIBLE IN ONE YEAR:
■ Genesis 29–30
■ Matthew 9:1-17

I like soup when it is steaming hot and a soft drink when it is icy cold. I can't stand either one lukewarm. Jesus has the same attitude toward people who profess to be His children. He detests lukewarmness. He said He wished they would be either cold or hot (Revelation 3:15).

Although some people believe the term *cold* refers to hostility toward Jesus and the gospel, I don't believe He prefers hostility to halfheartedness. Rather, in His message to the church in Laodicea, Jesus may have had in mind two springs in the region—the hot mineral springs at Hierapolis and the pure cold water springs in Colosse. The hot springs were seen as having healing powers. The cold springs provided refreshment. The Christians in the church at Laodicea brought neither healing to the spiritually ill nor refreshment to the weary. They were lukewarm and of no help to anyone.

You and I must ask ourselves these questions: Do I provide refreshment to the spiritually weary by bringing them encouragement, joy, and hope? Do I bring healing by challenging the careless, correcting the erring, and motivating the indifferent? Remember, we can't help anybody if we are lukewarm. The Lord wants us either cold or hot — whatever is needed at the moment.  — Herb Vander Lugt

*O God, grant me the strength of heart,*
*Of motive, and of will*
*To falter not but do my part*
*Your purpose to fulfill.* — Anon.

**A half-hearted Christian needs to regain
a heart for God.**

# LOOKING AHEAD

**READ:**
**Philippians 3:7-14**

---

*Forgetting those things which are behind . . . , I press toward the goal.*
—Philippians 3:13-14

---

THE BIBLE IN ONE YEAR:
■ Genesis 31–32
■ Matthew 9:18-38

The month of January is named after Janus, the Roman god of beginnings. He was symbolized as a man with two faces, one looking back and the other looking ahead.

Some people have trouble looking ahead with hope because they keep looking back and moping over the mistakes of the past. Their outlook for the future is dimmed, and their enthusiasm is dampened. But there is no use "crying over spilled milk." History is likely to repeat itself if they keep on brooding over failures of the old year, or continue complaining about the injustices they suffered during the last 12 months. Nothing is gained by continually grieving over the past.

On this day early in the new year, begin by confessing your sins to the Lord and accepting the gracious forgiveness He offers (1 John 1:9-10). Make right what needs correcting, and then, "forgetting those things which are behind," press onward with confidence and trust in your heavenly Father (Philippians 3:13-14). That was Paul's secret, and it worked.

Let's stop looking back and brooding over past failures. Rather, with a forward look, let's move ahead with hope and joy. — Richard De Haan

*THINKING IT OVER*
*What mistakes of the past are still burdening you?*
*Have you confessed them to God and accepted*
*His complete forgiveness? (1 John 1:9).*
*When you do, your future will hold great promise.*

---

**Instead of living in the shadows of yesterday,**
**walk in the light of today and the hope of tomorrow.**

# IN THE MORNING

**READ:**
Mark 1:23-39

In the morning . . .
He went out and
departed to a solitary
place; and there He
prayed. —Mark 1:35

THE BIBLE IN ONE YEAR:
■ Genesis 33–35
■ Matthew 10:1-20

Are you so rushed during the day that you find it hard to take even a few minutes to spend with God? Many people set aside time in the early morning before they get caught up in the hectic pace of the day.

I read about a very busy man who somehow manages to find time for giving the day a spiritual jump-start. He's Dr. Ben Carson, chief of pediatric neurosurgery at Johns Hopkins Children's Center, a position he assumed in 1984 when he was only 33 years old.

Here's Carson's testimony about the value of putting spiritual things first: "I've found that having a morning ritual — meditation or some quiet reading time — can set the tone for the whole day. Every morning, I spend a half-hour reading the Bible, especially the book of Proverbs. There's so much wisdom there. During the day, if I encounter a frustrating situation, I think back to one of the verses that I read that morning."

Jesus faced busy days filled with demanding crowds of people. In Mark's gospel we read, "In the morning, having risen a long while before daylight, He went out and departed to a solitary place; and there He prayed" (1:35).

Do you take time to read God's Word and pray? Try it in the morning. It can transform your day. — Vernon Grounds

*In the stillness of the morning,*
*Before a busy day of care,*
*How sweet to be alone with God*
*Through His holy Word and prayer.* —Anderson

---

**Let Christ be first in your thoughts in the morning,
and last in your thoughts at night.**

# LET'S NOT KID OURSELVES

**READ:**
James 1:19-25

---

Be doers of the Word, and not hearers only, deceiving yourselves.
—James 1:22

---

THE BIBLE IN ONE YEAR:
■ Genesis 36–38
■ Matthew 10:21-42

A child was told by his mother, "Go look in the mirror and wash your face." He insisted, "I already have!" But she replied, "You're only kidding yourself!" His dirty face proved to her that if he really had looked in the mirror, he ignored what it revealed. He may have seen the truth about himself, but he didn't act on it.

The apostle James taught that anyone who hears God's Word but does not obey it is kidding himself. He is like someone who looks at himself in a mirror but goes his way unchanged (James 1:22-24). He hears and reads God's Word, but then dismisses it, not letting the Scriptures change him. The person who looks into the mirror of God's Word, however, longing to be transformed by it, "is not a forgetful hearer" (v.25). He wants the Word to reveal his true needs and show him truths to obey. As he obeys, he progressively becomes more like Jesus. James said that kind of person "will be blessed in what he does" (v.25).

If we honestly want to become more like Christ in our attitudes, actions, and reactions, we must look into God's mirror, the Bible, regularly. But let's not kid ourselves — just looking isn't enough. God's Word will transform us, but only if we obey it.  — Joanie Yoder

> Lord, help me heed Your every word,
> Commands that I have read or heard;
> As You reveal Your will each day,
> Help me to follow and obey.  — Fitzhugh

---

**Open your Bible prayerfully,
read it carefully, and obey it joyfully.**

# NOTHING BUT THE TRUTH

**READ:**
**Proverbs 12:17-22**

---

Lying lips are an abomination to the LORD, but those who deal truthfully are His delight.
—Proverbs 12:22

---

THE BIBLE IN ONE YEAR:
■ Genesis 39–40
■ Matthew 11

Years ago I read some unusual and humorous explanations for auto accidents. The following are just a few that people submitted to an insurance company:

"An invisible car came out of nowhere, struck my car, and vanished."

"I had been driving my car for 40 years when I fell asleep at the wheel and had the accident."

"I pulled away from the side of the road, glanced at my mother-in-law, and headed over the embankment."

"The pedestrian had no idea which direction to go, so I ran over him."

"The telephone pole was approaching fast. I attempted to swerve out of its path when it struck my front end."

"The guy was all over the road. I had to swerve a number of times before I hit him."

"The indirect cause of this accident was a little guy in a small car with a big mouth."

These "excuses" may bring a smile, and some were probably meant to. But they also remind us of how prone we are to shade the facts, especially when it works to our advantage. The book of Proverbs tells us that "lying lips are an abomination to the LORD" (12:22).

So let's be careful at all times to speak the truth — and nothing but the truth! — Richard De Haan

*Deceit at first may have its sweets,*
*But these are brief, decaying,*
*So speak the truth as God directs,*
*For all your words He's weighing!* — Bosch

---

**A lie is a coward's attempt to get out of trouble.**

## SHOPPING STRATEGY

READ:
Malachi 1:6-14

---

"You bring the stolen, the lame, and the sick. . . . Should I accept this from your hand?" says the LORD.
—Malachi 1:13

---

THE BIBLE IN ONE YEAR:
■ Genesis 41–42
■ Matthew 12:1-23

"I have no pleasure in you." This was the Lord's stinging rebuke to His people through the prophet Malachi (1:10). God was angry with their careless, shoddy methods of worship. The animals they brought for sacrifice were not acceptable to Him because they were not the best of the herds and flocks. Instead, they offered stolen, lame, and sick animals (v.13).

While we may not be showing this degree of contempt toward God, sometimes we are too casual in our worship. A friend of mine made this observation about herself: "When I shop for simple things like soap or butter, I hardly think about it. But when I'm looking for a blouse to match a skirt, I shop very carefully. I go from store to store until I find exactly what I'm looking for." Then she added thoughtfully, "I should pay that same attention when I am worshiping God. But sometimes I approach Him as casually as if I were shopping for a box of Kleenex."

During worship services in our churches, we may fail to give God our full attention. We rush in late. Our thoughts wander. We need to discipline our minds so that we are not focusing on yesterday's cares or tomorrow's responsibilities. When we worship the Lord with all our heart, He will be pleased with us. — Dave Egner

> *Our very best we offer to You,*
> *Gracious God, Almighty King;*
> *As we come to You in worship,*
> *Let our lives Your praises sing.* —Sper

---

**At the heart of worship**
**is worship from the heart.**

# REALITY OR ILLUSION?

READ:
Malachi 2:13-17

---

You say, "Everyone who does evil is good in the sight of the LORD." —Malachi 2:17

---

THE BIBLE IN ONE YEAR:
■ Genesis 43–45
■ Matthew 12:24-50

I had just started to back the van away from the loading area. In my rearview mirror I saw two semi trucks side by side. I had plenty of clearance. Just then it appeared that one of the trucks was moving into my path. I stopped. But then I realized that the other truck was actually backing up, creating the illusion that the standing semi was moving forward.

An illusion, according to the dictionary, is an "erroneous perception of reality." Sleight-of-hand artists use it to "do the impossible." Most illusions are harmless, but some can be fatal. In a desert, chasing a mirage that looks like water can lead to death.

But the most dangerous illusions are the spiritual and moral ones that people are so prone to believe. In Malachi 2, the Israelites were breaking their marriage vows (vv.14-16). They knew that God hates divorce (v.16), yet they were saying, "Everyone who does evil is good in the sight of the LORD" (v.17).

Doesn't that sound like today's culture? People believe that things like abortion, extramarital sex, and divorce for other than biblical reasons are morally right. Even some Christians believe in such illusions.

It's crucial that we allow the Bible to be the standard by which we distinguish reality from illusion! — Dennis De Haan

> The Word of God declares what's right
> And what is pleasing in His sight;
> It also shows that deep within
> What we call good may be a sin. — Hess

---

**One of life's greatest illusions
is that sin has no consequences.**

# A WORK OF PEACE

READ:
James 3:13-18

---

The fruit of righteousness is sown in peace by those who make peace. —James 3:18

---

THE BIBLE IN ONE YEAR:
■ Genesis 46–48
■ Matthew 13:1-30

The small church in Umbarger, Texas, was an unlikely place for an international work of art. But toward the end of World War II, seven Italian prisoners of war, who were being held at a large camp nearby, were chosen to help decorate the church's plain brick walls.

The prisoners were reluctant to aid their captors, but they agreed on the condition that their efforts be considered a contribution toward Christian brotherhood and understanding. But as they worked on their paintings and a woodcarving of the Last Supper, one of the POWs later recalled, "A spontaneous stream of good feelings began almost at once to flow among us." No one spoke of the war or the past because "we were here for a work of peace and love."

Our lives are filled with unlikely settings for introducing God's peace. We can feel imprisoned by hard feelings, strained relationships, and confining circumstances. But peace has the power to break out anywhere. James reminded us that "the wisdom that is from above is . . . peaceable, gentle, willing to yield . . . . The fruit of righteousness is sown in peace by those who make peace" (James 3:17-18).

Wherever we are today, let's ask the Lord to use us as His peacemakers. — David McCasland

*O Prince of Peace, keep us, we pray,*
*From strife and enmity;*
*Help us to speak with loving words*
*That calm hostility.* —Branon

---

**The best peacemakers are
those who know the peace of God.**

# LIMITATION OR ADVANTAGE?

**READ:**
2 Corinthians 12:1-10

He said to me, "My grace is sufficient for you, for My strength is made perfect in weakness."
—2 Corinthians 12:9

THE BIBLE IN ONE YEAR:
■ Genesis 49–50
■ Matthew 13:31-58

We've been taught that when we ask God for something through prayer, His answer may be *yes*, *no*, or *wait*. We're told that even *no* is an answer, though obviously not the one we may want. It certainly wasn't the answer Paul wanted when he begged God three times to remove his "thorn in the flesh" (2 Corinthians 12:7-8).

Whatever Paul's thorn was, it weakened him. Because he wanted to be strong in his ministry, Paul asked God for deliverance. Although God didn't grant his request, He answered his prayer! He said to Paul, "My grace is sufficient for you, for My strength is made perfect in weakness" (v.9). The all-sufficient strength of Christ became Paul's new boast.

Author J. Oswald Sanders summarized Paul's attitude about his thorn like this: "At first he viewed it as a limiting handicap, but later he came to regard it as a heavenly advantage." Paul could therefore testify, "I take pleasure in infirmities, in reproaches, in needs, in persecutions, in distresses . . . . For when I am weak, then I am strong" (v.10).

Have you prayed for deliverance from something that weakens you, but deliverance hasn't come? Remember, God's grace is sufficient for you. He can transform your limitation into your "heavenly advantage." — Joanie Yoder

*There's advantage in our weakness,*
*There is blessing in our pain;*
*It is when we're feeling helpless*
*That God's grace and strength sustain.* — Fitzhugh

**Our weakness is a blessing**
**when we lean on God's strength.**

# WHAT DO YOU SEEK?

READ:
John 1:35-42

---

Jesus turned, and seeing them following, said to them, "What do you seek?"
—John 1:38

---

THE BIBLE IN ONE YEAR:
■ Exodus 1–3
■ Matthew 14:1-21

How would you answer if Jesus were to ask you, "What do you seek?" (John 1:38). Would you ask Him for health and fitness? A better job? A happier marriage? Financial security? Vindication from a false accusation? Salvation for a wayward loved one? An explanation of some difficult theological concept?

For two disciples of John the Baptist, this situation was more than an exercise in imagination. One day while they were with John, Jesus walked by and John announced, "Behold the Lamb of God!" (v.36). Instead of continuing to follow John, his two disciples started following Jesus.

When Jesus saw them, He asked, "What do you seek?" (v.38).

Apparently John had taught them well, because their answer indicated that they were not seeking something for themselves but Jesus Himself. They wanted to know where Jesus was staying. Not only did Jesus show them the place, He spent the remainder of the day with them.

I wonder how often we miss an opportunity to spend time with Jesus because we're seeking something other than His presence. I know from experience that the more time I spend with Jesus, the less desire I have for a lot of things that once seemed very important. — Julie Ackerman Link

*To walk in fellowship with Christ*
*And sense His love so deep and true*
*Brings to the soul its highest joy*
*As nothing in this world can do.* — D. De Haan

---

**Jesus longs for our fellowship
even more than we long for His.**

# A WITNESS OF HOPE

**READ:**
Acts 26:1-8,24-32

Always be ready to give a defense to everyone who asks you a reason for the hope that is in you. —1 Peter 3:15

THE BIBLE IN ONE YEAR:
■ Exodus 4–6
■ Matthew 14:22-36

As a child growing up in the former Soviet Union, Nickolas was the only one in his school who refused to join the political group for young people. Because of his faith in God, he was singled out for ridicule, given bad grades he did not deserve, and denied a recommendation to the university. Despite the opposition, he persisted, and in later years he led some of his persecutors to trust in Jesus Christ. Now he is the pastor of a thriving church in Belarus.

The apostle Paul also suffered persecution. His faith landed him in the court of King Agrippa, and he had opportunity to tell how God had changed his life. He testified, "Now I stand and am judged for the hope of the promise made by God to our fathers" (Acts 26:6). His witness to the king about salvation in Christ and the hope of resurrection was clear and convicting.

When we live out our faith in Christ, we're bound to attract the attention of others and may even face persecution. We know our sins are forgiven, and we look forward to being with Jesus forever in heaven. We want to share our faith with others, and some people will want to know the reason for our hope (1 Peter 3:15). When questions come, let's be ready to give a witness. — Dave Egner

*When witnessing, if people ask,*
*"How do you know it's true?"*
*Remember that they can't deny*
*What Christ has done for you.* — Sper

**Our witness for Christ is the light for a world in darkness.**

# THE FREEDOM OF STRUCTURE

READ:
1 John 5:1-13

This is the love of God, that we keep His commandments. And His commandments are not burdensome.
—1 John 5:3

THE BIBLE IN ONE YEAR:
■ Exodus 7–8
■ Matthew 15:1-20

Concert pianist Jeannette Haien believes that the structure of a fine musical composition actually provides great freedom for the person who plays it. "Within the strictures of so-called form," she says, "is all the freedom in the world."

It's easy to feel confined by structure in our faith because we have a natural resistance to rules. But God's commands are given to enhance our lives rather than restrict them.

First John 5:3 states, "This is the love of God, that we keep His commandments. And His commandments are not burdensome." Instead of weighing us down, they protect us from the burden of sin. As we follow His commands, we experience liberty.

Speaking of an excellent musical composition, Jeannette Haien says, "Under the laws of structure you have the freedom to work in the freest way imaginable. What [the composer] has written is that which I honor."

The Bible is our sheet music for living. Today, we can play the song of life as God has written it, and we can discover anew the promise of Jesus to those who believe in Him: "If you abide in My word, you are My disciples indeed. And you shall know the truth, and the truth shall make you free" (John 8:31-32). — David McCasland

*Lord, help us to value the freedom*
*Of life we receive from Your love,*
*A life of obedience and service,*
*Kept safe by Your hand from above.* — K. De Haan

**True freedom is found in obedience to Christ.**

## STEADFAST SERVICE

**READ:**
Acts 20:23-24

Be steadfast, immovable,
. . . knowing that your
labor is not in vain
in the Lord.
—1 Corinthians 15:58

THE BIBLE IN ONE YEAR:
■ Exodus 9–11
■ Matthew 15:21-39

**H**ow do we react to tragic events? When upsetting experiences come into our personal lives and create an atmosphere of darkness and gloom, how do we respond? We may tend to panic or lose heart. A man named Abraham Davenport can teach us a lesson in steadfastness.

On May 19, 1780, a mysterious phenomenon took place. Thick darkness (perhaps caused by smoke from forest fires combined with dense fog) covered areas of New England. Filled with fear, many people thought the world was coming to an end.

The Connecticut legislature was meeting that day, and many members were urging adjournment. Abraham Davenport, however, proclaimed to his colleagues, "I am against adjournment. The day of judgment is either approaching or it is not. If it is not, there is no cause for an adjournment; if it is, I choose to be found doing my duty. I wish therefore that candles may be brought."

The apostle Paul had a similar determination. Even though he had faced severe hardship and opposition, and he was hearing gloomy news about his future, he was determined to "finish [his] race with joy" (Acts 20:24).

Let us, then, with soul-quieting confidence in our Lord, remain steadfast in serving Him all our days. — Vernon Grounds

*We have an anchor that keeps the soul*
*Steadfast and sure while the billows roll,*
*Fastened to the Rock which cannot move,*
*Grounded firm and deep in the Savior's love.* — Owens

**To survive the storms of life,
be anchored to the Rock of Ages.**

# GOLDEN GODS

READ:
Exodus 12:29-36

---

You shall have no other gods before Me.
—Exodus 20:3

---

THE BIBLE IN ONE YEAR:
■ Exodus 12–13
■ Matthew 16

God had seized the attention of Pharaoh and the Egyptians with a series of plagues. Now they were dying to be rid of their Hebrew slaves. But God didn't want the Israelites to leave Egypt empty-handed. After all, they had 400 years of wages due them. So they asked their former masters for articles of silver, gold, and clothing, and they got them. Exodus 12:36 says that the Israelites "plundered the Egyptians."

It wasn't long, however, until God's people fell into idolatry. They used their gold to make a golden calf, which they worshiped while Moses was on Mount Sinai receiving the law (32:1-4).

This tragic experience highlights the tension that Christians are required to maintain in relation to their possessions. There is much in our society that we may enjoy, but material things can also pose grave dangers when we use them unwisely. Os Guinness says that we are "free to utilize" but "forbidden to idolize." We are "strangers and pilgrims on the earth" (Hebrews 11:13), and we must not become so enamored with "the treasures in Egypt" (v.26) that we grow complacent and forget our true calling.

Are we using our material blessings to serve the Lord — or have we become slaves to them?   — Haddon Robinson

> I have an old nature that noisily clamors
>     To satisfy empty desire;
>   But God in His goodness has sent me a Helper
> Who whispers, "Your calling is higher."   — Gustafson

---

**Gold can be a helpful servant
but a cruel master.**

# A TIME FOR ACTION

**READ:**
**Exodus 14:5-18**

---

The LORD said to Moses, "Why do you cry to Me? Tell the children of Israel to go forward." —Exodus 14:15

---

THE BIBLE IN ONE YEAR:
■ Exodus 14–15
■ Matthew 17

The woman chuckled as she told me about the time she woke her husband to tell him she was in labor and needed to go to the hospital. He jumped out of bed, dropped to his knees, and said, "Honey, let's pray." She told him that it was not the time to kneel and pray. It was time to get dressed and head for the hospital. It was time for action!

I think this was the type of message God gave Moses when He said of the Israelites, "Why do you cry to Me?" (Exodus 14:15). Not long before that, Pharaoh had permitted the Israelites to leave Egypt, but then he changed his mind (vv.5-6). Wanting to bring them back, he and his army chased after them (vv.7-9). The Israelites were terrified when they saw the Egyptians approaching. They were trapped at the shore of the Red Sea, with nowhere to go! But Moses assured Israel that God would deliver them. Now was a time for action — not crying to Him. It was time to "go on dry ground through the midst of the sea" (v.16).

There's a proper time for everything (Ecclesiastes 3:1), including a time to pray and a time to act. When we see someone who lacks food and clothes, it's right to provide what they need (James 2:15-16). Sometimes we need to trust God and take immediate action. — Herb Vander Lugt

*Lord, when I sense Your call to serve,*
*Help me to follow through;*
*I must not just stand by and pray*
*When there is work to do.* — Fasick

---

**If God has already told you what to do,**
**you don't need to ask Him again.**

# FROM BITTER TO SWEET

**READ:**
**Exodus 15:22-27**

The LORD showed him a tree. When he cast it into the waters, the waters were made sweet.
—Exodus 15:25

THE BIBLE IN ONE YEAR:
■ Exodus 16–18
■ Matthew 18:1-20

Joy and sorrow are often close companions. Just as the Israelites went from the thrill of victory at the Red Sea to the bitter waters of Marah just 3 days later (Exodus 15:22-23), our rejoicing can quickly turn into anguish.

At Marah, the Lord told Moses to throw a tree into the water, which made it "sweet" and drinkable (v.25). Another "tree," when "cast into" the bitter circumstances of our lives, can make them sweet. It is the cross of Jesus (1 Peter 2:24). Our outlook will be transformed as we contemplate His sacrificial death and His submission to the will of God (Luke 22:42).

Our pain may come from the ill-will of others, or worse, from their neglect. Nevertheless, our Lord has permitted it. We may not understand why, yet it is the will of our Father and Friend, whose wisdom and love are infinite.

When we say yes to God as His Spirit reveals His will to us through His Word, the bitter circumstances of our lives can become sweet. We must not grumble against what the Lord permits. Instead, we must do all that He asks us to do. Jesus said that we are to take up our cross daily and follow Him (Luke 9:23).

When we remember Jesus' cross and submit to the Father as He did, bitter experiences can become sweet. — David Roper

*Lord, I've not always understood*
*What plan You have for me;*
*Yet I will glory in Your cross*
*And bear mine patiently.* — Anon.

---

**God uses our difficulties to make us better—**
**not bitter.**

# CARING PRAYER

READ:
**Romans 15:30-33**

I beg you, . . . strive together with me in prayers to God for me. —Romans 15:30

THE BIBLE IN ONE YEAR:
■ Exodus 19–20
■ Matthew 18:21-35

I recently received an e-mail from someone I didn't know. It was from a teenager who set a great example we all can learn from. His e-mail showed how much he believed in the power of prayer.

He told about a teenage girl in his hometown who had become pregnant outside of marriage. Her parents were threatening to force her to get an abortion. When the young man heard about it, he got on his computer and sent an e-mail to more than 100 people, telling of the girl's predicament and saying over and over, "Please pray for this girl." His compassion for her was evident — as well as his faith in God to answer prayer.

This teenager could have spent time on his computer doing many other things: looking up information about cars, playing video games, sending jokes to his buddies. Instead, he took the time to compile all those e-mail addresses, then he wrote a caring, heartfelt note. In Romans 15:30-33, the apostle Paul showed that he knew the value of concerted prayer — whether it's for ourselves or for someone else in need.

What a lesson! It reminds us to cling to the Lord in prayer, and it shows us an example of the compassion that leads us to team up with others in caring prayer. — Dave Branon

*LEARNING TO PRAY*
*Unsure of how to develop an effective prayer life?*
*Read the booklet* Jesus' Blueprint For Prayer *at*
www.discoveryseries.org/hj891

**When you can't be there,
you can help through prayer.**

# LET'S TALK ABOUT IT!

READ:
**Matthew 18:15-20**

Let not mercy and truth
forsake you; bind them
around your neck,
write them on the
tablet of your heart.
—Proverbs 3:3

THE BIBLE IN ONE YEAR:
■ Exodus 21–22
■ Matthew 19

The police in San Diego received complaints from a woman who said she was getting annoying phone calls. In the middle of the night a person would phone her, bark like a dog, and then hang up. Police eventually discovered that the source of the calls was a neighbor. He said that whenever he was awakened by the barking of her dog, he wanted to make sure she was awake too.

The neighbor's approach certainly didn't express the wisdom of God. The Scriptures tell us that it is often necessary to face a problem head-on (Matthew 18:15-20). At the right time and for the sake of all parties involved, an honest discussion is part of the solution.

Yet such a loving, open approach is not usually followed among Christians. Rather than trusting God and walking into a tense situation with a clear conscience and a desire for peace, we tend to play games. Hints are dropped. Affection is withheld. Conversation is abbreviated. The air gets chilly, and ice forms around a situation that can only be melted by a wise combination of mercy and truth (Proverbs 3:3).

Our complaints against others cannot be smoothed over by burying our anger. If a problem is not small enough to overlook graciously, then let's talk about it.  — Mart De Haan

*If you can't forgive a brother*
*For the wrong he's done to you,*
*Go to him and talk it over —*
*That's the Christian thing to do.*  —D. De Haan

---

**The best way to destroy your enemy**
**is to make him your friend.**

# TURNAROUND EXPERT

READ:
Galatians 3:22–4:7

*When the fullness of the time had come, God sent forth His Son, born of a woman, born under the law.*
—Galatians 4:4

THE BIBLE IN ONE YEAR:
■ Exodus 23–24
■ Matthew 20:1-16

Members of The Turnaround Management Association are rarely asked to join successful companies. Instead, these skilled professionals are called into ailing businesses to help get them back on their feet.

The same need for dramatic change exists throughout society. People who can reverse the downward spiral in an individual's life, a relationship, or a team are constantly in demand.

But what about changing the world? Many people would say that only God can do that. And that's exactly what He sent His Son to do. The Bible describes humanity's downward spiral by saying that the entire world was imprisoned by sin and "in bondage" (Galatians 3:22; 4:3).

Into that hopeless situation Jesus came "to redeem those who were under the law, that we might receive the adoption as sons" (4:5). The personal turnaround for us begins when we accept God's offer of eternal life in Christ and receive His Spirit into our hearts (v.6). Rather than simply being given a new set of rules and sent off on our own, we are adopted into God's family.

Jesus Christ is the ultimate turnaround expert. He specializes in impossible cases. Will you invite Him into your life today? — David McCasland

*The Lord will turn your life around*
*If you'll invite Him in;*
*Then you'll at once be heaven-bound,*
*No longer chained by sin. — Hess*

**When we choose to follow Jesus,**
**our whole life changes direction.**

# TIME FLIES

READ:
**Psalm 90:10-17**

---

Teach us to number
our days, that we
may gain a heart of
wisdom.
**—Psalm 90:12**

---

THE BIBLE IN ONE YEAR:
■ Exodus 25 – 26
■ Matthew 20:17-34

Many metaphors are used in litera-
ture to describe life's brevity. It
is a dream, a swift runner, a mist, a
puff of smoke, a shadow, a gesture in
the air, a sentence written in the sand,
a bird flying in one window of a house
and out another. Another symbolic
description was suggested by a friend
of mine who said that the short dash
between the dates of birth and death
on tombstones represents the brief
span of one's life.

When we were children, time loi-
tered. But as we get closer to the end
of our lives, time moves with increasing swiftness, like water swirling
down a drain. In childhood we measured our age in small increments.
"I'm 6 ½," we would say, for it
seemed to take so long to get older. Now we have no time
for such childishness. Who claims to be 60 ½?

It's good to ponder the brevity of life now and then. Life
is too short to treat it carelessly. In Psalm 90, after describing
the shortness of life, Moses prayed, "Teach us to number our
days, that we may gain a heart of wisdom" (v.12).

To make the most of our earthly existence, we must lose
ourselves in the will of God (1 Peter 4:2). This we can do
even when time is running out. It's never too late to give
ourselves totally to God.  — David Roper

> *Lord, help us to redeem the time*
> *You give us every day —*
> *To take each opportunity*
> *To follow and obey.*  — Sper

---

**Don't just count your days, make your days count.**

# THE RESISTERS

READ:
Isaiah 30:8-17

---

This is a rebellious people, lying children, children who will not hear the law of the LORD.
—Isaiah 30:9

---

THE BIBLE IN ONE YEAR:
■ Exodus 27–28
■ Matthew 21:1-22

"I don't have to listen to you!" That's a sentence parents don't like to hear from their teenage children. It means they have decided not to obey their parents. Usually, it's spoken in anger and soon forgotten.

Sometimes, though, a teen might decide to make that attitude a way of life. When that happens, it's hard for everyone in the family. A child's refusal to obey authority creates ongoing turmoil in the home and saps the joy from life.

The teenager openly rebels, thinking he would be happier by resisting authority. But instead, he can actually become miserable in his heart.

The prophet Isaiah told about some resisters — rebellious, lying people who refused to listen to what God was saying (30:8-17). In effect, they said to Him, "We've heard enough. We don't have to listen to You!" Their heart of resistance turned them against God's truth.

Rebellion is not limited to teens or to the people of Isaiah's day. Sometimes we too wear the resister label. We read God's Word and decide it's too restrictive. Or we sense that God wants us to do something, and we run from it. That leads only to misery. Instead, if we obey God's Word, we will enjoy His peace in our hearts.  — Dave Branon

*If you've rebelled and turned away*
*From what you know is true,*
*Turn back to God — He will forgive;*
*He waits to pardon you.*  — Sper

---

**Obedience is the pathway to joy.**

# FREELY FORGIVE

READ:
**Colossians 3:12-17**

If anyone has a
complaint against
another; even as Christ
forgave you, so you
also must do.
—Colossians 3:13

THE BIBLE IN ONE YEAR:
■ Exodus 29–30
■ Matthew 21:23-46

Studies by a number of psychologists show that it is not great riches that make people happy, but friends and forgiveness. Commenting on these findings in a *USA Today* article, Marilyn Elias says, "The happiest people surround themselves with family and friends, don't care about keeping up with the Joneses next door, lose themselves in daily activities, and most important, forgive easily."

University of Michigan psychologist Christopher Peterson says that the ability to forgive others is the trait most strongly linked to happiness. He calls it "the queen of all virtues, and probably the hardest to come by."

An unforgiving spirit is often the last emotional fortress we yield to the power of God. Even as Christians, we may cling to anger and bitterness, feeling that those who have wronged us should suffer for their offenses. But when we realize how much God has forgiven us, we are compelled to extend mercy to others. The Bible urges us to "put on tender mercies, kindness, humility, meekness, longsuffering; . . . even as Christ forgave you, so you also must do" (Colossians 3:12-13).

Forgiveness is God's command to us and is part of a life of love, peace, thankfulness, and praise (vv.14-16). Freely we have been forgiven; let us freely forgive. — David McCasland

*Lord, help me be kind and forgiving —*
*Your loving forgiveness You've shown*
*To me for the sins I've committed;*
*Lord, grant me a love like Your own.* —Anon.

**When it seems you can't forgive,**
**remember how much you've been forgiven.**

# AGING GRACEFULLY

READ:
Psalm 139:13-18

---

I will praise You, for
I am fearfully and
wonderfully made.
—Psalm 139:14

---

THE BIBLE IN ONE YEAR:
■ Exodus 31–33
■ Matthew 22:1-22

**M**any people try to reverse the aging process. Those with wrinkles get facelifts, while others have injections to remove unwanted facial lines. Behind this current trend is the notion that an aging face is unacceptable.

But not everyone feels that way. An elderly woman being interviewed on television was asked, "Do you like your face?" She responded with conviction, "I love my face! It's the face God gave me, and I accept it happily."

In Psalm 139, David expressed the conviction that his entire being was fashioned by God and therefore is worthy of acceptance. He prayed, "I will praise You, for I am fearfully and wonderfully made" (v.14). He also believed that God fashioned all the days of his life (v.16).

Instead of fighting a losing battle against our waning youthful appearance, we should concentrate on cultivating inner qualities that last forever. One key attribute is a lifelong faith in God, who reassures His people: "Even to your old age, . . . and even to gray hairs I will carry you!" (Isaiah 46:4).

Myron Taylor wrote: "Time may wrinkle the skin, but worry, doubt, hate, and the loss of ideals wrinkle the soul." As we gracefully accept the passing of years, God will smooth out the wrinkles of our souls.  — Joanie Yoder

*The wrinkles on a time-worn face*
*Can be symbols of God's grace,*
*If through our laughter and our tears*
*His love has freed us from our fears.* — D. De Haan

---

**When you let God's love fill your heart,**
**it will show on your face.**

## "I Spy!"

READ:
John 21:1-7

---

That disciple whom
Jesus loved said to
Peter, "It is the Lord!"
—John 21:7

---

THE BIBLE IN ONE YEAR:
- Exodus 34–35
- Matthew 22:23-46

My wife and I have some friends who used to play a game with their children called "I Spy." If a family member saw what appeared to be God at work in their surroundings, he or she would call out, "I spy!" It might be a beautiful sunset or some special blessing. These experiences reminded them of God's presence in the world and in their lives.

That game reminds me of Jesus' disciples and their futile fishing endeavor recorded in John 21:1-7. Early in the morning they saw through the mist a man standing on the shore, but they didn't know it was Jesus. "Children, have you any food?" He asked. "No," they replied. "Cast the net on the right side of the boat," He said, "and you will find some." The disciples obeyed and their net was filled with so many fish they couldn't draw it in. "It is the Lord!" exclaimed John. It was an "I spy" moment, and it was John, "the disciple whom Jesus loved," who was the first to recognize Him.

Ask God to give you eyes to "see" Jesus, whether in the extraordinary events or the everyday affairs of your life. If you pay attention, you will see His hand at work where others see nothing. Try playing "I spy" today and let the Lord's presence reassure you of His love and care. — David Roper

*We cannot fully know God's greatness,*
*Wisdom, power, and care;*
*But it's enough to know that He*
*Is with us everywhere.* — Hess

---

**Eyes of faith can see God at work.**

**February 5**

# DOES HE CARE?

READ:
**Matthew 6:25-34**

I live by faith in the Son of God, who loved me and gave Himself for me.
—Galatians 2:20

THE BIBLE IN ONE YEAR:
■ Exodus 36–38
■ Matthew 23:1-22

If you are ever tempted to write yourself off as insignificant among the billions of people on earth, consider this: You are a one-of-a-kind creation of God (Psalm 139:13-14). That's true even of identical twins. There never has been and never will be another person exactly like you.

Even more important, God values you (Matthew 6:26-30) and has gone to great lengths to show His love. The Bible says that His Son Jesus loves you so much that He gave His life for you (Galatians 2:20).

If you were to ask a loving mother of a large family which child she would be willing to give up, I'm sure she would think your question was absurd. Susannah Wesley, for example, had 19 sons and daughters. Among them were John and Charles, who spearheaded the evangelical revival in 18th-century England. Yet if you were to read the letters she wrote to each of her children, you would marvel at her concern for their unique personalities and problems. It was as if each child was her one and only offspring.

That's a picture of how much God cares about you. If you are ever tempted to wonder if He knows you exist or cares what happens to you, remember what Jesus did for you on the cross. That's how much He loves you. — Vernon Grounds

*Not the nails, but His wondrous love for me,*
*Kept my Lord on the cross of Calvary;*
*Oh, what power could hold Him there —*
*All my sin and shame to bear!* —Keller

**God loves you as much as if
you were His only child.**

## FOCUS

READ:
**Colossians 3:1-11**

---

Set your mind on
things above, not on
things on the earth.
—Colossians 3:2

---

THE BIBLE IN ONE YEAR:
- Exodus 39–40
- Matthew 23:23-39

Missionary pilot Bernie May writes, "One of the most difficult lessons to teach new pilots about landing on short, hazardous airstrips is to keep their eyes on the good part of the strip rather than on the hazard. The natural tendency is to concentrate on the obstacle, the danger, the thing he is trying to avoid. But experience teaches us that a pilot who keeps his eye on the hazard will sooner or later hit it dead center."

This makes me think of a spiritual principle in the Bible. Instead of concentrating on the sins we want to avoid, we are told to focus on the positive actions Christ desires for us. Paul told the Christians at Colösse: "Set your mind on things above, not on things on the earth" (Colossians 3:2). We are to discard old ways of thinking and acting (vv.5-9) and "put on" new ways of living (vv.10-17).

Bernie May sums it up by saying that experienced pilots focus their attention solidly on the track they want the plane to follow, keeping the hazards in their peripheral vision only.

When Christ and His interests are the focus of our lives, the lure of the old life remains in the corner of our eye, while we aim to land squarely in the center of God's will. — David McCasland

### THINKING IT OVER

*What "hazards" sometimes divert your attention from Jesus? What positive, God-honoring actions can you concentrate on doing instead?*

---

**Those who fix their eyes on heaven
will not be distracted by the things of earth.**

# WITH GOD ALL THE TIME

**READ:**
2 Corinthians 5:1-10

---

If our earthly house . . .
is destroyed, we have a
building from God, . . .
eternal in the heavens.
—2 Corinthians 5:1

---

THE BIBLE IN ONE YEAR:
■ Leviticus 1–3
■ Matthew 24:1-28

It was the summer between Melissa's sophomore and junior years of high school. She and her friend Mandy were in Spain on a trip with their Spanish class, and they stayed up one night in their hotel room for a serious discussion. They had just seen a report on the BBC about some teens who had died in an accident, and they started talking about death.

Melissa told Mandy that she could not figure out why Christians were afraid to die. After all, she told her, when a Christian dies, he or she gets to be "with God all the time." *What could be better than that?* Melissa wondered.

How do I know about this conversation? Mandy shared this story with me and my wife shortly after we lost our precious 17-year-old daughter in a car accident in 2002. We have been comforted by this story, because it reminds us that Melissa knew she was saved, and she was confident that she would spend eternity with her Savior. We just never expected that she would be "with God all the time" so suddenly and so early in her life.

Do you have the assurance that Melissa had, that if you were to die you would be in God's presence forever? (2 Corinthians 5:6-8). Make sure of your salvation today. Then you won't need to be afraid to die.  — Dave Branon

*MAKING SURE*
*Admit that you are a sinner (Romans 3:23; 7:23).*
*Believe in Jesus for forgiveness (John 1:12; 3:16).*
*Confess that Jesus is Lord (Romans 10:9).*

---

**If you make room for Jesus in your heart,
He will make room for you in heaven.**

# HEARTS LIFTED UP

READ:
2 Chronicles 26

---

As long as he sought the LORD, God made him prosper.
—2 Chronicles 26:5

---

THE BIBLE IN ONE YEAR:
■ Leviticus 4–5
■ Matthew 24:29-51

It's tragic to witness someone starting out well in life and then finishing poorly. That's the life story of Uzziah. He had been appointed king at the tender age of 16. Despite being so young, we read that "he did what was right in the sight of the LORD . . . . He sought God in the days of Zechariah, who had understanding in the visions of God; and as long as he sought the LORD, God made him prosper" (2 Chronicles 26:4-5).

Uzziah's fame spread and his army grew stronger (v.8). He had 2,600 chief officers and 307,500 soldiers who helped him defeat his enemies (vv.12-13).

Sadly, we then read, "When he was strong his heart was lifted up, to his destruction" (v.16). Uzziah had failed to remember the One who had given him success and those who had given godly counsel. He sinned against the Lord when he burned incense in the temple, and God struck him with leprosy (vv.16-19). He remained "a leper until the day of his death" (v.21).

To finish well, we need to avoid having a heart that is "lifted up." Let's remind ourselves often of the warning in Proverbs 16:18, "Pride goes before destruction, and a haughty spirit before a fall." And let's keep seeking the Lord, obeying Him, and thanking Him for all He has done. — Albert Lee

*Blessed Savior, make me humble,*
*Take away my sinful pride;*
*In myself I'm sure to stumble,*
*Help me stay close by Your side.* — D. De Haan

---

**You won't get indigestion**
**by swallowing your pride.**

# WORK: A NARCOTIC

**READ:**
**Ecclesiastes 2:1-11**

My heart rejoiced in
all my labor . . . .
And indeed all was
vanity and grasping
for the wind.
—Ecclesiastes 2:10-11

THE BIBLE IN ONE YEAR:
■ Leviticus 6–7
■ Matthew 25:1-30

A friend told me that he feels closest to God when he's the busiest. He explained that when demands are the greatest, he finds himself most reliant on the Lord's strength. He pointed out, however, that unless he takes time for daily worship, his work can quickly become an escape.

Many people engage in activity for activity's sake and use busyness as a device to avoid facing reality. Just as alcohol can deaden the senses to personal relationships, family obligations, and community responsibilities, so also constant work can be a narcotic. It dulls our sensitivity to the deeper issues of life.

About 3,000 years ago, the author of Ecclesiastes discovered this. He sought satisfaction by busying himself with building houses and planting vineyards. But then as he thought about the work he had done, he realized it was full of emptiness (2:10-11).

We can make the same mistake, even in the name of the Lord. Could this be the reason some of us try to keep the church running by our own efforts but forget that fulfillment comes only from hearts full of God? Are we laboring without those vital times of worship and reflection? If so, it's time now to worship before we get caught again in the trap of working merely for work's sake. — Mart De Haan

*Lord, teach me how to work each day,*
*That every deed I do*
*May not be driven by false pride*
*But render service true.* — Anon.

---

**Never take on more work
than you have time to pray over.**

# IN GOD'S HANDS

**READ:**
**2 Samuel 16:5-14**

It may be that the LORD will look on my affliction, and that the LORD will repay me with good.
—2 Samuel 16:12

THE BIBLE IN ONE YEAR:
■ Leviticus 8–10
■ Matthew 25:31-46

In 2 Samuel 16:5-14 we read of King David being cursed by Shimei. This happened while David was fleeing from his son Absalom, who wanted to kill him.

Unlike David, we often want to silence our critics, insist on fairness, and defend ourselves. But as we grow in our awareness of God's protective love, we become less concerned with what others say about us and more willing to entrust ourselves to our Father. Like David, we can say of each critic, "Let him alone, and let him curse" (2 Samuel 16:11). This is humble submission to God's will.

We may ask our opponents to justify their charges, or we may counter them with steadfast denial. Or, like David (v.12), we can wait patiently until God vindicates us.

It is good to look beyond those who oppose us and look to the One who loves us with infinite love. It is good to be able to believe that whatever God permits is for our ultimate good—good, though we're exposed to the curses of a Shimei; good, though our hearts break and we shed bitter tears.

You are in God's hands, no matter what others are saying about you. He has seen your distress, and in time He'll repay you for the cursing you have received. So trust Him and abide in His love. —David Roper

*THINKING IT OVER*

*Read 1 Peter 2:20-23. How did Jesus respond to words spoken against Him? What did He do and not do? In what situations can you follow His example?*

**We can endure life's wrongs because we know that God will make all things right.**

# A SIGNIFICANT IMPACT

READ:
**Daniel 10**

---

We do not wrestle
against flesh and
blood, but against . . .
the rulers of the
darkness of this age.
—Ephesians 6:12

---

THE BIBLE IN ONE YEAR:
■ Leviticus 11–12
■ Matthew 26:1-25

---

John Wesley was convinced that the prayers of God's people rather than his preaching accounted for the thousands who came to Christ through his ministry. That's why he said, "God will do nothing except in answer to prayer." An overstatement? Yes. But the fact is that our praying is a powerful weapon in the war between God and Satan.

In today's Scripture reading, Daniel was so disturbed by a revelation about Israel's future that he could do nothing except fast and pray. Three weeks later a heavenly messenger appeared, saying that God had sent him when Daniel prayed, but that the prince of Persia had detained him (10:13). This "prince" was an evil spirit who sought to influence the rulers of Persia to oppose God's plan. He had detained God's messenger, until the archangel Michael came to his aid.

A cosmic conflict between good and evil is continually being fought in the invisible spirit world. Paul reminded us that it involves Christians. He listed the spiritual armor and weaponry we need for these battles (Ephesians 6:13-17), and then he added "praying always" (v.18).

Our prayers can have a significant impact on the outcome of those spiritual battles. May we, therefore, faithfully pray as we fight the good fight (1 Timothy 1:18). — Herb Vander Lugt

*Something happens when we pray,*
*Powers of evil lose their sway,*
*We gain strength and fear gives way —*
*Therefore, let us pray.* — Anon.

---

**Satan trembles when he sees
the weakest saint upon his knees.**

# OCEANS OF PRAISE

**READ:**
Psalm 104:24-30

O LORD, how manifold are Your works! In wisdom You have made them all. —Psalm 104:24

THE BIBLE IN ONE YEAR:
■ Leviticus 13
■ Matthew 26:26-50

Whenever I see the ocean (which is not often enough), I am awed by its sheer volume and beauty and power. Great ships loaded with oil or food or merchandise make long journeys across its vast surface. Fishing vessels, working near the shore or hundreds of miles at sea, harvest its rich provisions: lobster and crab, tuna and swordfish. Beneath its churning surface is a storehouse of wealth of all kinds, some still undiscovered.

The author of Psalm 104, recounting the works of God in a lofty hymn of praise, used the "great and wide sea" as an example of God's creative power and wisdom (vv.24-25). The Lord rules over all the "innumerable teeming things, living things both small and great" that inhabit the oceans (v.25). The psalmist referred in poetic terms to the ocean as the playground of Leviathan, a giant sea monster that God "made to play there" (v.26).

The surging ocean, both life-sustaining and dangerous, points us to the greatness of our God. He is awesome in His works, unlimited in His provision, and generous in His bestowal of all kinds of life.

Lord, truly Your works are magnificent! As I think of them, I join the psalmist in praising You. — Dave Egner

*I sing the mighty power of God*
*That made the mountains rise,*
*That spread the flowing seas abroad*
*And built the lofty skies.* — Watts

**All creation sings God's praise.**

# PERFECT LOVE

**READ:**
**1 John 4:15-18**

There is no fear in love; but perfect love casts out fear, because fear involves torment. But he who fears has not been made perfect in love. —1 John 4:18

THE BIBLE IN ONE YEAR:
■ Leviticus 14
■ Matthew 26:51-75

A wise man once wrote, "When love comes, fear goes."

I know so many Christians who are tormented by feelings of self-doubt, worthlessness, and sinfulness. They think they must do something to make God love them more. Yet the apostle John said that "as [Jesus] is, so are we in this world" (1 John 4:17). In other words, we share the same confidence that Jesus has in knowing that the Father loves us with perfect love.

Because Jesus accomplished our redemption on the cross, all judgment for sin is behind Him and us, and the sin question is forever settled. We now face no condemnation.

This removes fear. For as John wrote, "There is no fear in love; but perfect love casts out fear" (v.18). The "fear" of which John spoke is fear of judgment. But we have nothing to fear, for "there is therefore now no condemnation to those who are in Christ Jesus" (Romans 8:1). Fear is driven out by God's "perfect love."

We're forgiven for all our sins, held fast by God's love, and destined to enjoy eternal fellowship with Him, not because of anything we have done but because He has done everything for us. "In this is love, not that we loved God, but that He loved us" (1 John 4:10). That's perfect love! — David Roper

> *It was love that heard my pleadings*
> *When I cried out in my sin;*
> *It was love that gave me comfort;*
> *It was love that took me in.* — Bonney

**We won't fear God's judgment**
**when we know His forgiving love.**

# KEEP THE ROMANCE

**READ:**
Jude 17-23

---

Keep yourselves in
the love of God.
—Jude 21

---

THE BIBLE IN ONE YEAR:
■ Leviticus 15–16
■ Matthew 27:1-26

The great American statesman and lawyer William Jennings Bryan (1860–1925) was having his portrait painted. The artist asked, "Why do you wear your hair over your ears?"

Bryan responded, "There is a romance connected with that. When I began courting Mrs. Bryan, she objected to the way my ears stood out. So, to please her, I let my hair grow to cover them."

"That was many years ago," the artist said. "Why don't you have your hair cut now?"

"Because," Bryan winked, "the romance is still going on."

Is the romance still going on in our relationship with Jesus? When we first came in faith to Christ, we experienced the joy of knowing our sins were forgiven and we were adopted into His family. Our hearts were full and overflowing with love for the Lord. We longed to please Him.

As time passed, however, the zeal of our first love may have begun to cool. That's why we need to take to heart the words of Jude in his brief letter. He wrote, "Keep yourselves in the love of God" (v.21). Jesus used similar terms when He said, "Abide in My love" (John 15:9-10). We nurture that love when we focus on pleasing Him instead of ourselves.

Keep the romance going.  — Dave Egner

*"Keep yourselves in the love of God"*
*Is what He says to do;*
*Feeding on His Word each day,*
*You'll find His love anew.* — Hess

---

**To renew your love for Christ,
review His love for you.**

## STARTING OVER

READ:
Ephesians 2:1-10

If anyone is in Christ, he is a new creation; old things have passed away; behold, all things have become new.
—2 Corinthians 5:17

THE BIBLE IN ONE YEAR:
■ Leviticus 17–18
■ Matthew 27:27-50

The little boy looked up at his mother and asked, "Mama, do you know why God made us?"

Knowing that her son had his own explanation, she asked, "Well, Justin, do *you* know why?"

"Oh, that's easy. Because the people in the Bible were so bad, He wanted to start over."

When you think about it, it's easy to see how this first-grader could come up with such a conclusion. When he listens to the Bible stories in Sunday school, he hears about Adam and Eve, who messed things up for all of us. He hears about Jonah, who wouldn't obey God and was swallowed by a big fish. He hears about Judas, who betrayed Jesus for 30 silver coins.

The Bible is painfully realistic in its portrayal of people. It is no whitewashed version of the history of God's people. In its honest presentation of its characters, the Bible proves that we all need to be forgiven of our sins. The "bad" people of the Bible remind us that "all have sinned and fall short of the glory of God" (Romans 3:23).

But there's great news. God did provide a way to "start over." He sent Jesus, who died so that we could become new creations (2 Corinthians 5:17). Trust Jesus and be saved from your sin. Then you will be able to "start over." — Dave Branon

*The Savior is waiting to save you,*
*And cleanse every sin-stain away;*
*By faith you can know full forgiveness*
*And be a new creature today! — Bosch*

**For a new start, ask God for a new heart.**

# THE TESTS
# OF CRITICISM

READ:
Leviticus 19:15-18

---

Faithful are the
wounds of a friend,
but the kisses of an
enemy are deceitful.
—Proverbs 27:6

---

THE BIBLE IN ONE YEAR:
■ Leviticus 19–20
■ Matthew 27:51-66

After a church service in which the minister had preached about spiritual gifts, he was greeted at the door by a woman who said, "Pastor, I believe I have the gift of criticism."

He responded, "Do you remember the person in Jesus' parable who had the one talent? Do you recall what he did with it?"

"Yes," replied the woman, "he went out and buried it" (see Matthew 25:18).

With a smile, the pastor suggested, "Go, and do likewise!"

If criticism is not given lovingly and with an honest desire to help, it can be cruel and destructive. The words of Leviticus 19:17, "You shall surely rebuke your neighbor, and not bear sin because of him," are preceded by warnings against spreading slander and nursing hatred.

You can determine when you should criticize and when you shouldn't by asking yourself three questions:

1. Am I motivated by a desire to help the other person?
2. Am I planning to face him honestly, but gently?
3. Am I doing this for the Lord, or because I enjoy being critical?

If your goal is to help, if your motives are loving, and if your desire is to please God, then go ahead and criticize. If you can't pass these tests, keep quiet. — Richard De Haan

*We're building up or tearing down*
*In everything we do;*
*Are we in the construction gang*
*Or on the wrecking crew?* — Anon.

---

**He has the right to criticize who has
the heart to help.** —Abraham Lincoln

# THE BEST POLICY

READ:
Leviticus 19:32-37

You shall have honest scales, honest weights,
. . . I am the LORD your God.
—Leviticus 19:36

THE BIBLE IN ONE YEAR:
■ Leviticus 21–22
■ Matthew 28

A former chairman of the American Institute of Certified Public Accountants says that ethical behavior is the foundation of business success. Speaking to an audience of business and community leaders, Marvin Strait said, "People want to do business with people they can trust. Trust is what makes business work. It is the bedrock of the free-enterprise system."

In the wake of corporate scandals and eroding public confidence, his words remind us of the value of honesty. Without it, our lives and our work fall short of God's design.

The Old Testament law says, "You shall have honest scales, honest weights, . . . I am the LORD your God" (Leviticus 19:36). And the New Testament teaches that truth and honesty in all that we say and do should characterize those who have been redeemed by Christ (Ephesians 4:25-28).

A good way to evaluate our daily choices is to ask ourselves: "Would I be embarrassed if I read about this in the newspaper or if my family and friends knew about it? Am I excusing or profiting by the unethical acts of other people?"

Honesty is not only the best policy, it's God's policy for every aspect of our lives. Living with integrity honors and glorifies Him. — David McCasland

*Lord, help me to be honest*
*In all I do and say,*
*And grant me grace and power*
*To live for You each day.* — Fitzhugh

**Honesty is the best policy.**
—Benjamin Franklin

# OPEN AT THE TOP

READ:
Hebrews 4:14-16

We have a great High Priest who has passed through the heavens, Jesus the Son of God.
—Hebrews 4:14

THE BIBLE IN ONE YEAR:
■ Leviticus 23–24
■ Mark 1:1-22

A preacher was delivering a sermon before a large congregation. He pointed out that believers aren't exempt from trouble. In fact, some Christians are surrounded by trouble — trouble to the right, trouble to the left, trouble in front, and trouble behind. At this, a man who had served the Lord for many years, shouted, "Glory to God, it's always open at the top!"

This man's confidence in God is fully supported by Hebrews 4. Because our great High Priest, Jesus the Son of God, has ascended to heaven and is interceding there for us, we have good grounds for trusting Him in the midst of trouble (v.14). Jesus is able to sympathize with our weaknesses, for when He lived on earth He was tempted in every way that we are, yet He never sinned (v.15). His throne is completely approachable and is called "the throne of grace" (v.16).

In Hebrews we're urged to look up from our trials and to approach that throne boldly by faith. Through humble prayer, we will receive mercy for our failures and grace to help us in our time of need (v.16).

Are life's trials and temptations hemming you in? Has the tempter told you there's nowhere to go? Take heart. Keep looking up — it's always open at the top! — Joanie Yoder

*When life's afflictions batter you*
*Like waves upon the sand,*
*Remember to look up to God*
*And take His outstretched hand.* — Sper

**To improve your outlook, try the uplook.**

February 19

## "UNSUNG"

READ:
Romans 16:1-16

She has been
a helper of many,
and of myself also.
—Romans 16:2

THE BIBLE IN ONE YEAR:
■ Leviticus 25
■ Mark 1:23-45

James Deitz has produced paintings of airplanes and their crews that are so realistic they look like photographs. His works hang in many aviation galleries in the United States, including the Smithsonian Institution.

One of the paintings by Deitz, titled *Unsung*, depicts a crew of four mechanics who are working on a dive bomber. They are far below the flight deck of an aircraft carrier somewhere in the Pacific during World War II. The pale, serious-looking, grease-stained men are working tirelessly to get the plane ready to go back into battle.

We too may be performing unnoticed tasks as we support the church's mandate to spread the gospel and train believers. Without many volunteers, no church or mission agency could do its ministry effectively.

As the apostle Paul closed his letter to the believers in Rome, he listed several people who receive no other mention in Scripture. For example, Paul referred to Phoebe and said that she was "a helper of many" (16:2). Phoebe and the others were essential to the life and work of the early church.

Are you working "below the flight deck"? Remember, your service for Christ is essential. Even if no one shows appreciation for your hard work, you can be sure that one day the Lord will reward you (Colossians 3:23-24). — Dave Egner

*Our works of service in Christ's name*
*May not be noticed by our peers;*
*But what we've done in love for Him*
*Will be revealed when He appears.* — Sper

**No service for Christ goes unnoticed by Him.**

# AMAZING!

**READ:**
Mark 2:1-12

---

All were amazed
and glorified God.
—Mark 2:12

---

**THE BIBLE IN ONE YEAR:**
- Leviticus 26–27
- Mark 2

When Jesus healed a paralytic as proof of His authority to forgive the man's sins, the people who witnessed the event were amazed, and they "glorified God, saying, 'We never saw anything like this!'" (Mark 2:12). More than a dozen times in the gospel of Mark, we read accounts of people reacting in a similar way to the words and works of Jesus.

The word translated as "amazed" or "astonished" carries the meaning of "being thrown into a state of surprise or fear, or both." We may sometimes feel that way when we encounter Jesus Christ as we read God's Word. Like the disciples, we may be amazed when we read of Jesus saying, "How hard it is for those who have riches to enter the kingdom of God!" (10:23). So often we think that having lots of money would solve all our problems.

Those who saw a man delivered from a legion of demons reacted with amazement (v.20). But why? Did they think he was beyond God's power to save? Do we feel the same way when God saves certain people?

Jesus is not bound by our limitations or expectations. He speaks and acts with authority and wisdom far beyond ours. With reverence and awe, let's hear Jesus' words and look for the transforming touch of His mighty hand. — David McCasland

*I bow, O Lord, before Your throne*
*In awed humility*
*When I reflect on who You are*
*And all You've done for me.* —Sper

---

**Never measure God's unlimited power
by your limited expectations.**

# HOW WOULD YOU ANSWER?

READ:
1 Thessalonians 4:13-18

The Lord Himself will descend from heaven with a shout . . . .
And the dead in Christ will rise first.
—1 Thessalonians 4:16

THE BIBLE IN ONE YEAR:
■ Numbers 1–3
■ Mark 3

Sir Norman Anderson was invited to give a television talk on the evidence for Christ's resurrection, a subject that he had written much about. When his son died of cancer, the program producers offered to cancel his participation, saying, "You can't speak about the resurrection when you've just lost a son." But Anderson said, "I want to speak about it now even more." And so, sad in heart but with great assurance, he spoke of Christ's resurrection, and ours as believers.

The resurrection of Jesus is no myth — it's a historical, well-attested fact. Indeed, it's an eternal fact! Jesus declared, "I am He who lives, and was dead, and behold, I am alive forevermore" (Revelation 1:18).

Jesus spoke to His disciples about His own resurrection and reassured them, "Because I live, you will live also" (John 14:19). And Paul wrote of the Christian's resurrection, teaching that when a fellow believer dies we don't need to sorrow as those who have no hope (1 Thessalonians 4:13).

When Lazarus died, Jesus assured Martha that whoever believes in Him, though he dies, shall live again (John 11:25-26). He then asked, "Do you believe this?" Martha replied, "Yes, Lord, I believe that You are the Christ, the Son of God" (v.27). How would you answer? — Joanie Yoder

*All flesh, as grass, shall pass away*
*From this vile world of sin and strife;*
*The one who sleeps in Christ today*
*Will wake to resurrected life.* — Benson

**Christ's resurrection is the guarantee of our own.**

# GARDENING TIPS

READ:
Mark 4:1-9

These are the ones sown on good ground, those who hear the Word, accept it, and bear fruit.
—Mark 4:20

THE BIBLE IN ONE YEAR:
■ Numbers 4–6
■ Mark 4:1-20

I picked up a gardening book the other day and got some good advice: "Take care of the soil, and don't worry about the plants. If the soil is good, the seed will take root and grow."

In the parable of the sower in Mark 4, Jesus spoke of the importance of "good ground" (or good soil). He defined good soil as referring to those who "hear" God's Word, "accept it," and "bear fruit" (v.20). If we keep our heart soft and receptive, God's Word will take root, grow, and produce fruit.

In gardening, life is in the seed. Under the right conditions, it will grow until it reaches maturity and produces fruit. Similarly, if the seed of the Word is planted in the good soil of a receptive heart, it will grow until the character of Jesus is seen.

For the Christian, the power of the spiritual life comes from the indwelling Holy Spirit. As we open our heart to the Word with an eagerness to obey it, the Spirit causes us to grow and bear fruit (Galatians 5:22-23).

We can't make ourselves grow, any more than we can force growth from the seeds in our gardens. But we can tend the soil, keeping our hearts soft, receptive, and obedient to God's Word. Then we will yield the fruit of righteousness.

What kind of soil are you?   — David Roper

*Lord, I would be soil in which You can plant*
*Your Word with its promise of fruit;*
*I want to be open to You every day,*
*So what You have planted takes root.*   — Hess

---

**A heart open to God is soil in which**
**the seed of His Word can flourish.**

February 23

## SUBMISSIVE LEADERSHIP

READ:
2 Chronicles 10

---

. . . submitting to one another in the fear of God.
—Ephesians 5:21

---

THE BIBLE IN ONE YEAR:
■ Numbers 7–8
■ Mark 4:21-41

A mild-mannered man was reading a book on being self-assertive and decided to start at home. So he stormed into his house, pointed a finger in his wife's face, and said, "From now on I'm boss around here and my word is law! I want you to prepare me a gourmet meal and draw my bath. Then, when I've eaten and finished my bath, guess who's going to dress me and comb my hair." "The mortician," replied his wife.

King Rehoboam tried that kind of self-assertiveness and it turned Israel against him. When he came to the throne, the people pleaded for less oppressive taxation. His older advisors urged him to heed their request, but his young friends told him to be even more demanding than his father. As a result of listening to his peers, 10 of the 12 tribes of Israel seceded and formed a new kingdom (2 Chronicles 10:16-17).

Good leaders don't rely on domineering self-assertion — not at home, nor in church, nor in business. Rather, they balance self-assertiveness (which isn't wrong in itself) with the principle of submitting to one another (Ephesians 5:21). They listen respectfully, admit when they're wrong, show a willingness to change, and mix gentleness with firmness. That's submissive leadership — and it works! — Herb Vander Lugt

*Submissive leadership requires*
*A kind and gentle honesty*
*That will attend to others' needs*
*And win their love and loyalty.* — D. De Haan

---

**The only leaders qualified to lead
are those who have learned to serve.**

# A MYSTERIOUS EQUATION

READ:
Colossians 1:9-18

---

God demonstrates His own love toward us, in that while we were still sinners, Christ died for us. —Romans 5:8

---

THE BIBLE IN ONE YEAR:
■ Numbers 9–11
■ Mark 5:1-20

Professor John Nash of Princeton University is a math genius who has spent his life in the abstract world of numbers, equations—and delusions. Nash suffers from schizophrenia, a mental illness that can result in bizarre behavior and broken relationships. With medical help and the love of his wife, he learned to live with his illness and later won the Nobel Prize.

In the movie version of his life, Nash said: "I've always believed in numbers and the equations and logics that lead to reason. . . . My quest has taken me through the physical, the metaphysical, the delusional, and back. And I've made the most important discovery of my life. It's only in the mysterious equations of love that any logical reasons can be framed."

In Colossians 1, we read of "the mysterious equation of love" at its deepest level—God's love for us in Christ. Jesus is the image of the invisible God, and out of love He has created us and sustains us (vv.16-17). He has also provided deliverance from the powers of darkness (v.13) and the forgiveness of our sins (v.14). No wonder Paul said that such love "passes knowledge" (Ephesians 3:19). It takes us beyond logic into the very heart of who God is (1 John 4:16).

We are to live and show that love—always. —Dennis De Haan

*FOR FURTHER STUDY*
*How do we experience the love of Christ? (John 15:10).*
*What is the evidence of God's love in our lives?*
*(1 John 4:16-21). How can you show God's love today?*

---

**God's love cannot be explained—
it can only be experienced.**

# GRAFFITI

READ:
Luke 12:13-21

One's life does not consist in the abundance of the things he possesses.
—Luke 12:15

THE BIBLE IN ONE YEAR:
■ Numbers 12–14
■ Mark 5:21-43

Pastor and evangelist E. V. Hill went home to be with his Lord and Savior on February 25, 2003. He was much sought after as a conference speaker, and few have gained the attention and respect of people from all levels of society as he did.

Many years ago, Pastor Hill was invited to speak in a suburban church of a large southern city in the United States. In the introduction to his message, Pastor Hill commented on the difference between the affluent suburb and the poor urban area where he ministered. "I know what's missing," he said. "You folks don't have any graffiti anywhere. I'd like to volunteer to provide some for you. I'll get a bucket of paint and walk through your neighborhood, writing this one word on your million-dollar homes and expensive European cars: *temporary*. That's it — temporary. None of it will last."

We enjoy and take care of what we have, and that's as it should be. But Jesus said we shouldn't be possessed by our possessions, for they won't last into eternity (Luke 12:15-21). A house is just a box in which to stay warm and dry; a car is a way to get us from one place to another. Since we can't take them with us when we die, we're far better off to view them as E. V. Hill did — temporary.  — Dave Egner

*The riches of this world are vain,*
*They vanish in a day;*
*But sweet the treasures of God's love —*
*They never pass away.*  — Bosch

**The real measure of our wealth is
what will be ours in eternity.**

# IDOLS OF THE HEART

**READ:**
1 Corinthians 10:1-14

---

My beloved, flee
from idolatry.
—1 Corinthians 10:14

---

THE BIBLE IN ONE YEAR:
■ Numbers 15–16
■ Mark 6:1-29

In Old Testament times, idolatry was easy to recognize — dancing around the golden calves, bowing before the Baals. Even when the apostle Paul wrote to followers of Christ in first-century Corinth, pagan idolatry was openly practiced. He warned them to avoid any association with it (1 Corinthians 10:14).

Idolatry is still a danger to the people of God, though it isn't always so open or obvious. Idols are usually more subtle and hard to detect, for they set up their home in the hidden places of our heart.

If we want to know our idols, we need to consider our predominant thoughts, for what we think about most of the time may be an idol. Our last thought before we sleep, our first thought when we awake, our reveries throughout the day, are spent on the items and issues we treasure and trust. Any possession or person we put our hope in to bring us fulfillment, any goal or aspiration that becomes more important to us than God — these are the "gods" that attract our allegiance and subtly control our lives.

Only God can satisfy the deepest needs of our heart and make us truly alive. That's why we would be wise to heed the loving counsel of the apostle Paul: "My beloved, flee from idolatry." — David Roper

> *The dearest idol I have known,*
> *Whate'er that idol be,*
> *Help me tear it from Thy throne*
> *And worship only Thee.* — Cowper

---

**An idol is anything that takes
the place of God.**

# A GOOD NEIGHBOR

READ:
Luke 10:25-37

---

Which of these three do you think was neighbor to him who fell among the thieves?
—Luke 10:36

---

THE BIBLE IN ONE YEAR:
■ Numbers 17–19
■ Mark 6:30-56

When Fred Rogers died February 27, 2003, scores of newspapers carried the story as front-page news, and almost every headline included the word *neighbor*. As host of the long-running children's television show *Mr. Rogers' Neighborhood,* he was well known to millions of children and their parents as a kind, gentle, warm person who genuinely believed "each person is special, deep inside, just the way they are."

Mr. Rogers once told a journalist: "When we look at our neighbor with appreciative eyes, . . . with gratitude for who that person truly is, then I feel we are arm in arm with Christ Jesus, the advocate of eternal good." Because Rogers recognized the value of each person, he believed in being a good neighbor to all.

When Jesus was asked, "Who is my neighbor?" He told the parable of the Good Samaritan (Luke 10:29-35). At the conclusion of this story, the Lord asked, "Which of these three do you think was neighbor to him who fell among the thieves?" The answer? "He who showed mercy on him" (vv.36-37).

Who in our "neighborhood" needs a kind word, an arm of friendship, or an act of encouragement today? Jesus calls us to show love and compassion to others as we love God with all our heart, and our neighbor as ourselves. — David McCasland

*How many lives shall I touch today?*
*How many neighbors will pass my way?*
*I can bless so many and help so much*
*If I meet each one with a Christlike touch.* — Jones

---

**Your love for your neighbor
is proof of your love for God.**

# OLD SKINFLINT

**READ:**
1 Timothy 6:17-19

---

For God so loved the world that He gave His only begotten Son, that whoever believes in Him should not perish but have everlasting life. —John 3:16

---

THE BIBLE IN ONE YEAR:
■ Numbers 20–22
■ Mark 7:1-13

Some people will do anything to save a buck. Like the miserly uncle I read about who invited his nephews to hunt for arrowheads in the field behind his house. Before the search could begin, however, he told the excited youngsters they had to move all the rocks out of the field and clear away the underbrush. By the time they were finished, it was too late to search for arrowheads. Later, they learned that none had ever been found on his property. When they complained to their dad, he said, "My old skinflint brother bamboozled you out of a day's work." Those boys will not soon forget how they were taken advantage of.

There's nothing wrong with being frugal. It's a matter of good steward-ship. But there is something wrong with being so thrifty that you won't pay a boy what he's worth.

Stinginess at the cost of someone else's humiliation or hurt is not what our Lord wants. In 1 Timothy 6:18, we learn that we're to "do good" and be "ready to give, willing to share." We're to be fair, giving, and generous people.

God is the ultimate giver. He gave His Son, at unbeliev-able sacrifice, to offer us new life (John 3:16). Let's follow His example of love and generosity — then we won't be accused of being an "old skinflint."  — Dave Egner

*One grace each child of God can show*
*Is giving from a willing heart;*
*Yet, if we wait till riches grow,*
*It well may be we'll never start.*  — D. De Haan

---

**Because God gives us all we need,
let's give to others in their need.**

## STRENGTH FOR TODAY

READ:
Philippians 4:8-13

I can do all things
through Christ who
strengthens me.
—Philippians 4:13

THE BIBLE IN ONE YEAR:
■ Numbers 23–25
■ Mark 7:14-37

M ost people own a calendar or an appointment book in which they record details of future commitments. A Christian friend of mine uses one in the opposite way. He doesn't record key activities until *after* they've taken place.

Here's his approach: Each morning he prays, "Lord, I go forth in Your strength alone. Please use me as You wish." Then, whenever he accomplishes something unusual or difficult, he records it in his diary in the evening.

For example, he may write, "Today I was enabled to share my testimony with a friend." "Today God enabled me to overcome my fear through faith." "Today I was enabled to help and encourage a troubled person."

My friend uses the word *enabled* because he knows he couldn't do these things without God's help. By recording each "enabling," he is giving God all the glory. Relying constantly on God's strength, he can testify with the apostle Paul, "I can do all things through Christ who strengthens me" (Philippians 4:13).

As you enter each new day, ask God to strengthen and use you. You can be sure that as you look back on your day, you'll praise and glorify the Lord as you realize what He has enabled you to do. — Joanie Yoder

> Lord, give me strength for this day's task,
> Not for tomorrow would I ask;
> At twilight hour, oh, may I say,
> "The Lord has been my guide today." — Nillingham

**God always gives enough strength for the next step.**

# GOING OUT & COMING IN

**READ:**
**Numbers 27:15-23**

At his word they shall go out, and at his word they shall come in.
—Numbers 27:21

THE BIBLE IN ONE YEAR:
■ Numbers 26–27
■ Mark 8:1-21

The phrase "at his word" is used twice in Numbers 27:21 to emphasize how God would guide Israel. Joshua was to direct Israel to "go out" and "come in" based on what God told Eleazer the priest.

How often do we make a decision to go somewhere or do something based on our pride, personal ambition, or merely to keep busy? How often do we go only because someone we long to please asked us to go, rather than because we want to please the Lord? When we "go out" to pursue our own desires instead of following God's leading, we will be frustrated in our efforts and left empty and disappointed.

But when we go out at the Lord's prompting and direction, "at His word," He is responsible for the outcome. The result will be fruitful labor, whether we know it or not.

The time to "come in" is also ordered by the Lord. There are times to retreat — to pray, to fill our hearts with His Word, to rest our bodies.

We must come daily before our great High Priest, the Lord Jesus, and receive His instruction. If we bow before Him and ask for His guidance, He will help us to know what to do and when to do it. — David Roper

*We need to take the time each day*
*To read God's Word and pray,*
*And listen for what He might say*
*To guide us on our way.* — Sper

**You can't go wrong if you follow God's lead.**

# UNEXPECTED KINDNESS

READ:
1 Samuel 26:1-25

If your enemy is hungry, feed him; if he is thirsty, give him a drink. —Romans 12:20

THE BIBLE IN ONE YEAR:
■ Numbers 28-30
■ Mark 8:22-38

A missionary was teaching a class of young girls about kindness. She told them about Jesus, who said that a person who gives a cup of water in His name "will by no means lose his reward" (Mark 9:41).

The next day the missionary watched as a group of weary men walked into the village square, removed their heavy backpacks, and sat down to rest. A few minutes later, several little girls shyly approached the surprised men and gave them all a drink. Then they ran to the missionary. "Teacher!" they shouted. "We gave those men a drink in Jesus' name."

Although Mark 9:41 applies primarily to showing kindness to believers in Christ, we know that we are to "do good to all" (Galatians 6:10) and even give our enemy a drink (Romans 12:20).

In today's Bible reading, David had the chance for revenge against King Saul (1 Samuel 26:9). But because David revered God, he showed kindness to the king.

Showing unexpected kindness to strangers or enemies will not always change their hearts. But sooner or later someone will wonder why we were kind, and we will have an opportunity to tell about our Lord, who was kind even to His enemies (Romans 5:10). — Herb Vander Lugt

*Do a deed of simple kindness,*
*Though its end you may not see;*
*It may reach, like widening ripples,*
*Down a long eternity.* — Norris

**One act of kindness may teach more
about the love of God than many sermons.**

# HAPPY ADVERSITY?

**READ:**
James 1:1-12

---

Count it all joy when you fall into various trials. —James 1:2

---

THE BIBLE IN ONE YEAR:
- Numbers 31–33
- Mark 9:1-29

On the back of a wedding anniversary card were some wiggly lines drawn by our 3-year-old grandson. Alongside was a note from our daughter explaining that Trevor told her what he had written: "I'm writing a letter for your love and happy adversity."

Trevor's "mistake" has become our watchword, because "happy adversity" embodies the biblical principle of facing difficulties with joy: "Count it all joy when you fall into various trials, knowing that the testing of your faith produces patience" (James 1:2-3).

From our perspective, adversity is anything but happy. We have the idea that the Christian life is supposed to be trouble-free, and we see little value in hardship. But God sees it differently.

J. B. Phillips' translation of James 1:2-3 reads: "When all kinds of trials and temptations crowd into your lives, my brothers, don't resent them as intruders, but welcome them as friends! Realize that they come to test your faith and to produce in you the quality of endurance."

Affliction does not come as a thief to steal our happiness, but as a friend bringing the gift of staying power. Through it all, God promises us His wisdom and strength.

So don't be offended if I wish you "Happy Adversity" today. — David McCasland

> Be assured beyond all doubting,
> In the trial you're passing through,
> That the Lord's great love and mercy
> Is at work for good in you. — Anon.

---

**Life's burdens are designed not to break us
but to bend us toward God.**

# PRESSURING GOD

**READ:**
**Matthew 26:36-46**

O My Father, if this cup cannot pass away from Me unless I drink it, Your will be done.
—Matthew 26:42

THE BIBLE IN ONE YEAR:
■ Numbers 34–36
■ Mark 9:30-50

Under General George Patton's command in World War II, the Third Army had been driving back the Nazis until fog and rain forced the troops to stop. Patton telephoned a chaplain to ask, "Do you have a good prayer for weather?" Immediately the chaplain complied with the general's request. He wrote a prayer, which Patton ordered to be printed and distributed to the 250,000 soldiers under his command, directing them to pray for clear weather.

The Scriptures teach us that God wants us to bring our requests to Him, and we can be confident that He cares and will answer (Philippians 4:6; 1 John 5:14-15). But He is never obligated to answer in the way we want or just because many people are praying.

When the Son of God was agonizing in Gethsemane, He made His request in humble submission to His Father by saying, "Your will be done" (Matthew 26:42). That Gethsemane principle ought to govern all our praying.

The Father's will is always infused with infinite love and wisdom. So instead of trying to pressure God because we think He's obligated to us, we as trustful children gladly commit to Him our desires. Whatever He grants will prove in the end to be the best of blessings. — Vernon Grounds

*So lift up your heart to the heavens;*
*There's a loving and kind Father there*
*Who offers release and comfort and peace*
*In the silent communion of prayer.* — Anon.

---

**Instead of trying to twist God's arm,**
**put yourself in His hands.**

# A WASTED LIFE

READ:
Ephesians 4:17-29

You should no longer
walk as the rest of the
Gentiles walk, in the
futility of their mind.
—Ephesians 4:17

THE BIBLE IN ONE YEAR:
■ Deuteronomy 1–2
■ Mark 10:1-31

It's frustrating to talk to some people about God, Jesus, and salvation. They shrug you off by saying, "You have your belief and I have mine." Or, "I won't tell you how to live if you won't tell me how to live."

How do we respond to that? By telling them and showing them that our belief in Christ makes sense. It gives life meaning now and for eternity.

In the book *Papillon,* the main character dreams that he is on trial. The judge says he is being charged with the most terrible crime that a person can possibly commit. When Papillon asks what it is, he is told, "The tragedy of a wasted life." "Guilty!" says Papillon, weeping. "Guilty."

There are people all around us whose lives have no meaning or hope. They're caught in the web of sin, living "in the futility of their mind" (Ephesians 4:17). Our role, as followers of the Lord Jesus, is to demonstrate that the life of faith does make sense. In the midst of a world of aimlessness and despair, we are to live with purpose and hope.

When we show people the difference Jesus has made in our lives, they will see that life can have meaning and purpose. Then, if they turn to Jesus, they too will avoid the tragedy of a wasted life.  — Dave Egner

*People searching for an answer,*
*Looking for a better way,*
*Can discover truth and meaning*
*If God's love we will display.*  — Sper

**A Christlike life can be the world's Bible.**

# BEHIND THE THRONE

READ:
Esther 1

---

[God] changes the times and the seasons; He removes kings and raises up kings.
—Daniel 2:21

---

THE BIBLE IN ONE YEAR:
■ Deuteronomy 3–4
■ Mark 10:32-52

During my lifetime I have seen evil men rise to political and military power, make colossal blunders, and pass off the scene. Even good leaders leave a record that includes mistakes and weaknesses.

The first chapter of Esther shows us the pride of King Ahasuerus, head of the mighty Persian Empire. He hosted an elaborate festival designed to display his riches and splendor. After 7 days of partying, the king gave orders to his servants to bring Vashti, his queen, before the revelers so they could see her great beauty. But Queen Vashti refused to come, humiliating the great king of Persia (vv.12-18).

Ahasuerus was furious and sought counsel from the wise men of his kingdom. They advised him to remove Vashti as queen and "give her royal position to another who is better than she" (v.19). God used these unusual events to place a Jewish girl in a strategic position to preserve His people from destruction.

God's name is not mentioned in the entire book of Esther, but the message in chapter 1 comes through loud and clear: God can bring good out of everything, even when flawed and mistake-prone humans are involved. He is the real power behind the throne. — Herb Vander Lugt

*We comprehend Him not,*
*Yet earth and heaven tell,*
*God sits as sovereign on the throne,*
*And ruleth all things well.* — Gerhardt

---

**The most powerful ruler is but a pawn in the hand of the King of kings.**

# TOO MUCH AMBITION

READ:
Mark 10:35-45

The Son of Man did not come to be served, but to serve, and to give His life a ransom for many. —Mark 10:45

THE BIBLE IN ONE YEAR:
■ Deuteronomy 5–7
■ Mark 11:1-18

If you are familiar with the works of William Shakespeare, you know that Macbeth was one of his characters. Macbeth wanted so much to be king that he resorted to murder — and he paid for it with his life.

We are like that tragic character when we let our ambitions cloud our thinking and forget who is really in control of our lives. We don't use evil methods to achieve our goal, but we do allow ambition to cloud our thinking about the sovereignty of God. Instead of leaving matters in His hands, we take them into our own.

Another example of too much ambition is found in the conversation James and John had with Jesus in Mark 10. Their goal was to sit in the positions of greatest prestige and power in the kingdom. And because they weren't content to wait and see if Jesus would bestow that honor on them, they boldly requested it. They were too impatient to leave the whole matter in His hands.

Ambition is not always wrong. But when it consumes us so that we can't wait for God, we display a lack of faith as the disciples did.

When we submit our goals and desires to the Lord, we can be sure that He will give us what is best. — Dave Branon

*Lord, grant us now the grace to wait,*
*To trust alone in You,*
*Lest we set goals outside Your will*
*That we with zeal pursue.* — Anon.

---

**Be ambitious for the Lord,
but be cautious about your motives.**

# MONEY AND TIME

READ:
Mark 12:13-17,28-31

---

Render to Caesar the things that are Caesar's, and to God the things that are God's.
—Mark 12:17

---

THE BIBLE IN ONE YEAR:
■ Deuteronomy 8–10
■ Mark 11:19-33

During a trip to London, I visited the Bank of England Museum, then made my way to The Clockmakers' Museum. At some point, it struck me that both money and time have been very important commodities as far back as anyone can remember. Yet they present one of the great dilemmas of life. We trade our valuable time working for money, and then we spend our money to make the most of our time off. We seldom possess the two with any degree of balance.

In contrast, our Lord never seemed perplexed by money or time. When asked if it was lawful to pay taxes to Caesar, Jesus answered: "Render to Caesar the things that are Caesar's, and to God the things that are God's" (Mark 12:17). With great demands on His time, Jesus spent early mornings and late nights in prayer, seeking to know and do His Father's will.

Hymnwriter Frances Havergal wrote:

*Take my life, and let it be*
*Consecrated, Lord, to Thee;*
*Take my moments and my days,*
*Let them flow in ceaseless praise.*
*Take my silver and my gold,*
*Not a mite would I withhold;*
*Take my intellect and use*
*Every power as Thou shalt choose.*

We can properly balance time and money when we offer ourselves without reservation to God. —David McCasland

---

**Spend time and money wisely—**
**they both belong to God.**

# THE HIDING PLACE

**READ:**
**Psalm 34:4-8**

---

Oh, taste and see that the LORD is good; blessed is the man who trusts in Him!
—Psalm 34:8

---

THE BIBLE IN ONE YEAR:
■ Deuteronomy 11–13
■ Mark 12:1-27

In this world's misery there is only one sure refuge: God Himself. "He is a shield to all who trust in Him" (Psalm 18:30).

To "trust in" comes from a Hebrew word that means "to take refuge in" or "to hide in" or "to hide with." It suggests a secret place of concealment, a "hidey hole," as we used to say in Texas.

When we're exhausted by our efforts, when we're bewildered by our problems, when we're wounded by our friends, when we're surrounded by our foes, we can hide ourselves in God. There is no safety in this world. If we were to find safety here, we would never know the joy of God's love and protection. We would miss the happiness for which we were made.

The only safe place is God Himself. When storm clouds gather and calamities loom, we must run into His presence in prayer and remain there (Psalm 57:1).

George MacDonald said, "That man is perfect in faith who can come to God in the utter dearth of his feelings and desires, without a glow or an aspiration, with the weight of low thoughts, failures, neglects, and wandering forgetfulness, and say to Him, 'Thou art my refuge.'"

How safe and blessed we are! — David Roper

*O the sweet unfailing refuge*
*Of the everlasting arms;*
*In their loving clasp enfolded,*
*Nothing worries or alarms.* —Hennessay

---

**Safety is not found in the absence of danger**
**but in the presence of God.**

# THE BEACON

READ:
Mark 6:45-52

He came to them,
walking on the sea.
—Mark 6:48

THE BIBLE IN ONE YEAR:
■ Deuteronomy 14–16
■ Mark 12:28-44

When a helicopter crashed in a cold, mountainous wilderness, the pilots survived but were seriously injured. The frozen afternoon stretched toward an even more freezing night. The situation seemed hopeless — until a rescue helicopter appeared, its searchlights illuminating the darkness. It spotted the wreckage, landed nearby, and carried them off to safety.

"How did you know where we were?" an injured man asked.

"The homing device on your aircraft," the rescuers told him. "It went off automatically when you went down. All we had to do was follow it."

The disciples of Jesus also experienced the joy of being rescued. They had been struggling as they rowed their boat against wind and waves in the darkness of night on the Sea of Galilee (Mark 6:45-47). Then Jesus came to them, walking on the water, and calmed the sea (vv.48-51).

We may experience similar times when all is dark and foreboding. We can't help ourselves, and it seems that no one else can either. No one knows how terrified and exhausted we are. No one, that is, except Jesus.

When we're trapped, hurt, lonely, or discouraged, Jesus knows it. Our cries of grief are beacons that bring Him to our side — right when we need Him most.  — Dave Egner

*There is only One who knows*
*All the answers to my woes;*
*He will all my needs supply*
*When in faith to Him I cry.*  — Morgan

**Jesus hears even the faintest cry for help.**

# ONLY ONE OPTION

**READ:**
**Habakkuk 1:1–2:4**

---

Behold the proud, his soul is not upright in him; but the just shall live by his faith.
—Habakkuk 2:4

---

THE BIBLE IN ONE YEAR:
■ Deuteronomy 17–19
■ Mark 13:1-20

If you were to ask several people to draw a crooked line on a piece of paper, no two lines would be identical. There is a lesson in this: There are many ways to be crooked, but only one way to be straight.

The Lord tells us that the righteous person has only one option — to "live by his faith" (Habakkuk 2:4). In the chapter prior to this declaration from the Lord, the prophet Habakkuk had complained about the violence and injustice around him. It seemed as if the wicked were swallowing up the righteous (1:13).

God responded to Habakkuk by saying that His people were to be "just" and were to live by faith. They were not to be like the one who is "proud" and "not upright" (2:4). A proud and self-sufficient person will rationalize his faults and imperfections. He doesn't want to admit that he needs God. His ways are crooked.

Wickedness seems to prevail in our world. God urges us to live our lives in faith, taking to heart His assurance to Habakkuk that there will be a day of reckoning for the wicked.

The only way to please God now and to be ready for that day of reckoning is to live by faith. — Albert Lee

> *Lord, grant me grace throughout this day*
> *To walk the straight and narrow way,*
> *To do whatever in Thy sight*
> *Is good and perfect, just and right.* — *Huisman*

---

**The only right way is the straight and narrow way.**

## MESSAGE FOR ALL SEASONS

READ:
Acts 5:31-42

Lift up your eyes and look at the fields, for they are already white for harvest!
—John 4:35

THE BIBLE IN ONE YEAR:
■ Deuteronomy 20–22
■ Mark 13:21-37

I'm a novice at growing flowers. But I've learned to appreciate the difference between annuals and perennials. Every spring I usually buy trays of annual bedding plants. Once in the ground, they immediately take root. Their brief life always ends with the autumn frosts, and the soil lies barren until my next annual spring planting. I prefer to plant perennial flowers. They go on living from year to year, and regularly bloom, flower, and reproduce.

Writer Eugene Harrison describes the evangelistic efforts of New Testament believers as "perennial" in nature. They didn't pour all their energies into once-a-year evangelistic efforts. Instead, according to Harrison, sharing the good news of Christ was "the supreme concern of every believer, every day in the year, in every place." In Acts 5:42 and 8:4, the scope of their witness is clear: They shared Christ and the gospel in the temple, in their homes, and in the marketplace, using the Spirit-given methods of preaching, teaching, and personal testimony.

Jesus taught that the season for spiritual harvest is always *today* (John 4:35). And the apostle Paul said that "now is the day of salvation" (2 Corinthians 6:2).

Be assured, there's never a time when the harvest is out of season. The fields are white today. — Joanie Yoder

*Help us, Lord, to be a lifeline*
*To a dying world today,*
*Bringing hope to hopeless people*
*As we share salvation's way.* — Sper

**Witnessing for Christ is never out of season.**

# Costly Consequences

**READ:**
**1 Samuel 13:1-15**

---

You have not kept the commandment of the LORD . . . . Now your kingdom shall not continue.
—1 Samuel 13:13-14

---

THE BIBLE IN ONE YEAR:
■ Deuteronomy 23–25
■ Mark 14:1-26

I always knew that disobedience has consequences, but it came home to me forcibly in basic training during World War II. I had traveled beyond the distance allowed on my weekend pass to be with my wife Ginny, and I returned to camp late because the train had broken down. I paid for my rule-breaking — 20 hours of extra duty washing pots and pans!

King Saul also learned the high cost of disobedience. He faced the prospect of fighting a huge well-equipped Philistine army with his small band of frightened and untrained followers. While waiting for Samuel to come and offer a sacrifice before going to battle, Saul became impatient and offered the sacrifice himself, even though he knew that God had given that right only to the priests. It was a costly mistake.

Saul had begun his reign with humility and compassion, and he gave God the credit (1 Samuel 11). And the prophet Samuel told him that God would have kept the kingship in his family if he had obeyed God's command (13:13-14). But that one act of disobedience changed the course of his life. From that point on, it was a sad downhill journey.

Never forget that disobedience has consequences. And some of them may be very costly. — Herb Vander Lugt

*O help me, Lord, to be afraid*
*Of disobedient ways;*
*And may I seek what pleases You,*
*What gives You highest praise.* — Sper

---

**The way of obedience is the only way of blessing.**

# HEALTHCARE FOR THE HEART

READ:
Proverbs 4:20-27

Keep your heart with all diligence, for out of it spring the issues of life. —Proverbs 4:23

THE BIBLE IN ONE YEAR:
■ Deuteronomy 26–27
■ Mark 14:27-53

If you're over 40 years old, your heart has already beat more than 1.5 billion times. I know that when my heart stops, it will be too late to change my ways. So I've been trying to control my weight, get exercise, and watch not only what I eat but also what's eating me.

This last point relates to another vital organ called "the heart"—our spiritual heart. It too has throbbed millions of times with thoughts, affections, and choices. In the heart we determine how we will speak, behave, and respond to life's circumstances (Proverbs 4:23). Will we trust the Lord and choose to be gracious, patient, and loving? Or will we yield to pride, greed, and bitterness?

Today's Scripture reading emphasizes the importance of caring for our heart. Are we keeping spiritually fit?

- **Weight:** Do we need to lose the weight of unnecessary burdens and cares?
- **Pulse:** Are we maintaining a steady rhythm of gratitude and praise?
- **Blood pressure:** Is our trust greater than our anxiety?
- **Diet:** Are we enjoying the life-giving nutrients of the Word of God?

Have you checked your heart lately? — Mart De Haan

*O Lord, You see what's in the heart—*
*There's nothing hid from You;*
*So help us live the kind of life*
*That's filled with love for You.* — D. De Haan

**To keep spiritually fit, consult the Great Physician.**

# SEEK AND YOU WILL FIND

**READ:**
**Proverbs 2:1-6**

If you seek her as silver,
and search for her as
for hidden treasures;
then you will . . . find
the knowledge of God.
—Proverbs 2:4-5

THE BIBLE IN ONE YEAR:
■ Deuteronomy 28–29
■ Mark 14:54-72

Justin Martyr was a second-century man who eagerly sought for truth. He read the Greek classical writers, examining and analyzing every philosophy from all sides. He sought insight, especially the answer to his longings for sexual purity. But every effort was in vain. He wrote, "All at last did faithless prove, and late or soon betrayed love."

One day, aimlessly wandering on the seashore, he met an elderly man who spoke to his heart as no one had ever spoken before. He pointed him to God through Jesus Christ, and in that simple witness Justin found the knowledge he had sought all his life — "the knowledge of God" (Proverbs 2:4-5).

Perhaps you, like Justin Martyr, are searching for insight, looking everywhere for the answer to your longing for truth. You've read widely and thought earnestly about life, but you can find no answers that satisfy the deep needs of your soul. If so, read the Gospels, the first four books of the New Testament. As you read, cry out to God for understanding. He will hear you, and you too will find the knowledge of God through Jesus Christ (John 17:3).

God doesn't force truth on those who don't want it, but He hears the earnest cries of those who request it. As Jesus said, "Ask, and you will receive" (John 16:24). — David Roper

*Look not to reason's arguments*
*If God you seek to find;*
*Look only to His holy Word,*
*For sin has made us blind.* —D. De Haan

---

**To find truth, look to Christ.**

# LIFE'S SEASONS

READ:
Psalm 71:1-21

---

By You I have been
upheld from birth . . . .
My praise shall be
continually of You.
—Psalm 71:6

---

THE BIBLE IN ONE YEAR:
■ Deuteronomy 30–31
■ Mark 15:1-25

When we are young, we can't wait to grow up. When we are old, we look back longingly to former years. But God intends that we joyfully take each season of life as it comes. Whatever our age, He imparts what we need to be all that we can be. He asks us to commit our way to Him and accept the struggles He allows and the strength He provides.

A woman who was facing the difficulties of aging asked Bible teacher J. Robertson McQuilkin, "Why does God let us get old and weak?" McQuilkin replied, "I think God has planned the strength and beauty of youth to be physical. But the strength and beauty of old age is spiritual. We gradually lose the strength and beauty that is temporary so we'll be sure to concentrate on the strength and beauty that is forever. And so we'll be eager to leave the temporary, deteriorating part of us and be truly homesick for our eternal home. If we stayed young and strong and beautiful, we might never want to leave."

Are you in life's springtime? Trust God's timing to fulfill your dreams. Are you in life's summer or autumn? Face your daily challenges head-on. And if you feel winter's chill, draw close to the Lord. His presence can make every season of life one of strength and beauty. —Dennis De Haan

*Only this hour is mine, Lord —*
*May it be used for Thee;*
*May every passing moment*
*Count for eternity.* — Christiansen

---

**Whatever the season of life,
attitude makes all the difference.**

# FRIENDS LISTEN

**READ:**
Job 13:1-9

---

Oh, that you would
be silent, and it would
be your wisdom!
—Job 13:5

---

THE BIBLE IN ONE YEAR:
■ Deuteronomy 32–34
■ Mark 15:26-47

It is about 9 in the evening. My wife Ginny and I are sitting in our living room. I'm reading a book. Suddenly she says, "Honey, I want to talk with you for a few minutes." She begins to talk—then she abruptly asks, "Are you listening?"

I'm tempted to reply, "Of course I am. I'm only 2 feet away from you." But actually my mind is still on what I'm reading. I need to close the book and give my full attention to what Ginny is saying. She deserves that from me.

Job too was frustrated because his friends weren't paying attention to what he was saying to them. He sensed that while he was talking they were planning their next response. They were bent on trying to convince him that his suffering was punishment for sin in his life. They were not listening to the deep cry of Job's heart.

Many of us are poor listeners too. Teenagers can be frustrated because their parents always have a quick answer, when actually they just want someone to listen to their struggles and accept them. One teen said, "Sometimes I would just like to talk until I know what I want to say."

Deep relationships are built on acceptance, understanding, and being a good listener. — Herb Vander Lugt

*When our friends encounter suffering,*
*We can help them if we're near;*
*Some may need a word of comfort,*
*Others just a listening ear.* —Sper

---

**Listening may be the most loving
thing you do today.**

# BUTTERFLY MAN

**READ:**
**Galatians 5:13-26**

---

Walk in the Spirit, and
you shall not fulfill the
lust of the flesh.
—Galatians 5:16

---

THE BIBLE IN ONE YEAR:
- Joshua 1–3
- Mark 16

The Internet is one of the most remarkable developments of our time. How astounding that with a few keystrokes you can find out the address of Uncle Frank in Schenectady, New York, or the recipe for a Brazilian fish dish, or the statistics for your favorite athlete.

Of course, the Internet opens up a whole world of sinful choices as well. That's why many Internet providers offer a service to protect a family's computer from sites that promote immorality. One company used a comical-looking man dressed as a butterfly to represent the service, and in an advertisement showed him shielding children from various immoral activities.

Christians already have a similar resource, and it doesn't cost us a monthly fee. It's not the butterfly man — it's the Holy Spirit, who lives in the heart of each believer. As we seek guidance from God's Word and pray, He will enable us to detect and filter out the immoral. He can help us to keep from going where we shouldn't go, doing what we shouldn't do, and saying what we shouldn't say.

The world, like the Internet, has much we need to avoid. As we daily seek to "walk in the Spirit," relying on His wisdom and power, we can stay clean. — Dave Branon

*The Spirit gives us power to live*
*A life that's pleasing to the Lord;*
*He also guides us and provides*
*Direction in God's holy Word.* —Sper

---

**The Holy Spirit is our ever-present protector.**

# LISTEN TO THE CHILDREN

**READ:**
Matthew 21:1-17

---

Have you never read, "Out of the mouth of babes and nursing infants You have perfected praise"?
—Matthew 21:16

---

THE BIBLE IN ONE YEAR:
■ Joshua 4–6
■ Luke 1:1-20

The religious leaders were wrong about Jesus as He rode into Jerusalem (Matthew 21:15-16). They couldn't have been more off-base if they had tried. True, they knew a lot of theology, but they were dead wrong about who Jesus was.

The children, however, were right. They were the ones in the temple who shouted, "Hosanna to the Son of David!" (v.15). They believed that the Person riding that unbroken colt was the promised Son of David. They fulfilled the prophecy of Psalm 8:2 by giving praise to the Lamb who was about to die for the sins of the world. It was the children who responded with wholehearted joy, even though they may not have fully understood Jesus' mission to redeem mankind.

Yes, children can teach us a vital lesson about faith. In their openness and innocence, it's easy for them to trust the One whose pure character touches a responsive chord in their tender hearts.

As adults, we think we know so much. We try to be so mature, so correct, so religious. I wonder if we would even recognize the Savior if He walked among us, working the kind of miracles He performed long ago.

Lord, give us the faith of little children. — Dave Egner

*A child is blind to prejudice*
*But quick to see what's good and true;*
*Oh, how we need that childlike faith*
*In all we say and all we do!* — D. De Haan

---

**Big lessons can be learned from little children.**

# THORNS OR ROSES?

READ:
**Numbers 14:1-11**

---

When the people complained, it displeased the LORD.
—Numbers 11:1

---

THE BIBLE IN ONE YEAR:
■ Joshua 7–9
■ Luke 1:21-38

Two boys were eating some grapes. One of them remarked, "Aren't they sweet!" "I guess so," the other replied, "but they're full of seeds." Wandering into a garden, the first boy exclaimed, "Look at those big, beautiful red roses!" The other commented, "They're full of thorns!" It was a warm day, so they stopped at the store for a soft drink. After several swallows, the second youngster complained, "My bottle's half-empty already." The first quickly responded, "Mine's still half-full!"

Many people are like the negative-thinking boy in this story. They always look at life through dark glasses. Like the children of Israel in today's Scripture, they complain and grumble when they should be praising the Lord for His gracious provision. But thank God, not everyone is like that. There are people who concentrate on the bright side and are radiant, happy, and grateful. They are realistic about the somber side of life, but they don't pout and fret.

You can overcome negative thinking. No matter who you are or what your circumstances, there's always much to be grateful for. Think about God's love for you. Praise Him for His providential care. Then, instead of complaining about thorns, you'll be thankful for the roses. — Richard De Haan

*Some folks see so many thorns,*
*They scarce can see one rose,*
*While others count two blossoms*
*For every thorn that grows.* — Garrison

---

**Instead of grumbling because you don't get what you want, be thankful you don't get what you deserve.**

# MAKING A NAME

**READ:**
**Proverbs 10:1-17**

---

The memory of the righteous is blessed, but the name of the wicked will rot.
—Proverbs 10:7

---

THE BIBLE IN ONE YEAR:
■ Joshua 10–12
■ Luke 1:39-56

In the mid-1800s, Texas rancher Samuel Augustus Maverick refused to brand his cattle. When neighboring cowboys came upon a calf without a brand, they called it a "maverick." The word entered the English language and came to refer to a person who takes an independent stand and refuses to conform.

Other names have become words that describe a person's character and behavior: *Judas* and *Benedict Arnold* both mean "traitor." An *Einstein* is a genius, while a *Solomon* is a wise man.

Few of our names will become part of a language, but they signify who we are and how we have lived—today and for generations to come. Solomon said, "The memory of the righteous is blessed, but the name of the wicked will rot. . . . He who walks with integrity walks securely, but he who perverts his ways will become known" (Proverbs 10:7,9).

When we think of someone we know and admire, the words we associate with that person's name are usually the character traits we'd like to have as well. Honesty, generosity, and love often head the list. We see these in our Lord Jesus Christ, who allows us as Christians to bear His name.

Today, the Lord wants to work in us to make our name one that points to Him. — David McCasland

*I'd rather die than bring disgrace*
*Upon my Lord, His name debase;*
*So I will live my life each day*
*To honor Christ and walk His way.* — Hess

---

**When others think of you, do they think of Jesus?**

# FACING MY FEARS

READ:
**Psalm 138**

---

In the day when I cried out, You answered me, and made me bold with strength in my soul.
—Psalm 138:3

---

THE BIBLE IN ONE YEAR:
■ Joshua 13–15
■ Luke 1:57–80

After Bill and I married, I became overly dependent on him, rather than depending on God for my security and strength. Feeling very inadequate and fearful, secretly I worried, "What if one day I don't have Bill anymore?"

When our missionary work took Bill from home for weeks at a time, I began to depend on myself instead of Bill. Feeling even more inadequate, I reduced the risks of life whenever possible and lived within a cocoon of anxiety, even being afraid to go out in public.

Finally, at rock bottom, I followed David's example in Psalm 138:3. He said, "In the day when I cried out, You answered me, and made me bold with strength in my soul." I too cried out and God answered me. His answer gave me the understanding and strength to crack open the cocoon of fear and begin spreading my wings in dependence on God. Slowly but surely He made me a bold servant at Bill's side.

Years later, when Bill died, I recognized how compassionately God had dealt with my earlier fear: "What if one day I don't have Bill anymore?" Instead of removing my fear, God gave me the strength and ability to face it. And He will enable you as you depend on Him.  — Joanie Yoder

*I know not, but God knows;*
*Oh, blessed rest from fear!*
*All my unfolding days*
*To Him are plain and clear.*  — Flint

---

**To conquer your fears, surrender them to the Lord.**

# THE FEET OF JUDAS

READ:
John 13:1-20

I have given you an
example, that you
should do as I have
done to you.
—John 13:15

THE BIBLE IN ONE YEAR:
■ Joshua 16–18
■ Luke 2:1-24

When we read the story of Jesus washing the disciples' feet, we may think we understand why He was doing that for them. John, for instance, was a close friend. Then there were Peter and Andrew, who had been so faithful in following the Master.

Each of the disciples must have had something that endeared him to Jesus. But why did He wash the feet of Judas? Jesus knew that He was stooping down to serve the one who would soon stoop to perform history's worst act of treachery.

Jesus was performing the most menial of tasks for a person who treated the Creator of the universe as being someone worth no more than 30 pieces of silver. Knowingly, the One whose name is associated with giving life got His hands dirty to serve the one whose name would stand for betrayal and death for the rest of time.

Doesn't Jesus' example tell us something special about service? Doesn't it remind us that we are not called to serve only those who are like us, or even those who care for us? We are called to serve all people — the lovely and the unlovely, the friendly and the not-so-friendly.

When was the last time you "washed the feet" of someone like Judas? — Dave Branon

When Jesus took a servant's towel —
His honor set aside —
He humbly showed us how to serve,
And how to conquer pride. — Sper

**It's difficult to stand on a pedestal
and wash the feet of those below. —Colson**

# THE CROSS SPEAKS

READ:
Acts 2:22-39

Christ died for our
sins according to the
Scriptures, and . . . rose
again the third day.
—1 Corinthians 15:3-4

THE BIBLE IN ONE YEAR:
■ Joshua 19–21
■ Luke 2:25-52

Crosses decorate church steeples and designate burial places. Sometimes they mark the spot where people died in highway accidents. And they are often worn as jewelry.

Crosses remind people of Jesus Christ. I was made aware of this when a businessman, seeing a small gold cross on the lapel of my jacket, asked me, "Why are you a believer in Christ?" I was glad for the opportunity to share my faith with him.

Jesus died on the cross for us, but we don't worship a dead Savior. Our Lord's body was taken down from the cross and placed in a tomb, and then on the third day He emerged in a glorified body.

The cross speaks to us of the total picture — our Lord's atoning death to pay the price for our sins, as well as His glorious resurrection to deliver us from the power of death.

If it were not for what Christ did on the cross, we would all stand guilty before God and hopeless in the face of death. But through faith in Him, we receive the forgiveness of all our sins and the assurance that death cannot hold us.

Have you looked at the cross and placed your trust in the One who died there? It's the only sure and perfect remedy for guilt and fear.  — Herb Vander Lugt

*The cross upon which Jesus died*
*Is a shelter in which we can hide;*
*And its grace so free is sufficient for me,*
*And deep is its fountain — as wide as the sea.*  — Stanphill

**The cross of Christ—the crossroads to heaven or hell.**

# BEING USEFUL

**READ:**
Luke 3:21-22

---

A voice came from heaven which said, "You are My beloved Son; in You I am well pleased." —Luke 3:22

---

THE BIBLE IN ONE YEAR:
■ Joshua 22–24
■ Luke 3

Jesus emerged from obscurity and was baptized by John the Baptist. When He came out of the water, He heard His Father say, "You are My beloved Son; in You I am well pleased" (Luke 3:22).

What had Jesus been doing that merited such unqualified acceptance? He had not yet performed one miracle; He had not preached a single sermon; He had not cleansed one leper. In fact, He had not yet done anything that we normally associate with greatness. What had He been doing in Nazareth during those 30 silent years? He was growing "in wisdom and stature, and in favor with God and men" (2:52).

What's done in the silent place with God is what matters. It's in the quiet hours of fellowship with God that we're shaped and molded and made into men and women He can use — people with whom He can be well-pleased.

You might be thinking, *I'm in a place where I can't be useful.* You may feel limited and frustrated by the cramping restrictions of age, an illness, a difficult child, an uncooperative spouse. But your place, wherever it is, is a place to grow. Spend time in God's Word and in prayer. Grow and bloom where you are, and your Father will be pleased with you. — David Roper

*You'll go forth a little stronger*
*With a fresh supply of grace,*
*If each day you meet the Savior*
*In a secret, quiet place.* —Adams

---

**Fruitful service grows in the soil
of faithful worship.**

# LIVING WITH EXPECTATION

READ:
John 20:1-10

Peter therefore went out, and the other disciple, and were going to the tomb. So they both ran together.
—John 20:3-4

THE BIBLE IN ONE YEAR:
■ Judges 1–3
■ Luke 4:1-30

When the dark day of Jesus' crucifixion drew to a close, it seemed that the most wonderful of all lives had come to an end. For a few brief years, Christ had astounded the crowds and His followers with the wisdom of His teaching and the wonder of His miracles. But Jesus chose not to save Himself from the cross, and now His life was over. It seemed that nothing more could be expected of Him.

Hope returned, however, on that first resurrection morning. A painting by Eugene Burnand portrays Peter and John running to the tomb. Shortly after dawn, Mary Magdalene had told them that she and her friends had found the tomb empty. In Burnand's painting, the faces of Peter and John show contending emotions of anguish and relief, of sorrow and surprise, of despair and wonder as they race toward the tomb. Their gaze is eagerly fixed forward, turning the viewer's attention to the sepulcher. What did they find? An empty tomb — the Savior was alive!

Christ still lives. But many of us go from day to day as if He were still in the grave. How much better to look beyond the empty tomb to the One who can fill our lives with the power of His resurrection!  — Dave Egner

*Christ left the grave one glorious day*
*And vanquished death and sin;*
*He opened wide the gates of heaven*
*That we might enter in.*  — Anon.

---

**The victim of Good Friday became the victor of Easter.**

# Two Daughters

**READ:**
Luke 8:40-42,49-56

Someone came from the ruler of the synagogue's house, saying to him, "Your daughter is dead." —Luke 8:49

THE BIBLE IN ONE YEAR:
■ Judges 4–6
■ Luke 4:31-44

I had never thought much about Jairus before. Oh, I had heard the story about this synagogue ruler, and I knew he had begged Jesus to come to his house and heal his dying daughter. But I never understood the depth of his sorrow. I never understood how his heart must have shattered in pain when a messenger came to him and announced, "Your daughter is dead."

No, I never comprehended his grief and anguish — until I heard those same words from a police officer who came to our house on June 6, 2002.

Jairus' daughter was 12, and she died from an illness. Our daughter was 17, and it was an auto accident that broke our family's heart.

Jairus' daughter was restored to life by Jesus' touch. My daughter Melissa — though we ache to know she wasn't healed physically — was healed spiritually by Jesus' sacrifice of love when she trusted Him as Savior early in her life. Now our comfort comes from knowing that her eternal existence with the Lord has already begun.

Two daughters. The same Jesus. Two different results. His loving and compassionate touch is a miracle that can bring peace to grieving hearts — like Jairus', like mine, like yours. — Dave Branon

*God took that one. And in my lonely heart*
*He poured His special peace, His tender love;*
*I cannot doubt that God has drawn me near*
*To trust Him more until I'm drawn above.* — Morris

**In every desert of trial, God has an oasis of comfort.**

# WHERE WILL IT ALL END?

**READ:**
**1 Peter 2:18-25**

When [Jesus] suffered, He did not threaten, but committed Himself to Him who judges righteously.
—1 Peter 2:23

THE BIBLE IN ONE YEAR:
■ Judges 7–8
■ Luke 5:1-16

Four-year-old Angelo wakes up and discovers that his new beagle puppy has chewed up his plastic guitar. The little fellow has a fit of grief. Mom's nerves tighten. She snaps at husband Tony as he leaves for the office.

Still feeling the unhappy send-off, Tony greets his secretary with some cold and unreasonable instructions. She picks up the mood, and at coffee-break tells off a fellow secretary. At closing time the second secretary tells her boss she's ready to quit.

An hour-and-a-half later, after fighting heavy traffic, the boss walks into his house and blurts out an angry word to little Nelson, who had left his bike in the driveway. Nelson runs to his room, slams the door, and kicks his Scottish terrier.

Where does it all end? Each person may think he or she had reason to be upset. But what was needed in this imaginary situation was one person who would absorb unjust treatment without lashing out.

This is when Christians have a unique opportunity. By knowing the Father's will, by heeding the Son's example, and by relying on the Spirit's help, we can endure bad treatment and show others a better way. In chain reactions of frustration and anger, we can be where it all ends. — Mart De Haan

*It was a hasty, thoughtless word,*
*Sarcastic and unkind,*
*That chilled the day and dimmed its light*
*And left a sting behind.* — Anon.

**When you're wronged, don't do what comes naturally; do what comes supernaturally.**

# WAKE-UP CALL

**READ:**
**Revelation 3:1-6**

---

Be watchful, and strengthen the things which remain, . . . for I have not found your works perfect before God. —Revelation 3:2

---

THE BIBLE IN ONE YEAR:
■ Judges 9–10
■ Luke 5:17-39

On February 26, 1993, a powerful bomb exploded in the underground parking garage of the World Trade Center in New York City, killing six people and injuring more than a thousand. It sparked an aggressive investigation with many arrests. But few law enforcement authorities recognized it as part of an international terrorist plot. When the Trade Center towers were destroyed by terrorists in 2001, police commissioner Raymond Kelly looked back on the first attack and said, "It should have been a wake-up call for America."

The Lord told the church at Sardis that although they had a reputation for being spiritually alive, they were dead. He told them to wake up: "Be watchful, and strengthen the things which remain, that are ready to die, for I have not found your works perfect before God. Remember therefore how you have received and heard; hold fast and repent" (Revelation 3:2-3).

The call to every believer is to be vigilant toward the Lord rather than lax and indifferent. If the fire has gone out in our hearts, He pleads with us to stir the embers into flame again.

Ask yourself: Has there been a wake-up call in my life recently that I've missed? Is God trying to tell me something? Will I answer His wake-up call today? — David McCasland

> *Lord, grant to us a holy zeal*
> *That burns within our heart;*
> *A zeal like Yours for truth and right*
> *From which we'll not depart.* — D. De Haan

---

**To keep your heart from growing cold,**
**stay on fire for God.**

# HOW LONG?

**READ:**
Luke 19:41-44

---

As [Jesus] drew near,
He saw the city and
wept over it.
— Luke 19:41

---

THE BIBLE IN ONE YEAR:
- Judges 11–12
- Luke 6:1-26

It took years before she finally said yes. A Welshman had fallen in love with one of his neighbors and wanted to marry her. But they had quarreled, and she refused to forgive. Shy and reluctant to face the offended woman, the persistent suitor slipped a love letter under her door every week.

At last, after 42 years, he summoned up courage, knocked on her door, and asked her to become his wife. To his delight, she consented. So they were married at the age of 74!

God is also a persistent lover. Century after century He sent prophets, seeking the stubborn people of Israel. Then God sent His Son. In Luke 19, we read that Jesus looked out over the city of Jerusalem and wept because of their hardness of heart (vv.41-44).

Yet Jesus persisted in His loving pursuit. He opened the way for reconciliation by His redeeming sacrifice at Calvary. Today He is still asking sinners to come to Him, personally accept Him as Savior, and enjoy close fellowship with Him (Matthew 11:28).

If you have come to Him, rejoice that you are His. If you have not, however, you must realize that time may run out. Don't remain forever alienated from the Lover of your soul. Trust Him today. — Vernon Grounds

*Why trade the hope of heaven's light*
*For things that please the prince of night?*
*Eternal glories wait for all*
*Who turn and trust God's loving call.* — Branon

---

**God always knocks loud enough**
**for the seeking soul to hear.**

# ARRANGING YOUR MIND

READ:
**Philippians 4:4-9**

---

Rejoice in the Lord always. Again I will say, rejoice!
—Philippians 4:4

---

THE BIBLE IN ONE YEAR:
■ Judges 13–15
■ Luke 6:27-49

Several years ago I read a story about a 92-year-old Christian woman who was legally blind. In spite of her limitation, she was always neatly dressed, with her hair carefully brushed and her makeup tastefully applied. Each morning she would meet the new day with eagerness.

After her husband of 70 years died, it became necessary for her to go to a nursing home where she could receive proper care. On the day of the move, a helpful neighbor drove her there and guided her into the lobby. Her room wasn't ready, so she waited patiently in the lobby for several hours.

When an attendant finally came for her, she smiled sweetly as she maneuvered her walker to the elevator. The staff member described her room to her, including the new curtains that had been hung on the windows. "I love it," she declared. "But Mrs. Jones, you haven't seen your room yet," the attendant replied. "That doesn't have anything to do with it," she said. "Happiness is something you choose. Whether I like my room or not doesn't depend on how it's arranged. It's how I arrange my mind."

The Bible says, "Rejoice in the Lord" (Philippians 4:4). Remind yourself often of all that Jesus has given to you and be thankful. That's how to arrange your mind. — David Roper

*God takes delight when we rejoice*
*In all that He has done*
*And when we thank Him for the love*
*He shows us through His Son.* — D. De Haan

---

**The happiness of your life depends on the quality of your thoughts.**

# TWO REALMS

READ:
John 10:1-18

The thief does not come except to steal, and to kill, and to destroy. I have come that they may have life, and that they may have it more abundantly.
—John 10:10

THE BIBLE IN ONE YEAR:
■ Judges 16–18
■ Luke 7:1-30

How sad it is when a family watches a child walk away from the faith in which he or she grew up. And worst of all is to see sadness replace the joy that child once had.

One woman saw her daughter go from loving and trusting God to a life of sin and rebellion—but then back to the joy of a walk with Jesus. The daughter's sad, empty expressions during her time of running from God changed to an open, joyful happiness when she returned to fellowship with Him. The mother said the difference was like turning on a light that dispelled the darkness.

In John 10:10, we read of the contrast between the joy of life with Jesus and the anxiety of life in the realm of Satan. He comes deceptively as an "angel of light" (2 Corinthians 11:14), but he wants to ruin us. He is described as a thief who steals, kills, and destroys. But Jesus is presented as the One who gives life — abundant life.

These two realms are constantly in a battle for our hearts. We have this choice: the light of life with Jesus or the depths of darkness in the devil's lair. Life or death? Light or darkness? Contentment or anxiety? Both realms beckon us.

Whom will you choose to trust with your life? The thief or the Savior? — Dave Branon

*The devil is subtle, deceptive, and sly—*
*He's clever and tricks us to swallow his lie;*
*But his cunning methods we're sure to discern*
*If we make God's warnings our daily concern.* — D. De Haan

**God's truth is the best protection**
**against Satan's lies.**

# CHESS MASTER

READ:
Isaiah 48:17-22

---

He caused the waters
to flow from the rock
for them; He also split
the rock, and the
waters gushed out.
—Isaiah 48:21

---

THE BIBLE IN ONE YEAR:
■ Judges 19–21
■ Luke 7:31-50

An intriguing painting is on display in the Louvre in Paris. It portrays Faust (the legendary German magician who bartered away his soul to the devil) sitting across from Satan at a chessboard. Satan is gloating over what appears to be the checkmate of Faust's king. The magician's expression is that of a beaten man.

According to an often told story, a famous chess master visited the gallery one day and studied the painting with great care. All at once he startled everyone around him by shouting excitedly, "It's a lie! It's a lie! The king and the knight have another move."

Isaiah assured the people of Judah that God always provides a way of escape. Although they would be deported to Babylon because of their sinfulness, Isaiah prophesied that a future day of release would come when they would have to leave hurriedly. But they wouldn't have to worry. Just as God had provided water for the Israelites in the desert, He would also provide for them on their long trek homeward.

Many of us have experienced situations that appeared hopeless. We saw no way out, but we prayed and God opened a way. He made that "impossible" move. We can trust Him. He can never be checkmated. — Herb Vander Lugt

*When problems seem impossible*
*And we can't face another day,*
*The Lord extends His helping hand*
*And shows us He can make a way.* — Sper

---

**God is the only King who can never be defeated.**

# THE STONES CRY OUT

**READ:**
Luke 19:29-40

---

If these should keep silent, the stones would immediately cry out.
—Luke 19:40

---

THE BIBLE IN ONE YEAR:
■ Ruth 1-4
■ Luke 8:1-25

I received a letter from a woman who told me she had grown up in a troubled home. At an early age she ran away, began a life of crime, and spent time in jail. Later, ensnared by drugs, she felt that the only way out of her sin-darkened life was suicide.

At that point, because of the witness of two women who told her about Jesus, she put her trust in the Savior and found a reason for living. Soon she wanted to tell others about Jesus. She had some artistic ability, so she began to paint Bible verses and spiritual sayings on smooth stones she collected from beaches. She sold them and used the money to aid missionary causes. Those stones were her way of telling others about Jesus.

This woman's story reminds me of what Jesus said as He approached Jerusalem a few days before His crucifixion. The multitude declared, "Blessed is the King who comes in the name of the LORD!" (Luke 19:38). When the Pharisees told Jesus to quiet the crowd, He said that if the people were silenced, even the stones would cry out (v.40).

Of course, Jesus wasn't talking about painted stones, but it is still true that even if our verbal witness is silenced, there are all sorts of ways to tell others about Christ. What "stones" can you use to tell others of your Savior and King? — Henry Bosch

*Through transformed eyes, Lord, help us see*
*A world of people in despair,*
*And help us reach them with Your love,*
*To show them that we really care.* — Sper

---

**I'm just a nobody telling everybody**
**about Somebody who can save anybody!**

## LOVE THAT LIFTS

READ:
Psalm 40:1-3

They called upon the
LORD, and He answered
them. —Psalm 99:6

THE BIBLE IN ONE YEAR:
■ 1 Samuel 1-3
■ Luke 8:26-56

When King David looked back on his life, he remembered some painful experiences. In Psalm 40, he recalled one especially severe difficulty, a time when he felt as if he had sunk deep into "the miry clay" (v.2).

In his despair David kept pleading with God for deliverance, and graciously the Lord answered his desperate cries. Lifting him out of the "horrible pit," He set his feet on solid ground (v.2). No wonder David broke out into this hymn of praise and gratitude!

As you look back on your own life, do you remember any experience when you felt as if you had fallen into a pit? Perhaps it was the pit of failure, the pit of bereavement, the pit of painful illness, the pit of dark doubt, the pit of some persistent sin. Did you keep crying out to God, and did He mercifully deliver you?

If so, are you still praising the Lord for that answer to your cries and thanking Him for His grace? And are you now walking with Him in obedient fellowship?

You can confidently trust the Lord to help you in whatever experience comes your way in the days ahead. Rejoice that in His time He can — and will — bring you through and bring you out. — Vernon Grounds

*Why must I bear this pain? I cannot tell;*
*I only know my Lord does all things well.*
*And so I trust in God, my all in all,*
*For He will bring me through, whate'er befall.* —Smith

**God can bring showers of blessing**
**out of storms of adversity.**

## VALLEY OF THE SHADOW

READ:
Psalm 23

---

Though I walk through the valley of the shadow of death, I will fear no evil; for You are with me. —Psalm 23:4

---

THE BIBLE IN ONE YEAR:
- 1 Samuel 4–6
- Luke 9:1-17

Darkness upon darkness. Sorrow upon sorrow. Pain upon pain. Anguish upon anguish. That's death.

Death is a fearful visitor, snatching away people who are precious to us and leaving us behind to mourn, grieve, and wonder. It blocks the light that before had shined so freely and easily on our lives.

Whether we're facing the prospect of dying, or dealing with the death of a loved one, death can be devastating. It can sap our energy, change our plans, overwhelm our soul, alter our outlook, test our faith, steal our joy, and challenge our assumptions about life's purposes.

When we walk through the deep valley, we feel swallowed up by the shadow and come face-to-face with fear. The frantic emptiness of our loss threatens the comfort that previously originated from our trust in God, and so we grow afraid. Afraid of our future. Afraid to enjoy life again.

Yet in that valley, under that shadow, we can say to the Lord, "I will fear no evil; for You are with me" (Psalm 23:4). His loving arms never let us go. He is always with us.

Slowly at first, but most assuredly, He provides comfort and release from the darkness. He gives light. He leads us out. Eventually, we escape the valley of the shadow. — Dave Branon

*We need not ponder death with fear,*
*Though what's ahead we cannot see;*
*For we who put our faith in Christ*
*Look forward to eternity.* —Sper

---

**Death separates us for a time;**
**Christ will reunite us forever.**

# KEEP ON ASKING

**READ:**
Luke 11:1-13

---

I say to you, ask, and it will be given to you.
—Luke 11:9

---

THE BIBLE IN ONE YEAR:
■ 1 Samuel 7–9
■ Luke 9:18-36

I heard a woman say that she never prayed more than once for anything. She didn't want to weary God with her repeated requests.

The Lord's teaching on prayer in Luke 11 contradicts this notion. He told a parable about a man who went to his friend's house at midnight and asked for some bread to feed his unexpected visitors. At first the friend refused, for he and his family were in bed. Finally he got up and gave him the bread—not out of friendship but because the caller was so persistent (vv.5-10).

Jesus used this parable to contrast this reluctant friend with our generous heavenly Father. If an irritated neighbor will give in to his friend's persistence and grant his request, how much more readily will our heavenly Father give us all we need!

It's true that God, in His great wisdom, may sometimes delay His answers to prayer. It's also true that we must pray in harmony with the Scriptures and God's will. But Jesus moved beyond those facts to urge us to persist in prayer. He told us to ask, seek, and knock until the answer comes (v.9).

So don't worry about wearying God. He will never tire of your persistent prayer! —Joanie Yoder

> Don't think true prayer escapes God's ears,
> He hears your every plea;
> Though hope's deferred, believe—believe!
> The answer you will see. —Anon.

---

**God never tires of our asking.**

# BEARING HIS CROSS

**READ:**
**Mark 15:16-21**

They compelled a certain man, Simon a Cyrenian, the father of Alexander and Rufus, to bear His cross.
—Mark 15:21

THE BIBLE IN ONE YEAR:
■ 1 Samuel 10–12
■ Luke 9:37-62

In the eyes of most people in the crowd, Jesus was a common criminal going to the place of execution. So to help Him bear His cross was both degrading and humiliating.

Simon of Cyrene was pressed into this service (Mark 15:21). Yet this was perhaps the most glorious day in his life. It is possible that he believed in the Savior, and that his wife and children did also. Some Bible teachers come to that conclusion because many years later, when the apostle Paul sent his greetings to the Christians in Rome, he referred to a man named Rufus and his mother (Romans 16:13). I believe that he was the son of Simon mentioned by Mark in his gospel (15:21), which probably was written in Rome. This is likely the reason Mark said that Simon was the father of Rufus and Alexander.

When we walk with Jesus and "take up the cross" (Luke 9:23), we too will experience the ridicule of the world for identifying ourselves with the Savior. Yet through it all, like Simon of Cyrene, our lives will be transformed, and our testimony will have an influence on the lives of family and friends around us.

Simon was "compelled" to bear the cross (Mark 15:21), but Jesus invites us to take up our cross. Have you? — Henry Bosch

*"Take up thy cross and follow Me,"*
*I hear the blessed Savior call;*
*How can I make a lesser sacrifice*
*When Jesus gave His all?* — Ackley

---

**Following Jesus costs more than anything—
except not following Him.**

# THREE CROSSES

**READ:**
Luke 23:32-38

They crucified Him,
and the criminals, one
on the right hand and
the other on the left.
—Luke 23:33

THE BIBLE IN ONE YEAR:
■ 1 Samuel 13–14
■ Luke 10:1-24

In many paintings of the crucifixion of Jesus, the center cross on which He hung is taller or higher on a hill than the other two. We can appreciate an artist's desire to give Christ a place of preeminence, but we have no reason to believe that Jesus was given an elevated or exalted position — higher than that of the two thieves. Those who crucified Jesus considered Him to be a common criminal, so the crosses were most likely on the same level.

As I think about this, I realize that Jesus was not out of reach — way above the poor sinners on the other crosses. I also think it is likely that the three crosses were very close together. The two thieves could carry on a conversation with each other above the shouting and tumult of the mob around them. In fact, if the dying thief's hand had not been nailed to the cross, he might very well have been able to reach over and put his hand on Jesus' hand. This I believe is significant. Jesus is within reach of all who will look to Him and touch Him with the hand of faith!

Yes, anyone can come to Him and receive forgiveness and new life. Have you reached out in faith to the One who died on a cross for you? — M. R. De Haan, M.D.

> They nailed His hands, they pierced His brow
> As they cried with a fiendish glee,
> "If Thou be the Son of God, come down!"
> But He stayed on the cross for me! — Crooks

**Nothing speaks more clearly of God's love
than the cross.**

# MAKE PEACE

READ:
2 Corinthians 5:17-20

God . . . has given
us the ministry of
reconciliation.
—2 Corinthians 5:18

THE BIBLE IN ONE YEAR:
■ 1 Samuel 15–16
■ Luke 10:25-42

It was a dramatic story of forgiveness. In December of 2000, on the Battleship Missouri Memorial, a dozen American survivors of the attack on Pearl Harbor embraced three of the Japanese pilots who had flown attacking planes. The reconciliation ceremony had been arranged by the American-Japan Friendship Committee.

That moving scene is only a dim reflection of what God's grace does for us. Although we are sinful, we can be brought into a relationship with God through simple faith in Jesus. Because He died on the cross in our place, God blots out the record of our sins and makes us right with Him.

The Lord in His amazing love has not only forgiven us but has also given to us "the ministry of reconciliation" (2 Corinthians 5:18). We have the honor of sharing the good news with others so that they too can be at peace with God. And when we are right with God, we are also to do what we can to live at peace with everyone (Romans 12:18).

Have you accepted God's offer of forgiveness in Christ? Are you telling others about His love? And are you an agent of God's grace in your relationships? Start today—make peace. —Vernon Grounds

> *God has a purpose and plan for your life*
> *When from your sin He has given release;*
> *You're an ambassador for Jesus Christ—*
> *Go and tell others of His perfect peace.* —Hess

**When we experience peace with God,
we can share His peace with others.**

# A Sure Hope

Christ is risen from the dead, and has become the firstfruits of those who have fallen asleep.
—1 Corinthians 15:20

Konrad Adenauer, former chancellor of West Germany, said, "If Jesus Christ is alive, then there is hope for the world. If not, I don't see the slightest glimmer of hope on the horizon." Then he added, "I believe Christ's resurrection to be one of the best-attested facts of history."

Christ's resurrection and ours go together. So reasoned the apostle Paul in 1 Corinthians 15. And if Christ didn't rise from the grave, what's left? Empty preaching (v.14), false witnesses (v.15), a futile faith (v.17), unforgiven sins (v.17), no life after death (v.18), and hopelessness (v.19).

But Christ did rise from the grave. Paul asserted the proof for the resurrection in verses 1 through 11, listing many credible witnesses who saw the risen Lord: Peter (v.5), 500 people (v.6), all the apostles (v.7), and Paul himself (v.8).

When the Greek philosopher Socrates lay dying, his friends asked, "Shall we live again?" He could only say, "I hope so." In contrast, the night before author and explorer Sir Walter Raleigh was beheaded, he wrote in his Bible, "From this earth, this grave, this dust, my God shall raise me up."

If we trust in Christ as our Savior, we won't say, "I hope so" about our own resurrection. Jesus' resurrection gives us a sure hope. — Dennis De Haan

*Rejoice in glorious hope!*
*Our Lord the Judge shall come*
*And take His servants up*
*To their eternal home.* — Wesley

**Christ's resurrection is the guarantee of our own.**

# LOSS AND GAIN

READ:
Luke 24:13-35

---

Their eyes were
opened and they knew
Him; and He vanished
from their sight.
—Luke 24:31

---

THE BIBLE IN ONE YEAR:
■ 1 Samuel 19–21
■ Luke 11:29-54

A Texas high school football team began the 2002 season with a 57-game winning streak and hopes for an unprecedented fifth consecutive state championship. In spite of losing their longtime coach and competing against larger schools, the Celina Bobcats remained undefeated through the regular season. But then they lost a quarterfinal playoff game by one point. It felt like the end of the world — even though they had won 68 straight games and 5 state championships in 7 years.

When our dreams are shattered and our hearts are broken, we may feel that all has been lost and nothing has been gained. It takes the touch of God to open our eyes to the greater glory of His plan.

When the crucified and risen Christ joined two disciples on the road to Emmaus, they were grieving over His death. "We were hoping that it was He who was going to redeem Israel" (Luke 24:21), they told Jesus, whom they didn't recognize. But Jesus said, "Ought not the Christ to have suffered these things and to enter into His glory?" (v.26). Later they realized they had been talking with Jesus. He was alive!

In our time of loss, the risen Lord comes to us with comfort and peace, revealing His glory and the eternal gain that is ours because of His cross.  — David McCasland

*When circumstances overwhelm*
*And seem too much to bear,*
*Depend upon the Lord for strength*
*And trust His tender care.*  — Sper

---

**Present pains can lead to permanent gains.**

# FINDING GOD

READ:
1 Chronicles 28:1-10

If you seek Him, He
will be found by you.
—1 Chronicles 28:9

THE BIBLE IN ONE YEAR:
■ 1 Samuel 22–24
■ Luke 12:1-31

Tourists rarely take great photo-graphs. They seldom make the effort to be at the right spot at the right time to get the right angle of light in the right weather conditions. To capture beautiful outdoor pictures, professional photographers are careful to view the scene from different angles, during different seasons, and at different times of day.

This makes me wonder if the reason some people don't have a clear picture of the beauty and glory of God is that they make snap judgments. They come to wrong conclusions about God based on a bad church experience, or an encounter with someone who claims to be a Christian but isn't living like one. They misjudge what the Lord is like and turn away from Him, feeling disillusioned.

The pursuit of God involves more than casual observation. King David told his son Solomon, "If you seek Him, He will be found by you" (1 Chronicles 28:9). The psalmist said, "Blessed are those who . . . seek Him with the whole heart!" (Psalm 119:2). And the author of Hebrews wrote that God rewards "those who diligently seek Him" (11:6).

To see and know God in all His fullness and glory, we can't approach Him like tourists. We need to seek Him at all times, with all our heart.  — Julie Ackerman Link

*Lord, I am seeking You with all my heart,*
*With all my soul and all my mind;*
*For wondrous blessings You alone impart—*
*In seeking I will surely find.* —Hess

**To find God, we must be willing to seek Him.**

# FAITHFULNESS REQUIRED

**READ:**
**1 Corinthians**
**4:1-5, 14-20**

It is required in
stewards that one
be found faithful.
—1 Corinthians 4:2

THE BIBLE IN ONE YEAR:
■ 1 Samuel 25–26
■ Luke 12:32-59

Much of our attention and praise is directed toward highly visible and successful people. But occasionally we read about an ordinary, obscure person being honored for many years of faithful service. It may be a school custodian, a cafeteria worker, a handyman, or a clerk in a store who has served others in a dependable and unselfish way.

That kind of reliability often goes unnoticed, but I believe it's a powerful picture of how we are to live. Although consistency may not be flashy, days add up to a life of great significance to God.

Paul wrote, "It is required in stewards that one be found faithful" (1 Corinthians 4:2). If we live faithfully for Christ, God has promised to reward us at His appointed time. When the Lord comes, He "will both bring to light the hidden things of darkness and reveal the counsels of the hearts. Then each one's praise will come from God" (v.5).

When we long for success, God says, "*I* will reward you."

When we ache for recognition, God says, "*I* see you."

When we are ready to quit, God says, "*I* will help you."

Whether our service is public or private, our responsibility is the same — to be faithful. — David McCasland

*In all the little things of life,*
*Yourself, Lord, may I see;*
*In little and in great alike,*
*Help me to faithful be!* — Anon.

**God doesn't ask us to be successful**
**but to be faithful.**

# THE TONGUE THAT DEFILES

**READ:**
James 3:5-12

He who guards his mouth preserves his life, but he who opens wide his lips shall have destruction.
—Proverbs 13:3

THE BIBLE IN ONE YEAR:
- 1 Samuel 27–29
- Luke 13:1-22

My words have an effect on others; they also have an effect on me. When I speak evil, I not only reveal the sin in my own heart (Luke 6:45), I also reinforce that evil and cause it to grow. Jesus said it's not what goes into my mouth that defiles me, but what comes out. James put it another way: "The tongue . . . defiles the whole body" (James 3:6). My untamed tongue corrupts me.

On the other hand, when I refuse to give expression to impure, unkind, ungodly thoughts, I begin to choke and strangle the evil in my soul.

That's why the wise man said in Proverbs 13:3 that we must guard our mouth. When we do that, we starve the evil that is gnawing insidiously at the root of our soul. Do we want to put an end to the evil that so easily rises within us? With God's help, we must learn to control our tongue.

You may say, "I've tried to, but I have no power to subdue it." James agreed: "No man can tame the tongue" (James 3:8). But Jesus can. Ask Him to "keep watch" over your mouth (Psalm 141:3), and hand the bridle of your tongue to Him.

Let's echo the prayer of the hymn by Frances Havergal: "Take my lips and let them be filled with messages for Thee." — David Roper

> *Lord, set a guard upon my lips,*
> *My tongue control today;*
> *Help me evaluate each thought*
> *And watch each word I say.* — Hess

---

**Whoever guards his mouth and tongue keeps his soul from troubles.** —Proverbs 21:23

# FLEE!

**READ:**
James 4:1-10

Submit to God. Resist
the devil and he will
flee from you.
—James 4:7

THE BIBLE IN ONE YEAR:
■ 1 Samuel 30–31
■ Luke 13:23-35

I didn't see the movie *The Exorcist,* but I do recall its impact on my community. It left a lasting impression on many people about Satan's power. Even many Christians began to live in fear, swayed by the vivid images of evil. It seemed as if the devil was almost as powerful as God.

Is this perspective biblically sound? Of course not. God is the Creator, and all others, including demons, are just created beings. Only God is almighty.

It's easy to blame the devil when things go wrong. Although he does propagate wickedness and sin, we must be careful not to conclude that we are powerless against him. We are told in the Bible that the Holy Spirit within us "is greater than he who is in the world" (1 John 4:4).

The Bible also says we have a role to play in overcoming evil and doing what is good. We are to "flee sexual immorality" (1 Corinthians 6:18-20), "flee from idolatry" (10:14), "flee" from the love of money (1 Timothy 6:10-11), and "flee also youthful lusts" (2 Timothy 2:22).

James said that our attitude toward the devil should be to "resist" him (James 4:7). How do we do this? By submitting ourselves to God, allowing Him to direct our lives. Then it will be the devil who will flee from us. — Albert Lee

*When Satan launches his attack,*
*We must take heart and pray;*
*If we submit ourselves to God,*
*He'll be our strength each day.* —Sper

**To defeat Satan, surrender to Christ.**

# LEAVE
# IT BURIED

READ:
Colossians 2:6-14

---

I will forgive their
iniquity, and their sin
I will remember
no more.
—Jeremiah 31:34

---

THE BIBLE IN ONE YEAR:
■ 2 Samuel 1–2
■ Luke 14:1-24

A 10-year-old boy wanted to be a pastor when he grew up. One day, when the family's black cat died, he had an opportunity to do some "practice preaching" by conducting a funeral.

The boy found a shoebox and put the kitten inside it. When he placed the cover on the box, however, the tail wouldn't fit in. So he cut a hole in the lid so that the long furry tail could stick out. Then he rounded up his friends, preached a short sermon he had carefully prepared, and buried the cat in a shallow grave.

When the service was over, he noticed that the tip of the pet's tail was still sticking out of the ground. Every 2 or 3 days curiosity would get the better of him, and he would secretly pull up the cat by the tail and then rebury it. Eventually the tail came off, and the body finally remained buried!

How many of us do this with our forgiven sins? We confess our sins, but we continue to drag them up and weep over them, even though God considers the ugly things buried once and for all (Jeremiah 31:34; Colossians 2:13-14; 1 John 1:9). As a result, we are not joyful or productive in our Christian life and service.

Please — leave the "cat" buried!  — Henry Bosch

*God has buried my sins where no mortal can see;*
*He has cast all of them in the depths of the sea —*
*In the deep, silent depths, far away from the shore*
*Where they never may rise up to trouble me more.*  — Anon.

---

**The only sure place to bury sin
is at the foot of the cross.**

## OUR LIFE IN HEAVEN

**READ:**
**Revelation 22:1-5**

---

There shall be no more curse, but the throne of God and of the Lamb shall be in it, and His servants shall serve Him.
—Revelation 22:3

---

THE BIBLE IN ONE YEAR:
■ 2 Samuel 3–5
■ Luke 14:25-35

The following words were inscribed on a gravestone: "Don't weep for me now, don't weep for me ever; for I'm going to do nothing forever and ever." Some people think heaven will be a boring place. Others, after years of exhausting work, look forward to doing nothing in heaven — the ultimate retirement!

It's true that in heaven we will rest from earthly labors (Revelation 14:13), but it's not a place of inactivity. When John saw a vision of the New Jerusalem with the throne of God and the Lamb, and populated with God's redeemed people, he stated plainly, "His servants shall serve Him" (22:3).

If we know Christ as Savior, we will be raised up with resurrection power to serve Him in heaven. Never again will we serve Him half-heartedly and sporadically as we often do now. Instead, we'll serve enthusiastically and continually (7:15). In unimaginable ways, we will be involved creatively with God without the agonies of decline and death (21:4). We'll happily spend eternity basking in God's redeeming love and exploring endless pleasures at His right hand (Psalm 16:11).

Heaven certainly isn't a boring place with nothing to do — it's a place where we'll see Christ's face and joyfully serve Him forever! — Joanie Yoder

*Face to face! O blissful moment!*
*Face to face — to see and know;*
*Face to face with my Redeemer,*
*Jesus Christ, who loves me so.* — Breck

---

**Jesus is preparing a place for us**
**and preparing us for that place.**

# MAINTAINING CHARACTER

**READ:**
**Romans 12:1-21**

---

Do not be conformed to this world, but be transformed by the renewing of your mind.
—Romans 12:2

---

THE BIBLE IN ONE YEAR:
■ 2 Samuel 6–8
■ Luke 15:1-10

News reporting is a tough business that tends to make reporters hard and unfeeling. That's what Barbara Bradley, a correspondent for National Public Radio, tells aspiring journalists. But she also believes it doesn't have to be that way. "I made a strategic decision when I first fell in love with journalism," Bradley says, "that if I found myself beginning to get tough I would leave the business. It's just a career, and why mortgage your character for a career? Maintaining your character counts for something and you can do it; it's just a decision you have to make."

In every high-pressure situation, we can react like most people or we can choose to be different. J. B. Phillips translates Romans 12:2 this way: "Don't let the world around you squeeze you into its own mold, but let God remold your minds from within, so that you may prove in practice that the plan of God for you is good, meets all His demands, and moves toward the goal of true maturity" (*The New Testament in Modern English*).

When we feel pressure to conform, character can stand firm on the bedrock of conviction, saying, "This is God's way and it is best." Maintaining our character begins and continues with a decision. Let's make it today. — David McCasland

*O Lord, You see what's in my heart—*
*There's nothing hid from You;*
*So help me live the kind of life*
*That's loving, kind, and true.* —D. De Haan

---

**Beautiful character begins in the heart.**

# LOST IN THE FOG

**READ:**
Proverbs 3:1-6

Trust in the LORD with all your heart, and lean not on your own understanding.
—Proverbs 3:5

THE BIBLE IN ONE YEAR:
■ 2 Samuel 9–11
■ Luke 15:11-32

The fog was as thick as pea soup. Visibility was limited to a few feet, and the lake was as smooth as glass. The only sound to break the silence was the laughing of a loon across the lake.

I rowed for an hour around the shore, trying to catch fish in different areas, but the fish weren't biting! So I decided to go back to my cabin for a cup of coffee. I was at the mouth of a small inlet, which I knew was directly across the lake from the cottage. So I set out across the lake on a straight course (I thought) toward the dock.

The minutes went by — and after an hour I was surprised when I arrived back at the mouth of the little stream from which I started. I had been going in a circle in the fog. I was so sure I knew where I was going, but after an hour I had gotten nowhere! If I had only taken my compass — instead of relying on my own sense of direction.

Proverbs 3:5 comes to mind: "Lean not on your own understanding." Without the Lord as your guide through the fog of life, and His Word as your compass, you will wander aimlessly.

So be sure to make Proverbs 3:6 your lifelong motto: "In all your ways acknowledge Him, and He shall direct your paths." — M. R. De Haan, M.D.

*My Lord is ever with me*
*Along life's busy way;*
*I'll trust in Him completely*
*For guidance day by day. — Anon.*

**To avoid going wrong, follow God's leading.**

# WHO PACKED YOUR CHUTE?

READ:
1 Samuel 30:1-25

As his part is who goes down to the battle, so shall his part be who stays by the supplies; they shall share alike.
—1 Samuel 30:24

THE BIBLE IN ONE YEAR:
- 2 Samuel 12–13
- Luke 16

Charles Plumb was sitting in a restaurant when a man came up to him and said, "You're Plumb. You flew jet fighters in Vietnam. You were on the aircraft carrier *Kitty Hawk*. You were shot down!" "How in the world did you know all that?" asked Plumb. The man, who had been on the same ship, replied, "I packed your parachute." Then he added, "I guess it worked." "Indeed it did," said Plumb.

That night Plumb thought of this man who had stood at a table in the belly of the ship carefully folding parachutes for men whose lives might depend on them. Plumb was saddened and humbled as he thought, *How many times might I have passed this man but didn't even say good morning because I was a jet pilot and he was a low-ranking sailor?*

This story brings to mind David's words in today's Bible reading. Two hundred of his men became too weary to march farther to fight the Amalekites. So they stayed behind to guard the supplies. When David returned from battle, he made no distinction between them and his fighting men. He said, "They shall share alike" (1 Samuel 30:24).

In God's service there are no high and low people, no high and low tasks. We all depend on one another. Let's never forget those who packed our parachute. — Herbert Vander Lugt

*Lord, help us to appreciate*
*The work that others do,*
*The service given from their hearts,*
*Their sacrifice for You.* —Sper

**No service for Christ is insignificant.**

# UNLIMITED POWER

READ:
Isaiah 40:25-31

---

[God] brings out their host by number;
He calls them all by name. —Isaiah 40:26

---

THE BIBLE IN ONE YEAR:
■ 2 Samuel 14–15
■ Luke 17:1-19

"**W**hy don't the stars fall down?" A child may ask that question, but so does an astronomer. And they both get essentially the same answer: A mysterious power or energy upholds everything and prevents our cosmos from collapsing into chaos.

Hebrews 1:3 tells us that it is Jesus who upholds all things by the word of His power. He is the source of all the energy there is, whether the explosive potential packed inside an atom or the steaming kettle on the kitchen stove.

That energy is not simply a mindless force. No, God is the personal power who created everything out of nothing, including the stars (Genesis 1; Isaiah 40:26); who divided the Red Sea and delivered the Israelites from Egyptian bondage (Exodus 14:21-22); who brought to pass the virgin birth of Jesus (Luke 1:34-35); and who raised Him from the dead and conquered death (2 Timothy 1:10). Our God, the one and only true God, has the power to answer prayer, meet our needs, and change our lives.

So when life's problems are baffling, when you face some Red Sea impossibility, call upon the wonder-working God who upholds all things. And remember that with our almighty God, nothing is impossible. — Vernon Grounds

*Thou art coming to a King —*
*Large petitions with thee bring;*
*For His grace and power are such*
*None can ever ask too much.* — Newton

---

**God is greater than our greatest problem.**

# A Storm
# Is Coming!

**READ:**
**Proverbs 1:20-33**

It is appointed for men to die once, but after this the judgment.
—Hebrews 9:27

THE BIBLE IN ONE YEAR:
■ 2 Samuel 16–18
■ Luke 17:20-37

We were in a small boat on the far side of the lake and the fish were biting when we heard a rumble of thunder in the distance. Looking up, we saw a mass of dark clouds in the west.

I ignored the suggestion of my fishing partner that it might be wise to start back to the cottage — I wanted to keep fishing. Then it happened! The storm was suddenly upon us. We tried to start the motor but it wouldn't go! My friend tried to row, but the rain came in sheets and the waves tossed our little aluminum boat. We survived, but I learned a lesson. Don't delay when a storm is brewing.

Another type of storm is coming — a day of judgment. It may seem far off, and you don't feel you have to hurry to prepare. You may be in good health and in the prime of life. But listen, the storm may come upon you unexpectedly.

Proverbs 1 says that disaster will strike the person who foolishly ignores all warnings (v.27). And the author of Hebrews warned, "It is appointed for men to die once, but after this the judgment" (9:27).

To heed God's warnings is true wisdom. Have you sought shelter in Christ? If you haven't, it's time to stop "fishing" and seek safety before it's too late. Turn from your sin to Christ. Do so today.  — M. R. De Haan, M.D.

*Oh, turn to Christ while still you may;*
*Too late, it soon will be —*
*A glorious life you then will have*
*Throughout eternity.  — Anon.*

---

**Those who reject Christ as Savior
will face Him as Judge.**

# THE WORST DEFEAT

**READ:**
2 Kings 25:1-21

---

Because of the anger of the LORD this happened in Jerusalem and Judah.
—2 Kings 24:20

---

THE BIBLE IN ONE YEAR:
■ 2 Samuel 19–20
■ Luke 18:1-23

There have been some horrendous defeats in sports history, but none more convincing than Cumberland's 222-0 loss to Georgia Tech in 1916. It was the worst college football defeat ever, and the young men of Cumberland must have been devastated.

Another kind of loss happened to the people of Jerusalem in 586 BC, and it was much worse than any sports defeat. Because of God's punishment for their sin of worshiping other gods, they were defeated by the Babylonian army (2 Kings 24:20).

Led by Nebuchadnezzar, the Babylonians laid siege to the Holy City and left it in ruins. They burned the majestic temple, the palace of the king, and the people's homes.

It was perhaps the worst defeat in the long, often tragic history of God's people. Their continued disobedience to Him had devastating consequences. Through it all, He urged them to repent and turn back to Him.

It's sobering to me to see how much the Lord longs for His people to live in a way that glorifies Him. I need to remind myself often of my duty to live as God wants me to live because of how much it means to Him.

Judah's worst loss can challenge us all to live in obedience to God. — Dave Branon

*O help me, Lord, to be afraid*
*Of disobeying You;*
*And may I bring You highest praise*
*In everything I do.* — Sper

---

**The more you love God, the more you hate sin.**

# GIVE HIM YOUR BURDEN

**READ:**
**Psalm 55:16-23**

---

Cast your burden on the LORD, and He shall sustain you.
—Psalm 55:22

---

THE BIBLE IN ONE YEAR:
■ 2 Samuel 21–22
■ Luke 18:24-43

A poor man in Ireland was plodding along toward home, carrying a huge bag of potatoes. A horse and wagon finally drew up alongside him on the road, and the driver invited the man to climb aboard. After getting on the wagon, he sat down but continued to hold the heavy bag.

When the driver suggested that the man set the bag down in the wagon, he replied, "I don't want to trouble you too much, sir. You are giving me a ride already, so I'll just carry the potatoes."

"How foolish of him!" we say. Yet sometimes we do the same thing when we attempt to bear the burdens of our lives in our own strength. No wonder we become weary and overwhelmed with anxiety and fear.

In Psalm 55, David spoke of the anxiety he felt because his enemies were attacking him (vv.1-15). But then he gave his concerns to the Lord and was filled with renewed hope and confidence (vv.16-23). That's why he could write, "Cast your burden on the LORD, and He shall sustain you" (v.22).

When you recall the story of the man and his bag of potatoes, remember the simple lesson it illustrates: Rather than trying to bear your burdens by yourself, set them down in God's hands. —Henry Bosch

*Give Him each perplexing problem,*
*All your needs to Him make known;*
*Bring to Him your daily burdens —*
*Never carry them alone! —Adams*

---

**God invites us to burden Him
with what burdens us.**

**April 26**

# PAIN AND GAIN

**READ:**
Hebrews 12:1-11

---

No chastening seems
to be joyful for the
present, but painful;
nevertheless, afterward
it yields the peaceable
fruit of righteousness.
—Hebrews 12:11

---

THE BIBLE IN ONE YEAR:
■ 2 Samuel 23–24
■ Luke 19:1-27

Years ago I was an extremely anxious Christian. When I began spiraling downward emotionally, God didn't intervene, for He knew I needed to reach the end of myself. When I finally hit rock bottom, the "rock" on which I fell was Jesus Christ.

The Lord immediately began rebuilding me, applying truths from His Word to teach me trust and faith. Gradually He changed me into the joyful, God-dependent person He intended me to be. Through this painful but profitable experience, I learned that when God disciplines us, our greatest gain isn't what we get but what we become.

In Hebrews 12, we read that our heavenly Father loves us too dearly to let us remain immature. Like any loving father, He disciplines, corrects, and trains us — often through difficult situations. God uses our times of struggle to help us grow and make us more holy (vv.10-11).

Many people are motivated to live for health, wealth, and ease, and they try to avoid pain at all costs. But the abundant life that God intends for His people isn't trouble-free. Growth and change are often unsettling, but the gain is worth the pain.  —Joanie Yoder

*We shrink from the purging and pruning,*
*Forgetting the Gardener who knows:*
*The deeper the cutting and paring*
*The richer the cluster that grows.*  —Anon.

---

**God uses setbacks to move us forward.**

# A GOOD WILL

**READ:**
1 Peter 1:3-12

God . . . has begotten us again to a living hope through the resurrection of Jesus Christ. —1 Peter 1:3

THE BIBLE IN ONE YEAR:
- 1 Kings 1–2
- Luke 19:28-48

Perhaps you know someone who didn't receive the inheritance intended by a parent because of a faulty will. In an article titled "Money & The Law," attorney Jim Flynn says that if you want your estate to go to your chosen recipients instead of to members of the legal profession, you should avoid do-it-yourself wills. Such documents are usually legal but they are often unclear and fail to make provisions for unforeseen situations. Flynn advises having a formal will to be sure your wishes are carried out.

Man-made wills can fail, but there is no ambiguous language about the inheritance God has in store for us. The apostle Peter affirmed that God "has begotten us again to a living hope through the resurrection of Jesus Christ from the dead, to an inheritance incorruptible and undefiled and that does not fade away, reserved in heaven for you" (1 Peter 1:3-4).

No fluctuation in the economy can reduce this inheritance. It is not subject to review by the courts nor to debate by squabbling families. No amount of suffering or trials can diminish or change what God has in store for us. Our inheritance is certain and eternal (Hebrews 9:15). And as we live for Him, we are assured that His will for our lives today is "good and acceptable and perfect" (Romans 12:2). — David McCasland

*Why do we live like paupers,*
*When riches we possess?*
*We have become joint heirs with Christ*
*With blessings measureless.* — Sper

**The Christian's inheritance is guaranteed forever!**

## STILL TRUSTING

READ:
Psalm 139:1-16

In Your book they all
were written, the days
fashioned for me.
—Psalm 139:16

THE BIBLE IN ONE YEAR:
■ 1 Kings 3–5
■ Luke 20:1-26

How could this happen? How could God allow our beautiful daughter Melissa to be taken from us in a car accident at age 17? And it's not just us. It's also our friends Steve and Robyn, whose daughter Lindsay, Melissa's friend, died 9 months earlier. And what about Richard and Leah, whose son Jon — another of Melissa's friends — lies in a gravesite within 50 yards of both Lindsay and Melissa?

How could God allow these three Christian teens to die within 16 months of each other? And how can we still trust Him?

Unable to comprehend such tragedies, we cling to Psalm 139:16 — "In Your book they were all written, the days fashioned for me." By God's design, our children had a specific number of days to live, and then He lovingly called them home to their eternal reward. And we find comfort in God's mysterious words, "Precious in the sight of the LORD is the death of His saints" (116:15).

The death of those close to us could rob us of our trust in God — taking with it our reason for living. But God's unfathomable plan for the universe and His redemptive work continue, and we must honor our loved ones by holding on to His hand. We don't understand, but we still must trust God as we await the great reunion He has planned for us.  — Dave Branon

*Though tragedy, heartache, and sorrow abound*
*And many a hardship in life will be found,*
*I'll put all my trust in the Savior of light,*
*For He can bring hope in the darkest of night.*  —D. De Haan

---

**Don't let tragedy steal your trust in God.**

# DRONES

READ:
1 Timothy 5:8-16

There are some who
walk among you in a
disorderly manner,
not working at all,
but are busybodies.
—2 Thessalonians 3:11

THE BIBLE IN ONE YEAR:
■ 1 Kings 6–7
■ Luke 20:27-47

As I sat looking at my beehives, I was especially interested in the activities of a considerable number of bees that seemed to be busybodies. They were always buzzing, going in and out of the hive, but doing no apparent work. These nonproductive ones are called drones. They are male bees — much larger than a worker or even the queen. Their only function is to fertilize a queen and then die.

While waiting for a new queen to emerge, the drones spend their time visiting one hive after another. But they do no work; they make no honey; they build no comb; they can't even sting. And they're noisy! You should hear them buzz, but it's all bluff.

For a while drones are privileged characters, but when fall comes and the honey flow slackens, the worker bees will kill every drone! Not a one lives through the winter. The time of reckoning comes, and they are denied the reward of the workers.

In the apostle Paul's letter to Timothy, he warned about people who are active in the wrong kinds of activities — going from house to house as busybodies, stirring up trouble instead of serving others (1 Timothy 5:13).

Don't be a drone if you want to share in the heavenly treasures reserved for the faithful. — M. R. De Haan, M.D.

*In service true of any kind,*
*Lord, happy I shall be,*
*If by my help some soul may find*
*The path that leads to Thee.* — Anon.

**God's house should be a hive for workers—
not a nest for drones.**

# GO LIGHT YOUR WORLD

READ:
Zechariah 4:1-6

---

"Not by might nor by power, but by My Spirit," says the LORD of hosts.
—Zechariah 4:6

---

THE BIBLE IN ONE YEAR:
■ 1 Kings 8–9
■ Luke 21:1-19

Do you feel as if you're burning out in your service for God? You may want to supply spiritual light to your dark world till the end of your life, but you wonder if you can. You won't burn out if you understand and apply the truth of Zechariah 4:1-6.

The prophet saw two olive trees that supplied oil to a bowl that fed seven lamps on a golden lampstand. As we think about the reality behind this symbolism, we can be encouraged. You and I are not the source of light that enlightens the world. We can only receive the oil of the Holy Spirit that fuels the living flame He produces. If we burn steadily through the long, dark hours, it is because we have learned to yield our lives to the Spirit's unlimited supply of power and strength. This comes only through continual fellowship with Jesus our Savior.

It needs to be said again and again: It's not what we do for the Lord, but what He does through us that enlightens and enriches others. We must be satisfied to be a bright and shining lamp, drawing from the hidden resources of the indwelling Spirit of Christ. Our role is to help others see the glory of His light. And we must remember daily that every demand placed upon us is a demand placed upon Him. —David Roper

*Help me, dear Lord, to be honest and true*
*In all that I say and all that I do;*
*Give me the courage to do what is right,*
*To bring to the world a glimpse of Your light.* —Fasick

---

**Let your light shine—whether you're a candle in a corner or a lighthouse on a hill.**

# LIVING PEACEFULLY

**READ:**
**Genesis 26:14-22**

---

If it is possible, as much as depends on you, live peaceably with all men.
—Romans 12:18

---

THE BIBLE IN ONE YEAR:
- 1 Kings 10–11
- Luke 21:20-38

Isaac lived among the Philistines, who proved to be ornery neighbors. He had grown so rich and powerful that they feared him and asked him to leave their territory. Being "much mightier" than they (Genesis 26:16), Isaac could have refused, but he acquiesced and moved into a nearby valley where his father Abraham had dug some wells years before.

The Philistines had stopped up the wells after the death of Abraham. Each time Isaac reopened a well they claimed it for themselves, even though they had not been using it. They were just being contentious. But Isaac kept moving on till he entered an area where the Philistines no longer contested his right to the water.

I've encountered people like that. When my brothers and I played catch as young boys, we had to be very careful about our throws, because the neighbor would confiscate any balls that went into his yard.

It's difficult to like such people, but Jesus went so far as to say that we must love them, pray for them, and be good to them (Matthew 5:44). It may not be easy, and those ornery persons may not change. Yet, according to Romans 12:18, we must still do all we can to live peacefully with everyone. —Herb Vander Lugt

*We know there will be times of stress*
*With people who must have their way;*
*But we should always choose to love,*
*To live at peace, and for them pray.* —D. De Haan

---

**Try to live at peace with others**
**even though they want to fight with you.**

## May 2

# SO NEAR AND YET SO FAR

**READ:**
Numbers 14:26-35

---

Whoever calls on the name of the LORD shall be saved.
—Romans 10:13

---

THE BIBLE IN ONE YEAR:
■ 1 Kings 12–13
■ Luke 22:1-20

**B**ack in Canada's early days, pioneers were taking shelter in Fort Babine. When supplies were nearly exhausted, Victor Clark and a young guide left the fort and walked to the town of Hazelton to get food.

On their way back to the fort, snow began to fall. Soon the two travelers were chilled to the bone by a stinging wind and were unable to follow the trail in the darkness. Forced to stop, they built a fire and spent a miserable night. Then as light slowly dawned, they saw the fort with its warmth and comfort — only a few hundred yards away from where they had stopped. So near and yet so far!

The Israelites were at the very border of the Promised Land (Numbers 13). Caleb and Joshua, the two courageous spies, had brought back the lush foods of Canaan and encouraged the people to take possession of the land (vv.26,30). But the people doubted and condemned themselves to 40 years of wandering and death in the desert (14:28-30). They too were so near and yet so far away!

Have you heard many times about Jesus' love for you but remain uncommitted to Him? Are you near yet so far away? Choose now to cross over into the "promised land" of salvation found in Jesus. —Vernon Grounds

*A PRAYER*

*Dear Jesus, I admit that I am a sinner, and I ask for Your forgiveness. I believe that You died and took my punishment. I trust You as my Savior and Lord.*

---

**Now is the time to choose the Lord—
later may never come.**

# THE POWER OF TWO

**READ:**
1 Samuel
20:12-17,41-42

Jonathan again caused David to vow, because . . . he loved him as he loved his own soul.
—1 Samuel 20:17

THE BIBLE IN ONE YEAR:
■ 1 Kings 14–15
■ Luke 22:21-46

In G. K. Chesterton's novel *The Man Who Was Thursday*, an undercover policeman infiltrates a lawless group that is dedicated to throwing the world into chaos. He is gripped with fear until he discovers an ally within the group.

Chesterton writes of the policeman's feelings at finding a friend: "Through all this ordeal his root horror had been isolation, and there are no words to express the abyss between isolation and having one ally. It may be conceded to the mathematicians that four is twice two. But two is not twice one; two is two thousand times one."

When David was being pursued by the jealous and irrational King Saul, he had a friend who risked great danger to stand with him. Jonathan, Saul's own son, pledged his loyalty to David and warned him of his father's intention to kill him (1 Samuel 20:31-42). Later, when Saul pursued David into the wilderness, Jonathan "arose and went to David in the woods and strengthened his hand in God" (23:16).

What a wonderful gift we give by standing faithfully with a friend in need! There is incredible encouragement and power when two people are allied in life. Whose hand can you strengthen by being a friend today? — David McCasland

*Lord, help me be the kind of friend*
*That makes my friend secure;*
*So he can find new strength and hope*
*His trials to endure.* — D. De Haan

---

**A true friend helps you keep going**
**when you feel like giving up.**

# THE DISCUS THROWER

**READ:**
1 Peter 5:6-10

May the God of all grace, . . . after you have suffered a while, perfect, establish, strengthen, and settle you. —1 Peter 5:10

THE BIBLE IN ONE YEAR:
■ 1 Kings 16–18
■ Luke 22:47-71

A Scottish athlete in the 19th century made an iron discus based on a description he read in a book. What he didn't know was that the discus used in official competition was made of wood with only an outer rim of iron. His was solid metal and weighed three or four times as much as those being used by other discus throwers.

According to author John Eldredge, the man marked out the record distance in a field near his home and trained day and night to match it. For years he labored until he could break the record. Then he took his iron discus to England for his first competition.

When he arrived at the games, he was handed the official discus. He easily set a new record, a distance far beyond those of his competitors. He remained the uncontested champion for many years. This man trained under a heavy burden and became better for it.

When we are given a heavy burden to bear, we need to learn to bear it in Jesus' strength and for His sake. Whatever the burden or suffering, God will use it to "perfect, establish, strengthen, and settle" us, as 1 Peter 5:10 says.

Our burdens can make us better than we ever imagined — stronger, more patient, more courageous, more gentle, and more loving than we could otherwise be. —David Roper

*Without my trials and hardships*
*I would never know the way*
*That You turn burdens into blessings*
*With every passing day.* —Oglesby

**Today's burdens can strengthen you for tomorrow.**

# THE MIRACLE GOES ON

READ:
2 Chronicles 30:21-27

Their voice was heard; and their prayer came up to His holy dwelling place, to heaven.
—2 Chronicles 30:27

THE BIBLE IN ONE YEAR:
■ 1 Kings 19-20
■ Luke 23:1-25

Did you ever think of a prayer meeting as a miracle? That thought came to my mind one evening at church after we divided into small prayer groups. As someone in each group prayed, I heard several people talking to God at the same time. It sounded like a jumble of words. But that's the miracle. God was hearing each prayer — along with millions of others being lifted to Him around the world in many different languages.

For those of us who reach frustration levels when two children are talking to us at the same time, it is indeed a miracle that God can hear so many of His children simultaneously.

Consider the story of Hezekiah's Passover celebration. He called for the Israelites to join him in Jerusalem for praise and prayer (2 Chronicles 30:1). Multitudes came for what turned into a 2-week-long worship service. Huge numbers of people rejoiced and praised God at the same time (v.25). As the religious leaders prayed, "their voice was heard; and their prayer came up . . . to heaven" (v.27).

The miracle goes on. Today, throughout the world, millions of people are praying to God. Let's rejoice in knowing that He hears each prayer.  — Dave Branon

God hears us when we call to Him,
He does not miss one voice;
The knowledge that He always hears
Should cause us to rejoice.  — Sper

**You'll never get a busy signal
on the prayer line to heaven.**

# MOUNTAINS CAN MOVE!

**READ:**
Mark 11:20-24

---

Jesus answered and said to them, "Have faith in God."
—Mark 11:22

---

THE BIBLE IN ONE YEAR:
■ 1 Kings 21—22
■ Luke 23:26-56

A familiar slogan about prayer is, "Prayer changes things." But prayer doesn't do this — God does. Some people think that prayer itself is the source of power, so they "try prayer," hoping "it will work" for them. In Mark 11, Jesus disclosed one of the secrets behind all true prayer: "Have faith in God." Not faith in faith, not faith in prayer, but "faith in God" (v.22).

Jesus told His disciples they could command a mountain to be cast into the sea, and if they believed it would happen, it would. Jesus then gave them His meaning behind that astonishing promise. He said, "Whatever things you ask when you pray, believe that you receive them, and you will" (v.24). Jesus was speaking about answered prayer. We can ask and receive answers only if our asking is directed to God in faith and according to His will (1 John 5:14).

I've often wished that I could move mountains by faith. Having once lived in Switzerland, I'd like God to move the Alps into my backyard in England. But He has done something much more important: He has removed mountains of worry, fear, and resentment from my heart and cast them into oblivion through my faith in Him. He is still in the mountain-moving business! Have faith in God and pray! — Joanie Yoder

> *When the Spirit prompts the asking,*
> *When the waiting heart believes,*
> *Then we know of each petition —*
> *Everyone who asks receives.* — Anon.

---

**Faith is the key to answered prayer.**

# WAKE-UP CALLS

READ:
Daniel 4:28-34

I, Nebuchadnezzar, praise and extol and honor the King of heaven, all of whose works are truth, and His ways justice.
—Daniel 4:37

THE BIBLE IN ONE YEAR:
■ 2 Kings 1–3
■ Luke 24:1-35

A strong, young brute often swaggered around town boasting that he could walk a barbed wire fence in his bare feet with a wildcat under each arm. So goes the story according to the *Iron County Miner*. The braggart got a rude awakening, however, when he married a strong-willed little lady who made him wash the dishes twice a day.

Another rude awakening occurred when a platoon sergeant roused a new recruit after his first night in an army barracks. "It's four-thirty!" bellowed the sergeant. "Four-thirty!" gasped the rookie. "Man, you'd better go to bed. We have a big day tomorrow!"

We are all inclined to dream our way through life until someone or something confronts us with the real world. For Nebuchadnezzar, king of ancient Babylon, the wake-up call lacked humor. Before his encounter with God, he thought he had life well in hand. Suddenly he found himself on his hands and knees eating grass like an animal (Daniel 4:33). After 7 long years (v.32) he learned that in the real world everyone must live under authority, everyone is on God's time, and everything we possess is a gift from His gracious hand.

Father, wake us up today. Make us aware of what it means to live under Your wise and loving authority. — Mart De Haan

*When life is all sunshine and days are bright,*
*Our thoughts of the Lord may take wings of flight;*
*But God is still ruler, His kingdom stands,*
*And we all are subject to His commands.* — K. De Haan

---

**A person who thinks too much of himself
thinks too little of God.**

# A WINNING COMBINATION

READ:
1 Timothy 1:18-20

---

. . . having faith and a good conscience, which some having rejected, concerning the faith have suffered shipwreck.
—1 Timothy 1:19

---

THE BIBLE IN ONE YEAR:
■ 2 Kings 4–6
■ Luke 24:36-53

A new believer slipped into his old ways by attending a party and getting drunk. When he arrived home, his wife would not let him in. Instead, she called their pastor, who found the man sleeping in his car.

The pastor took him to a motel to sleep off his drunkenness. He knew him well and was confident that a strong rebuke would not be needed. Instead, he asked God to convict the man and bring him to repentance. In this case the pastor chose the right course. The young man later said that he had learned a valuable lesson through this experience and that the Lord had "taken all the fun out of sin."

A "good conscience" will disturb us when we do something we know is wrong. We keep it "good" by heeding it and turning away from sin. Paul said the faith of Hymenaeus and Alexander "suffered shipwreck" because they rejected the voice of their good conscience (1 Timothy 1:19-20). By doing so, they had deadened their conscience and then apparently twisted the truth to justify their conduct.

True faith and a sensitive conscience will take all the fun out of sinning and remove the desire to twist the truth to justify what is wrong. Faith and a good conscience are a winning combination. Let's keep them strong. — Herb Vander Lugt

*Our conscience is a gift from God,*
*It is a guiding light;*
*And when aligned with faith and truth,*
*It tells us wrong from right. — Sper*

---

**Conscience is a safe guide when
guided by God's Word.**

# INDISPENSABLE

**READ:**
2 Timothy 1:1-5

---

I call to remembrance
the genuine faith that
is in you, which
dwelt first in your
grandmother Lois and
your mother Eunice.
—2 Timothy 1:5

---

THE BIBLE IN ONE YEAR:
■ 2 Kings 7–9
■ John 1:1-28

A talented stay-at-home mother wrote a delightful essay in which she vividly describes (without complaining) the frustrations, sacrifices, and loneliness that accompany her chosen lifestyle. It's not glamorous to deal with a fussy 18-month-old who is teething, to settle quarrels between an irrational 3-year-old and a pushy 5-year old, and to listen to the incessant chatter of small children. Yet she concludes that her role is indispensable for the total well-being of her children. How true!

The importance of a godly mother's role in the life of a child cannot be overemphasized. Think of Timothy, for example, the young man the apostle Paul considered his spiritual son and a valuable partner in ministry. In his second letter to him, Paul recalled how Timothy had been influenced by "the genuine faith" of his grandmother Lois and his mother Eunice (2 Timothy 1:5). God used two generations of loving mothers to prepare Timothy for the crucial work he would have in spreading the gospel and establishing congregations of believers in Christ.

Let's praise the Lord for mothers who not only care for their children physically but also nurture them spiritually. Mothers like that are indispensable! — Herb Vander Lugt

*God has conferred on motherhood*
*A true nobility,*
*And she who gladly fills that role*
*Can shape man's destiny.* — D. De Haan

**No man is poor who has had a godly mother.**
—Abraham Lincoln

# POSTCARD CHRISTIANITY

READ:
Psalm 13

---

How long will You hide Your face from me? —Psalm 13:1

---

THE BIBLE IN ONE YEAR:
- 2 Kings 10–12
- John 1:29-51

When my husband and I visited Mt. Rainier, the highest point in the continental United States, I expected to see some spectacular sights. But for 2 days the mountain remained shrouded in clouds. So instead of taking pictures, I bought postcards.

Our vacation caused me to question the way I portray my faith to people around me. Do I present a "postcard" view of Christianity? Do I give the false impression that my life is always sunny — that my view of God is always clear?

That's not what David did. In the passion-filled poetry of Psalm 13, he admitted that he couldn't see God and didn't understand what He was doing (v.1). But by the end of his prayer, he was certain that what he couldn't see was nevertheless there because he had seen it before in God's bountiful care (vv.5-6).

Christians are like people living at the foot of Mt. Rainier. They've seen the mountain before, so they know it exists even when clouds are covering it.

When suffering or confusion obscures our view of God, we can be honest with others about our doubts. But we can also express our confidence that the Lord is still there by recalling times we've witnessed His grandeur and goodness. That's better than postcard Christianity. — Julie Ackerman Link

*God, give us wings to rise above*
*The clouds of trial that block the sun,*
*To soar above gray skies and see*
*The love and goodness of Your Son.* —Sper

---

**When living under clouds of adversity,**
**remember that the sun is still shining.**

## WHEN YOU'RE DOWN

READ:
Psalm 6

Depart from me, all
you workers of
iniquity; for the LORD
has heard the voice
of my weeping.
—Psalm 6:8

THE BIBLE IN ONE YEAR:
■ 2 Kings 13–14
■ John 2

Sometimes it doesn't take much to get us down, does it? An unkind remark from a friend, bad news from the auto mechanic, a financial setback, or a misbehaving child can put a cloud of gloom over everything, even on the sunniest day. You know you should be joyful, but everything seems to be against you, making simple tasks a struggle.

David must have been feeling that way when he wrote Psalm 6. He felt weak and sickly (v.2), troubled (v.3), forsaken (v.4), weary (v.6), and grief-stricken (v.7). But he knew what to do when he was down. He looked up and trusted God to take care of him and to see him through.

When we look up and focus on God, something good happens. We get our eyes off ourselves and gain a new appreciation of Him.

Next time you're down, try looking up to God. He is sovereign (Psalm 47:8); He loves you (1 John 4:9-10); He considers you special (Matthew 6:26); He has a purpose for your trials (James 1:2-4).

Yes, life can seem unbearable at times. But don't let it keep you down. Meditate on God's goodness, talk to Him, and know that He hears you (Psalm 6:9). That will give you strength to get up when you're down. —Dave Branon

*Come, ye disconsolate, where'er ye languish —*
*Come to the mercy seat, fervently kneel;*
*Here bring your wounded hearts, here tell your anguish:*
*Earth has no sorrow that heav'n cannot heal.* —Moore

**When life knocks you to your knees,
you're in a good position to pray.**

# RUNNING FOR OTHERS

**READ:**
**Philippians 2:1-11**

Let nothing be done
through selfish ambition
or conceit, but . . .
let each esteem others
better than himself.
—Philippians 2:3

THE BIBLE IN ONE YEAR:
■ 2 Kings 15–16
■ John 3:1-18

Tom Knapp never won a race during his entire high school track career. Tom was a "pusher." It was his task to set the pace for his fellow team members, who would then beat him to the finish line. When he ran a successful race, he was enabling a fellow teammate to win. Even though Tom never had enough reserve energy for the final sprint to victory, the coach considered him a valuable member of the team.

In a similar way, the New Testament tells us to run our race of faith with the success of others in mind. "Let nothing be done through selfish ambition or conceit, but in lowliness of mind let each esteem others better than himself. Let each of you look out not only for his own interests, but also for the interests of others" (Philippians 2:3-4). Our example of such living is Jesus Christ, who left the glory of heaven to share our humanity and die on the cross so that we can have eternal life (vv.5-8).

If the encouragement of our example helps another person to flourish and be successful, we should rejoice. When the eternal prizes are awarded for faithful service to God, a lot of "pushers" will be wearing blue ribbons. Until then, let's keep running so that others can win. — David McCasland

*Oh, to see the needs of others*
*More important than our own,*
*Following our Lord's example*
*When He left His heavenly throne.* —Sper

**You can't lose when you help others win.**

# BEARING A GRUDGE

**READ:**
**Genesis 27:35-41**

You shall not . . . bear any grudge against the children of your people, but you shall love your neighbor as yourself.
—Leviticus 19:18

THE BIBLE IN ONE YEAR:
■ 2 Kings 17–18
■ John 3:19-36

English essayist and critic Charles Lamb (1775-1834) had this to say about a person he did not want to meet: "Don't introduce me to that man! I want to go on hating him, and I can't hate someone I know."

Harboring malice robs us of close relationships with others. Jacob cheated his brother and stole his birthright. Understandably, Esau was angry. But what he did with his anger became a serious problem, not only for Jacob but for Esau himself. For years he harbored a deep resentment that robbed him of a warm relationship with his brother.

Grudges can also create a cold, icy environment in churches, and this often keeps people away. Pastor George Gardiner asked the members of a congregation he visited why their church wasn't growing. He received this reply: "There's an elder in this church who holds a grudge."

Instead of bearing a grudge, we must bare it before God in confession and ask for deliverance. We must begin praying for the person toward whom we have negative feelings and, if possible, take practical steps to resolve our differences. We must find ways to show love.

Resentment will fade when the object of our ill will becomes the special object of our goodwill. — Dennis De Haan

*When anger lingers in our heart,*
*It poisons all we think and do;*
*But faith seeks ways to show God's love*
*And keeps our spirit strong and true.* —D. De Haan

---

**A grudge is one thing that does not get better when it is nursed.**

# HE IS A FIRE

READ:
Hebrews 12:25-29

---

Let us have grace, by which we may serve God acceptably with reverence and godly fear. For our God is a consuming fire.
—Hebrews 12:28-29

---

THE BIBLE IN ONE YEAR:
■ 2 Kings 19–21
■ John 4:1-30

On December 5, 2002, the headline announced:

**RING OF FIRE ENCIRCLES SYDNEY**

A firestorm was raging outside the Australian city. Many people feared that this bushfire would prove to be Sydney's worst in decades. Fanned by strong winds, high temperatures, and low humidity, the fire jumped across roads and rivers, consuming everything in its path.

When we think about the destructive power of that kind of inferno, we gain a better understanding of the startling words of Hebrews 12:29, "Our God is a consuming fire."

Why did the author of Hebrews use such graphic imagery to describe the Lord? In his letter he was dealing with spiritual life-and-death issues — what his readers believed and the reality of their faith. Their response would reveal whether they were investing their lives in the kingdom that will last forever, or in the one destined for destruction.

We too need to remember that this world and all we possess are only temporary. If our faith and hope are in Jesus Christ, we are part of a kingdom that cannot be destroyed (v.28). Knowing that our days on earth are numbered and that "our God is a consuming fire," let us serve Him and invest in things that are imperishable. — Albert Lee

*Our God is a consuming fire*
*And will destroy earth's temporal things;*
*He seeks to purify our lives*
*For service to the King of kings.* —D. De Haan

---

**Hold tightly to what is eternal
and loosely to what is temporal.**

# THE LOST BOOK

**READ:**
2 Kings 22:8-13

---

I have found the Book of the Law in the house of the LORD.
—2 Kings 22:8

---

THE BIBLE IN ONE YEAR:
- 2 Kings 22–23
- John 4:31-54

Two US Senate staffers were cleaning out a storeroom underneath the Capitol when they spotted a partially opened door nearby. Curious, they stepped inside and found a small room jammed with dusty old brochures and payroll records. A leatherbound book with gold lettering caught their attention: *Senators' Compensation and Mileage*. It bore the dates 1790–1881.

What a find! It was a one-of-a-kind record of every dollar paid to senators during the Senate's first 90 years. Plus, the book contains the handwritten signatures of founding fathers Thomas Jefferson and John Adams. "The book speaks volumes," says historian Richard Baker. "There is nothing that comes remotely close to it in the archives of the Senate."

I imagine that Hilkiah the high priest felt even more excitement when he discovered the long-lost "Book of the Law" in some hidden cranny in the temple (2 Kings 22:8). King Josiah recognized its value and ordered it to be read aloud to all the people of Judah (23:1-2).

Maybe it has been a while since you've read portions of the Bible such as Leviticus, Zechariah, or Philemon. Dust them off and try reading them. They speak volumes — and their message may be just what you need. — Dave Egner

*I entered the world's great library doors;*
*I crossed their acres of polished floors;*
*I searched and searched their stacks and nooks,*
*And settled at last on the Book of books.* —Anon.

---

**The Bible is old, but its truths are always new.**

# FINE CRYSTAL

**READ:**
Psalm 127

Children are a heritage from the LORD, the fruit of the womb is a reward. —Psalm 127:3

THE BIBLE IN ONE YEAR:
■ 2 Kings 24–25
■ John 5:1-24

I have a friend — call her "Mary" — who tells me that her fondest memory is of the morning she broke her mother's "priceless" crystal.

Mary's mother was having a party. She had taken her fine crystal from the cupboard and carefully washed it and placed it on the table. The crystal represented the only valuable material possession her mother owned, and it was used only on special occasions.

In her rush to get things ready for her guests, Mary's mother said to her young daughter, "Would you please find some place that's not underfoot?" So Mary crawled underneath the table. Unfortunately, she kicked the leg of the table and the crystal crashed to the floor. "Crystal exploded like shrapnel," she recalls. She had destroyed the most elegant thing her mother possessed.

"I'm so sorry," the little girl sobbed. Her mother gathered her in her arms and whispered, "Don't cry, honey. You are far more valuable to me than mere crystal."

Children are indeed our most valuable possession, more precious than anything we could ever buy or earn. They are "a heritage from the LORD" and "a reward" (Psalm 127:3).

Do your children know how precious they are to you? Why not tell them today. — David Roper

*Our children are a heritage,*
*A blessing from the Lord;*
*They bring a richness to our lives —*
*In each, a treasure stored. — Fasick*

**Little children are of great value to God.**

# PUTTING LOVE INTO PRACTICE

READ:
**Matthew 5:11-16**

Let your light so shine before men, that they may see your good works and glorify your Father in heaven.
—Matthew 5:16

THE BIBLE IN ONE YEAR:
■ 1 Chronicles 1–3
■ John 5:25-47

In his book *Christians in the Marketplace*, Bill Hybels says that people outside the faith often say, "Show me" before they say, "Tell me."

I knew a young man in Germany named Wolfgang who modeled Hybels' principle at a building site where he worked. As an enthusiastic believer, Wolfgang always read his Bible during lunch. Though his fellow workers jeered, he didn't stop his daily reading. He simply prayed for a way to demonstrate Christ's love to them.

When the workers went home at night, they always left their muddy boots behind. Wolfgang began staying late after work to clean their boots. The men were puzzled at first but then realized that Wolfgang was the only one among them who would perform this humble service. Not only did they come to respect him, but sometimes they even asked him to read the Bible to them. Only eternity will reveal the full effect of Wolfgang's shining life. But this we know: When his co-workers saw his good works, they started listening to his God.

Jesus said, "Let your light so shine before men, that they may . . . glorify your Father in heaven" (Matthew 5:16). If you long to lead the people around you to Jesus, radiate His love by doing practical deeds for God's glory alone. — Joanie Yoder

*My life was dark until the Light shone in,*
*That Light was Christ, who saved me from my sin;*
*His light that I've received I long to share*
*In loving deeds for people everywhere.* — Hess

---

**A Christian's life is a window**
**through which others can see Jesus.**

# UNEXPECTED ALLIGATORS

READ:
Matthew 13:18-23

When tribulation or persecution arises because of the word, immediately he stumbles.
—Matthew 13:21

THE BIBLE IN ONE YEAR:
■ 1 Chronicles 4–6
■ John 6:1-21

A friend of actress and comedienne Gracie Allen once sent a small, live alligator to her as a gag. Not knowing what to do with it, Gracie put it in the bathtub and then left for an appointment. When she returned home, she found a note from her maid. "Dear Miss Allen: Sorry, but I have quit. I don't work in houses where there is an alligator. I would have told you this when I started, but I never thought it would come up."

Some people who say they'll serve Christ are quick to leave when trouble comes. In Jesus' parable of the soils, He pictured the various responses that people have to the gospel. For example, a person may seem to accept God's truth, but he stumbles in his faith when difficulties arise (Matthew 13:20-21). Such troubles test the sincerity of one's faith and expose the weakness of one's commitment to Christ.

But someone may say, "Shouldn't our Lord tell us up front what is involved in following Him?" He does. He appeals to us with one invitation: "Trust Me." If we let trouble or disillusionment shake our faith, we are breaking the spirit of the trust that brought us to Christ in the first place.

Father, when life brings us the unexpected and we feel like quitting, help us to be faithful to You. — Mart De Haan

*Day by day and with each passing moment,*
*Strength I find to meet my trials here;*
*Trusting in my Father's wise bestowment,*
*I've no cause for worry or for fear.* — Berg

**Tough times can teach us to trust.**

## SEE YOU NEXT TIME?

READ:
1 Chronicles 16:23-36

Sing to the LORD, all the earth; proclaim the good news of His salvation from day to day.
—1 Chronicles 16:23

THE BIBLE IN ONE YEAR:
■ 1 Chronicles 7–9
■ John 6:22-44

It was a Sunday afternoon several years ago. The whole family was gathered around the table for dinner. Our 4-year-old son Stevie led off our pre-meal prayer: "Dear heavenly Father, thank You for this nice day. Thank You that we could go to church and Sunday school today." Then, to our surprise, he said, "And we'll see You again next week."

What Stevie said in his prayer is how we often view the Christian life, I'm afraid. We easily fall into a see-you-next-time attitude about God. We forget about Him as we fulfill our daily responsibilities. We go for days at a time trying to pay the bills, keep the boss happy, and give attention to each family member. But we neglect to give God the time He deserves.

First Chronicles 16 gives us some facts about God's power and majesty that we can think and talk about "from day to day" (v.23). We can "declare His glory" (v.24) and recognize His hand of creation in the heavens (v.26). We can talk of His honor and majesty, the strength He possesses, and the gladness He gives us (v.27).

Each day brings new reasons to pray to God, to praise His name, and to proclaim His love. Let's make our worship of Him something we do "from day to day." — Dave Branon

*Worship, praise, and adoration*
*Render now to Jesus' name;*
*Freely give your heart's devotion,*
*Constantly His love proclaim.* — Anon.

**No day is complete without worship.**

# HEADLINE EVENT

**READ:**
John 13:33–14:3

---

Behold, He is coming
with clouds, and every
eye will see Him.
—Revelation 1:7

---

THE BIBLE IN ONE YEAR:
■ 1 Chronicles 10–12
■ John 6:45-71

Did you know that the largest type used by most newspapers for headlines of astounding events has been called "second coming" type? These heavy, black letters are reserved for only the most amazing front-page news stories. This dramatic type has been used to announce the beginning and end of wars, moon landings, presidential election winners, natural disasters, and other significant events.

One day mankind will witness the great event for which the "second coming" type was named — the return of Jesus Christ. And what a day that will be! The One who ascended to heaven long ago will return to this earth. When our Lord comes back, it will be such a phenomenal occurrence that it will command worldwide attention.

The day Jesus told His disciples that He would be leaving them, Peter was filled with questions (John 13:36-37). Jesus didn't explain when He would return, but He reassured His disciples that He was going to prepare a place for them and one day "come again" (14:2-3).

When the Savior comes back, His return will command the attention of all earth's inhabitants. It will be a headline event! — Dave Egner

*When Christ the Lord returns to reign,*
*The world will know of that event,*
*For everyone shall see His face*
*And know the reason He was sent.* — Hess

---

**Even so, come, Lord Jesus!**
—Revelation 22:20

# NEW HOPE

READ:
Romans 15:5-13

---

May the God of hope
fill you with all joy
and peace in believing,
that you may abound
in hope by the power
of the Holy Spirit.
—Romans 15:13

---

THE BIBLE IN ONE YEAR:
■ 1 Chronicles 13–15
■ John 7:1-27

Grant Murphy of Seattle was the active type, a man who ran at full throttle. Idling and coasting were not in his nature. "One might even call him hyperactive," recalled a dear friend.

Then multiple sclerosis began to slow Grant down. First he needed crutches to get around. Then he was limited to sitting in a chair. Finally he was confined to a bed.

Near the end, he was hardly strong enough to talk. His friend recalls, however, that "he expressed only joy and thankfulness with a constant anticipation of being in the Lord's presence." Not long before he died, Grant whispered Romans 15:13 to a friend. He repeated the words "in believing," then added, "I can't *do* anything now."

It's when we can't do anything that *God does everything*. And herein lies a profound paradox of the Christian's experience. Faith is simultaneously an exercise of our will and the impartation of divine strength. And from that marvelous mixture spring joy and peace and an abundance of hope.

Are you in a totally helpless situation? Strength gone? All options exhausted? If you have trusted Jesus as your Savior, God will strengthen you to keep on believing. As you trust Him, He'll give you not only joy and peace, but also hope when all hope is gone. — Dennis De Haan

*When we are weak and in despair,*
*Our mighty God is near;*
*He'll give us strength and joy and hope,*
*And calm our inner fear.* — Sper

---

**No one is hopeless whose hope is in God.**

# MASTER OF REDEMPTION

**READ:**
1 Samuel 21:10–22:2

---

Everyone who was in distress . . . gathered to [David]. So he became captain over them.
—1 Samuel 22:2

---

THE BIBLE IN ONE YEAR:
■ 1 Chronicles 16–18
■ John 7:28-53

As I glanced through the mail, some words on a card from a charitable organization caught my eye: WE NEED YOUR DISCARDS! The meaning was straightforward and simple: Whatever you don't want, we'll take. Those household items you call rubbish, rejects, throwaways, and junk, we'll use to help people in need.

While thinking about such a collection of castoffs, I recalled something I had read in the book of 1 Samuel. A company of desperate men gathered around an uncrowned king who was running for his life. The 400 men who joined David at the cave of Adullam were in distress, in debt, and discontented. Each one faced difficulty and discouragement. "So [David] became captain over them" (1 Samuel 22:2).

In many ways, Christians are a collection of desperate people who have answered the invitation of Jesus: "Come to Me" (Matthew 11:28). By faith, we acknowledge Christ as our Captain, Savior, Leader, and Lord. We come as we are so that we can become what He wants us to be.

If you feel like a moral or spiritual discard, come to Jesus. Loners and losers are welcome at the door. The crucified and risen Christ is the master of redemption for all who turn to Him. — David McCasland

*Christ asks thee for nothing —*
*Come just as thou art;*
*Come sinful, come guilty,*
*Come give Him thy heart.* — Anon.

---

**Jesus came to save the lost, the last, and the least.**

# THE UPSIDE OF DYING

READ:
John 17:20-26

Father, I desire that they also whom You gave Me may be with Me where I am, that they may behold My glory. —John 17:24

THE BIBLE IN ONE YEAR:
■ 1 Chronicles 19–21
■ John 8:1-27

A Sunday school teacher asked some 5-year-olds a series of questions to help them realize that trusting in Jesus is the only way to get to heaven. He asked, "If I sell everything I have and give the money to the church, would that get me into heaven?" "No," they answered. "How about if I keep everything clean in and around the church?" Another "No." "If I love my family, am kind to animals, and give candy to every child I meet, will that get me to heaven? Another unanimous "No!" Then he asked, "What will get me into heaven?" A little boy shouted, "You have to be dead!"

This was hardly the answer the teacher expected, but the youngster was right. The Bible tells us that we all must leave our flesh-and-blood bodies (1 Corinthians 15:50-52). Unless we are alive when Jesus returns, we all must die before entering His presence.

British preacher Charles Haddon Spurgeon captured this truth in a sermon titled "Why They Leave Us." He pointed out that Jesus' prayer in John 17:24 is answered every time a Christian dies. The person leaves his body and enters the presence of his Savior, where he beholds His glory. What a comfort for the believer! It reveals the upside of dying. Is that your confidence? — Herb Vander Lugt

*The death of people whom we love*
*Brings sorrow and deep pain;*
*But if our loved ones know the Lord,*
*Our loss becomes their gain.* — Sper

**When Christians die, they have just begun to live.**

# TOO MUCH TO DO?

**READ:**
Luke 10:38-42

One thing I have desired of the LORD, . . . that I may dwell in the house of the LORD all the days of my life. —Psalm 27:4

THE BIBLE IN ONE YEAR:
- 1 Chronicles 22–24
- John 8:28-59

I'm usually a happy person. Most of the time I can take on as much work as anyone can give me. But some days there just seems to be too much to do. The schedule may be so full of meetings, appointments, and deadlines that there's no room to breathe. Life often contains too much work, parenting, home improvement, and other responsibilities for one person to handle.

When that happens to me — as it may happen to you — I have some options. I can retreat into a shell of inactivity and leave everyone who is depending on me out in the cold. I can slug my way through, moaning as I go and making everyone wish I had chosen option one. Or I can get my perspective realigned by reminding myself what Jesus said to Martha (Luke 10:38-42).

Jesus told Martha that she had become "distracted with much serving" (v.40). He reminded her that her sister Mary had chosen the one thing that would never be taken away (v.42). Like many of us, Martha got so wrapped up in her service that she forgot the most important thing — fellowship with her Lord.

Are you overwhelmed? Don't lose sight of your priorities. Spend time with the Lord. He will lift your load and give you the right perspective. — Dave Branon

*The many tasks we face each day*
*Can burden and oppress,*
*But spending time with God each day*
*Can bring relief from stress.* — Sper

---

**To keep your life in balance, lean on the Lord.**

# WHO CALLS THE GAME?

READ:
Job 40:1-14

Shall the one who
contends with the
Almighty correct Him?
—Job 40:2

THE BIBLE IN ONE YEAR:
■ 1 Chronicles 25–27
■ John 9:1-23

During an afternoon baseball game when American League umpire Bill Guthrie was working behind home plate, the catcher for the visiting team repeatedly protested his calls.

According to a story in the *St. Louis Post Dispatch,* Guthrie endured this for three innings. But in the fourth inning, when the catcher started to complain again, Guthrie stopped him. "Son," he said gently, "you've been a big help to me calling balls and strikes, and I appreciate it. But I think I've got the hang of it now. So I'm going to ask you to go to the clubhouse and show them how to take a shower."

Job also had been complaining about calls he didn't think were fair. In his case, the umpire was God. After listening to Job's objections, the Lord finally spoke out of a violent storm. Suddenly things came into perspective for Job. God was gentle, but He was also firm and direct. The Lord asked him the kind of questions that bring finite man back down to size. Job listened, gave up his complaining, and found peace in surrendering to God.

Father, we don't make sense when we complain about Your fairness. Help us to be like Your Son Jesus, who trusted You without complaining, even to the point of dying on the cross. — Mart De Haan

*When troubles come and we complain*
*Because we do not understand,*
*The problem is our narrow view*
*That fails to see God's loving hand.* — K. De Haan

**When you feel like complaining,**
**think of all that Jesus endured.**

# GOD IS ALIVE!

READ:
Psalm 30

O LORD my God,
I will give thanks to
You forever.
—Psalm 30:12

THE BIBLE IN ONE YEAR:
■ 1 Chronicles 28–29
■ John 9:24–41

The great 16th-century theologian Martin Luther once experienced a long period of worry and despondency. One day his wife dressed in black mourning clothes.

"Who has died?" asked Luther.

"God," said his wife.

"God!" said Luther, horrified. "How can you say such a thing?"

She replied, "I'm only saying what you are living."

Luther realized that he indeed was living as if God were no longer alive and watching over them in love. He changed his outlook from gloom to gratitude.

Occasionally we too live as if God were dead. When we are discouraged, we can turn to the Psalms. Some of the writers faced bleak and barren times, but they had one habit in common that kept them from being soured: giving thanks to God. For example, David wrote, "You have turned for me my mourning into dancing . . . . O LORD my God, I will give thanks to You forever" (Psalm 30:11-12).

Meeting every situation with thanksgiving isn't a denial of trouble. It helps us see those situations from God's perspective — as opportunities to discover His power and love.

Every time you express gratitude to God in a difficult situation, you're declaring, "God is alive!" — Joanie Yoder

*When things go wrong, I would not be a grumbler,*
*Complaining, seeing everything as grim;*
*For when I think of how the Lord has blessed me,*
*I cannot help but give my praise to Him.* — Hess

---

**Instead of complaining about the thorns on roses,
be thankful for the roses among the thorns.**

# CALAMITY

**READ:**
Luke 13:1-5

Do you think that they were worse sinners . . . ? I tell you, no; but unless you repent you will all likewise perish.
—Luke 13:4-5

THE BIBLE IN ONE YEAR:
■ 2 Chronicles 1–3
■ John 10:1-23

Some Christians are quick to declare that a public disaster (such as a terrorist attack, an earthquake, or a flood) is the result of divine judgment. In reality, a complex array of factors lie behind most disasters.

In Luke 13, Jesus was asked about some people who were cruelly murdered, and about 18 people who died when a tower collapsed on them. The people asking the questions were wondering if those who died were worse sinners than others. "I tell you, no," said Jesus, "but unless you repent you will all likewise perish" (vv.3,5).

Instead of reading divine judgment into tragedies, we should see them as a call to personal repentance. This is especially true for unbelievers, but it is also true for Christians. Acts of terrorism, for example, challenge us to learn about the injustices that in part motivate people to commit such horrible atrocities. And we can pray earnestly for the conversion and the good of the desperate people who commit such acts.

Calamities in themselves are never good, but they can fulfill God's purposes when they serve as a wake-up call to believers, and when they bring unbelievers to repentance and faith in Jesus. Let's not ask, "Who's to blame?" but "Lord, what are You saying to me?"  — Herb Vander Lugt

*When great calamity befalls,*
*We wonder why it's sent;*
*But God says, "Ask not who has sinned—*
*Just hear My call, 'Repent!'"*  —D. De Haan

---

**In alarming situations,
listen for God's wake-up call.**

# RESTORING
# GOD'S IMAGE

**READ:**
Colossians 3:8-17

---

We all . . . are being
transformed into the
same image from glory
to glory.
—2 Corinthians 3:18

---

THE BIBLE IN ONE YEAR:
■ 2 Chronicles 4–6
■ John 10:24-42

As a young boy, theologian Alister McGrath enjoyed experimenting with chemicals in his school's laboratory. He liked to drop a tarnished coin into a beaker of diluted nitric acid. He often used an old British penny bearing the image of Queen Victoria. Because of the accumulated grime, Her Majesty's image couldn't be seen clearly. But the acid cleansed away the grime and the Queen's image reappeared in shining glory.

We know, to be sure, that we were created in the image of God (Genesis 1:26), but that image has been defaced by our sin. We are still His image-bearers, however.

Once we invite Jesus to enter our lives as Savior, He goes to work to restore the original image. He transforms us to make us like Himself (2 Corinthians 3:18). This process is described as putting off some behaviors and putting on others. For example, we are to "put off all these: anger, wrath, malice, blasphemy, filthy language" (Colossians 3:8) and to "put on love" (v.14).

Unless and until our sin-tarnished souls are cleansed by Jesus' forgiveness, God's image is obscured in our lives. But when we trust Jesus' sacrifice on the cross, we are forgiven and the restoration begins. — Vernon Grounds

*Restore in me Your image, Lord,*
*So tarnished by my sin and shame;*
*And cleanse whatever may conceal*
*The shining glory of Your name.* — D. De Haan

---

**Drawing close to Christ**
**produces a growing Christlikeness.**

# TRUE GREATNESS

**READ:**
Luke 9:28-29, 34-42

---

Now it happened on the next day, when they had come down from the mountain, that a great multitude met Him. —Luke 9:37

---

THE BIBLE IN ONE YEAR:
■ 2 Chronicles 7–9
■ John 11:1-29

On the 50th anniversary of Sir Edmund Hillary's historic ascent of Mt. Everest, a television newsman said that much of Hillary's status as a hero in Nepal was "not about what he did when he stood on top of the world, but what he did when he came back down." After conquering the world's highest mountain with his climbing companion Tenzing Norgay in 1953, Edmund spent the next five decades helping to build schools, hospitals, and bridges for the Sherpa community.

The contrast between Edmund Hillary's moment on the mountain and his service in the valley brought to mind Jesus' experience on the Mount of Transfiguration (Luke 9:28-36). It was a pinnacle of blessing when our Lord's appearance became radiant and the Father said, "This is My beloved Son. Hear Him!" (v.35).

But Jesus didn't stay on the mountain. He came down to the crowd, where He freed a boy from an evil spirit. He was determined to go to Jerusalem and fulfill His mission, where He would willingly die on the cross for our sins.

Jesus told His disciples, "He who is least among you all will be great" (v.48). Our Lord's life shows us that true greatness is found in humbly serving God and others in the valley of need.  — David McCasland

*Whether on the mountaintop*
*Or the valley down below,*
*True greatness is in serving*
*Wherever we may go.*  — D. De Haan

---

**In God's eyes, true greatness is serving others.**

# THE BEST CONSOLER

**READ:**
John 14:16-21, 24-27

I will pray the Father, and He will give you another Helper, that He may abide with you forever. —John 14:16

THE BIBLE IN ONE YEAR:
■ 2 Chronicles 10–12
■ John 11:30-57

When two uniformed men came to my door on Memorial Day afternoon, I thought they were collecting for charity. Instead, they told me that my sister and her husband had been killed in an accident earlier that day.

Just over a year after that shattering event, our church choir sang "Veni, Sancte Spiritus" ("Come, Holy Spirit") on Pentecost Sunday (Whitsunday). It brought a wave of peace over my still-aching soul. One verse says: "Thou best of Consolers, sweet guest of the soul, sweet refreshment. In labor, Thou art rest; in heat, the tempering; in grief, the consolation."

On Pentecost Sunday, many churches celebrate the Holy Spirit's coming in power on the disciples (Acts 2:1-21). But the Spirit came also as the Comforter promised by Jesus: "I will pray the Father, and He will give you another Helper, that He may abide with you forever" (John 14:16). The Spirit lives within each Christian, bringing the peace of Christ along with encouragement and alleviation of grief.

Pentecost and Memorial Day seldom fall next to each other as they do in 2004. But the "sweet guest of the soul" is always with us on any day we remember our loved ones who have died. In grief, the Spirit is our consolation, the light of our hearts, the giver of everlasting joy. — David McCasland

*O spread the tidings 'round wherever man is found,*
*Wherever human hearts and human woes abound;*
*Let every Christian tongue proclaim the joyful sound:*
*The Comforter has come!* — Bottome

---

**In every desert of trial,**
**the Holy Spirit is our oasis of comfort.**

# Remember

**Read:**
John 19:1-8

When we were still
without strength, in
due time Christ died
for the ungodly.
—Romans 5:6

THE BIBLE IN ONE YEAR:
■ 2 Chronicles 13–14
■ John 12:1-26

Prime Minister Winston Churchill was honoring members of the Royal Air Force who had defended Britain during World War II. Recounting their brave service, he declared, "Never in the history of mankind have so many owed so much to so few."

A similar sentiment appears on a memorial plaque in Bastogne, Belgium, where raged the famous Battle of the Bulge, one of the bloodiest conflicts of the Second World War. The inscription, in honor of the US 101st Airborne Division, reads: "Seldom has so much American blood been shed in the course of a single action. Oh, Lord, help us to remember!"

Those are fitting and well-deserved tributes to the courageous men and women who sacrificed so much for their country.

As I think about them, I also remember the One whose selfless sacrifice resulted in benefits for people of all nations. Jesus Christ, the sinless One, died on a cross and shed His blood to pay the penalty for our sins. In so doing, He guaranteed our freedom — freedom from the penalty, power, and someday even the presence of sin. Of Jesus it can be said: Never in the history of mankind have so many owed so much to one Man. Yes, His was the greatest sacrifice.

Lord, help us to remember!  — Richard De Haan

*'Twas not a martyr's death He died,*
*The Christ of Calvary;*
*It was a willing sacrifice*
*He made for you — for me.*  — Adams

---

**The memory of Jesus' death**
**calls us to a life of praise.**

## VICTORY OVER TEMPTATION

**READ:**
Matthew 4:1-11

God . . . will not allow
you to be tempted
beyond what you are
able, but . . . will also
make the way of escape.
—1 Corinthians 10:13

THE BIBLE IN ONE YEAR:
■ 2 Chronicles 15–16
■ John 12:27-50

Wanda Johnson, a single mother with five children, was on her way to the pawn shop, where she was hoping to get a loan of $60 for her TV set. Then something bizarre happened. As an armored truck filled with sacks of money drove past her, its rear door flew open, and a bag dropped out. Wanda stopped and picked up the sack. When she counted the cash, she found that it totaled $160,000.

A battle raged in her soul. That money would pay all her bills and provide for the needs of her children. But it wasn't hers to keep.

After a fierce 4-hour struggle with her moral convictions, Wanda called the police and turned in the money. Her sense of doing the right thing won a victory over the temptation to keep what wasn't hers.

How strong is your ethical fiber? Will it break down if you are faced with an enticing chance to do something wrong? Adam and Eve, as well as Jesus, were attacked by Satan on three fronts: the lust of the flesh, the lust of the eyes, and the pride of life (1 John 2:16). Our first parents succumbed to the serpent's solicitation (Genesis 3:1-6). Jesus did not (Matthew 4:1-11).

No matter what evil is pressuring us, let's follow Jesus' example and do what's right.   —Vernon Grounds

*Yield not to temptation, for yielding is sin—*
*Each victory will help you some other to win;*
*Fight manfully onward, dark passions subdue,*
*Look ever to Jesus—He will carry you through.*   —Palmer

**To withstand temptation, stand with Christ.**

## PORCUPINE PEOPLE

READ:
1 John 4:16-21

---

This commandment we have from Him: that he who loves God must love his brother also.
—1 John 4:21

---

THE BIBLE IN ONE YEAR:
■ 2 Chronicles 17–18
■ John 13:1-20

Deep in a Wyoming canyon I came across the biggest porcupine I've ever seen. As he lumbered toward me, I watched him closely and gave him plenty of room. I was not about to get near a guy whose quills looked like missiles. No wonder he was alone!

But he's not alone all the time. Every November and December, porcupines get close enough to produce offspring. During that time they choose to relax their quills, then they return to their prickly selves.

In nearly every church, there will be a porcupine or two, with sharp quills of criticism or sarcasm or arrogance. We want to avoid them, but God places us in communities of believers for fellowship. He commands us to love one another—including the porcupine types. And in our honest moments, we have to admit that we have quills too.

John wrote, "He who loves God must love his brother also" (1 John 4:21). To do this, we need to ask God to help us "relax our quills," even when other people are prickly. The Holy Spirit will help us stop being so defensive or critical or controlling, and enable us to love our Christian brothers and sisters. It's the way we show the world that we love God (John 13:35). — Dave Egner

*Some people can be difficult to love*
*And so we do not even try to care,*
*But God says, "Love them just as I've loved you—*
*You'll bring Me glory as My love you share." —Cetas*

---

**God loves you and me—let's love each other.**

# DEATH CLOCK

READ:
1 Peter 4:7-11

---

**The end of all things is at hand; therefore be serious and watchful in your prayers.**
—1 Peter 4:7

---

THE BIBLE IN ONE YEAR:
■ 2 Chronicles 19–20
■ John 13:21-38

There is a Web site that claims to predict when you will die. After you answer a series of questions, your projected date of death appears along with a digital clock counting down the number of seconds you have left to live. It's all based on current life-expectancy charts, but seeing it on a computer screen makes it more vivid. As the site says, it's "the Internet's friendly reminder that life is slipping away."

God in His wisdom doesn't tell us the day of our death. Nor do we know the day of Christ's return. The Bible urges us to live for Christ and be prepared for either event. Peter wrote, "The end of all things is at hand; therefore be serious and watchful in your prayers. . . . Have fervent love for one another . . . . Be hospitable to one another without grumbling. As each one has received a gift, minister it to one another, as good stewards of the manifold grace of God" (1 Peter 4:7-10).

Jesus said, "Be ready, for the Son of Man is coming at an hour you do not expect. . . . Blessed is that servant whom his master will find so doing when he comes" (Luke 12:40,43).

As Christians, we need not panic as we see our time slipping away. Instead, let's live every moment for Christ and be prepared to meet Him today. —David McCasland

*The godless ponder death with fear—*
*For what's ahead they cannot see;*
*But those who put their faith in Christ*
*Anticipate eternity.* —Sper

---

**Be ready for your last moment**
**by being ready every moment.**

# THE REBUKE FROM A FRIEND

**READ:**
**Galatians 2:11-20**

---

Faithful are the wounds of a friend, but the kisses of an enemy are deceitful.
—Proverbs 27:6

---

THE BIBLE IN ONE YEAR:
■ 2 Chronicles 21–22
■ John 14

Never will I forget the rebuke I received from a friend when I was 17. He walked into the back of the butcher shop where I worked and saw me laughing at an indecent cartoon. He said he had admired my Christian character, and was surprised that I would laugh at something sinful and degrading. Instantly a wave of embarrassment swept over me. I shamefully admitted that I had sinned.

It's not pleasant to be rebuked, nor is it easy to rebuke another person. So I can imagine that the apostle Paul didn't like confronting Peter (Galatians 2:11). But he felt he had to, because Peter's hypocritical behavior was hurtful and confusing to the Gentile converts at Antioch. Peter had freely eaten with them, but after some Jews from Jerusalem came to the Antioch church, he shunned the Gentiles, fearing the Jews' disapproval. I imagine that he felt shame, but he apparently accepted the rebuke gracefully and changed his ways. He knew that Paul was a true friend who loved him. And in later years he referred to him as "our beloved brother Paul" (2 Peter 3:15).

If you must rebuke someone, do it gently. If you are rebuked, avoid an angry response. You may be getting a needed "faithful wound" from a friend. — Herb Vander Lugt

*A friend will gently say what's true,*
*Although it may cause pain;*
*He's really thinking of our good*
*And what we stand to gain.* —D. De Haan

---

**A true friend will put a finger on your faults
without rubbing them in.**

# THE PRUNING

READ:
John 15:1-11

Every branch that bears
fruit He prunes, that it
may bear more fruit.
—John 15:2

THE BIBLE IN ONE YEAR:
■ 2 Chronicles 23–24
■ John 15

In every vineyard, a vinedresser prunes the branches so they will produce more fruit. In a spiritual sense, our heavenly Father must deal with us in a similar way at times—by pruning our lives. It isn't only the dead branches that have to go, but sometimes even the living and vital ones must be cut back so that better and more bountiful fruit may grow.

Many different circumstances may serve as a pruning knife in the hands of the Master Vinedresser. It may be the rejecting gesture, the unkind word, or no word at all. It could be the frustration of living in a constant state of noise and confusion, with daily duties and no chance to find a quiet place to call our own. Or it might be waiting for God to intervene when everything seems hopeless and we have no friends to help us.

But the pruning knife is guided by a loving set of hands. The Master Vinedresser knows what we can take, and He knows what we can become—more loving, joyful, tranquil, tolerant, kind, dependable, gentle, poised—stronger and better than we are today.

We must not shrink from the knife but trust the hand that holds it. Our Father in heaven has a purpose—to produce good fruit in us. —David Roper

*The Master is seeking a harvest*
*In lives He's redeemed by His blood;*
*He seeks for the fruit of the Spirit,*
*And works that will glorify God.* —Lehman

**Fruitbearing + Pruning = More Fruit**

# THE RING

**READ:**
**Philippians 1:12-17**

---

The things which
happened to me have
actually turned out
for the furtherance
of the gospel.
— Philippians 1:12

---

THE BIBLE IN ONE YEAR:
■ 2 Chronicles 25–27
■ John 16

I'm not much for jewelry. A wedding ring was all I ever wanted—until now. Next to my wedding ring, on the little finger of my left hand, rests a simple silver band. It's my daughter Melissa's.

Soon after Mell died in a car accident in June 2002, just 6 weeks short of her 18th birthday, I was in her bedroom when I found the ring. I recalled having seen it on her beautiful hand.

I slipped it on and was surprised that it fit. Now I wear it all the time. Here's why: I can look at it or touch it and feel close to my precious daughter. Knowing that it graced her finger warms my heart when I miss her the most.

But there's another reason I wear her ring. I want people to notice it and ask me about it. Then I can tell them of Melissa and her life of love, faith, and fun. I hope it opens conversations that will allow me to introduce people to Melissa's Savior, and mine.

The apostle Paul used his chains—his imprisonment—to advance the gospel (Philippians 1:12). It wasn't that he enjoyed being incarcerated, but he knew it could be turned to good purposes. It's like the ring. I wish it wasn't mine; I wish Melissa was still enjoying it. But she's not, and I want this tragic circumstance to bring glory to God.

Is there a loss in your life that God can use? — Dave Branon

*Our God works to transform us*
*Till life on earth is done;*
*He uses trials and testings*
*To make us like His Son.* — Sper

---

**God can transform a tragedy into a triumph.**

# VALUE TEST

**READ:**
Luke 6:46-49

Why do you call Me "Lord, Lord," and not do the things which I say? —Luke 6:46

THE BIBLE IN ONE YEAR:
■ 2 Chronicles 28–29
■ John 17

Robert Ginnett, a researcher at the Center for Creative Leadership in Colorado Springs, has found that the values we claim to have are not as closely linked to our actual behavior as we might like to believe.

One business executive, who said his 5-year-old daughter was the most important part of his life, realized that he usually went to work before she got up in the morning and often returned home after she was in bed at night. So to spend time with her, he took her to work with him one Saturday. After looking around his office, she asked, "Daddy, is this where you live?" He may have acknowledged that his daughter was important, but his behavior revealed what he truly valued.

In our relationship with Christ, He asks for our obedience, not a warm feeling or a statement of belief. He asked those following Him, "Why do you call Me 'Lord, Lord,' and not do the things which I say?" (Luke 6:46). Jesus illustrated His point with the parable of the wise and foolish builders (vv.47-49). The rock-solid foundation of the wise builder's house illustrates the result of our obedience to God. This honors Christ and enables us to withstand the storms of life.

What we *do,* more than anything we *say,* reveals what we truly value the most. —David McCasland

> *Fill up each hour with what will last;*
> *Buy up the moments as they go;*
> *The life above, when this is past,*
> *Is the ripe fruit of life below.* —Bonar

---

**To show that you value eternity,
make good use of your time.**

# PEACEMAKERS

**READ:**
1 Samuel 25:14-35

Blessed are the
peacemakers, for they
shall be called sons of
God. — Matthew 5:9

THE BIBLE IN ONE YEAR:
■ 2 Chronicles 30–31
■ John 18:1-18

Abigail was a remarkable woman! She was a true peacemaker whose courage spared the future king of Israel from committing a terrible sin. Here's her story:

David had been forced to live in the countryside to escape King Saul's jealous wrath. A group of about 600 men and their families had gathered around him. For several months they camped near Carmel where the flocks of Nabal (Abigail's husband) were grazing. David's men had helped Nabal's shepherds protect the sheep from robbers. Now the shearing time had come, and David sent messengers to request some compensation from Nabal, who was a wealthy man. But he refused and treated David's men with disdain.

In anger David rashly decided to kill Nabal and all the men in his household. When Abigail heard what had happened, she quickly gathered a large supply of food, intercepted David and his fighting men, and humbly apologized for her husband's surly behavior. David immediately realized that she had prevented him from carrying out a vengeful decision, and he praised God (1 Samuel 25:32).

Are we as quick to resolve a conflict? Jesus said, "Blessed are the peacemakers, for they shall be called sons of God" (Matthew 5:9). —Herb Vander Lugt

*How blest are those who persevere*
*To bring a conflict to an end;*
*And if the peace of Christ takes hold,*
*An enemy becomes a friend.* —D. De Haan

**You can be a peacemaker
if you have God's peace in your heart.**

# FRIENDSHIP WITH GOD

**READ:**
John 15:13-15

---

I have called you friends, for all things that I heard from My Father I have made known to you.
—John 15:15

---

THE BIBLE IN ONE YEAR:
■ 2 Chronicles 32–33
■ John 18:19-40

**P**age through an old-time hymnal and notice how often the songwriters referred to the blessing of God's friendship. Stop and think about what that really means.

Yes, it's a blessing to have human friends who enrich our lives. A devoted friend, as Proverbs 17:17 tells us, "loves at all times," standing with us steadfastly through life's sunshine and storm.

Indeed, some of us know gratefully by our own experience that "there is a friend who sticks closer than a brother" (Proverbs 18:24). We identify with David and Jonathan when we read about the bond between them (1 Samuel 18:1).

Friendship on a human level is wonderful, but what about friendship with God? It's an incredible blessing to have the Creator and Sustainer of our universe as a friend. Although worshiped by countless heavenly hosts, He takes great joy in His relationship with us.

Are we neglecting the privilege of walking with God, the greatest of all friends? Today, with gratitude and awe, let's spend time with Him in prayer and in reading His Word.

Remember that Jesus called His followers friends (John 15:15). What an honor that we can enjoy friendship with God! —Vernon Grounds

*I've found a Friend, oh, such a Friend!*
*He loved me ere I knew Him;*
*He drew me with the cords of love,*
*And thus He bound me to Him.* —Small

---

**When you spend time with God,
you invest in a forever friendship.**

# ENOUGH OF EVERYTHING

READ:
2 Corinthians 9:6-15

God is able to make all grace abound toward you, that you . . . may have an abundance for every good work.
—2 Corinthians 9:8

THE BIBLE IN ONE YEAR:
■ 2 Chronicles 34–36
■ John 19:1-22

Randy, our first child, went off to kindergarten with a 10-cent coin in his pocket to buy a carton of milk to go with his lunch. When he came home that afternoon, his mother asked if he had purchased the milk. "No," he replied, bursting into tears. "The milk was 5 cents and I only had a dime."

How often I have responded to demands placed upon me with the same childish understanding. According to God's Word, I have all the resources I need at my disposal—more than enough to meet my needs—and yet I'm reluctant to act because I fear that I won't have enough. But the Bible assures me that God has provided me with every blessing in abundance. By His grace, I have everything I need (2 Corinthians 9:8).

The apostle Paul was not saying that we have enough grace to do anything we want to do. God does not offer us a blank check. No, Paul was giving us the assurance that we have enough grace to do whatever God has called us to do—whether it is to give money for the cause of the gospel, as the Corinthians were doing (v.7), or to give love to a difficult teenager, an indifferent spouse, or an aging parent.

Whatever the task, God will make sure we have "an abundance for every good work" (v.8). —David Roper

*God uses us to do His work*
*If we will just obey;*
*He freely gives His love and power*
*To serve Him every day.* —Sper

**God's call to a task includes His strength to complete it.**

# STAY WITHIN GOD'S LIMITS

**READ:**
Ephesians 5:15-21

---

See then that you walk circumspectly, not as fools but as wise.
—Ephesians 5:15

---

THE BIBLE IN ONE YEAR:
■ Ezra 1–2
■ John 19:23-42

One of life's greatest enjoyments for Suzannah Worl is riding her Harley-Davidson motorcyle. In a devotional article for Covenant Publications, she wrote about cruising the streets of Chicago with her friends late one summer night. They were riding along the shore of Lake Michigan, enjoying the bright moonlight and gentle breeze off the water.

Suddenly the lead motorcyclist took off and several of the group went with him, reaching speeds of 100 miles an hour. Suzannah was tempted to join them—but she didn't. She knew it was not safe and it was against the law. So she held back, continuing at normal speed.

Sometimes the way others live seems far more attractive and exciting than our Christian life. We're tempted to disobey God's commands or compromise principles from His Word. But we are called to live each day with self-discipline and spiritual discernment. The apostle Paul said, "Walk circumspectly, not as fools but as wise" (Ephesians 5:15).

We need to ask the Lord for His help so that we'll see situations through His eyes and make wise choices. As we obey Him and stay within His limits, we will find true joy and lasting satisfaction. — Dave Egner

*Living for Jesus a life that is true,*
*Striving to please Him in all that I do;*
*Yielding allegiance, glad-hearted and free,*
*This is the pathway of blessing for me. —Chisholm*

---

**The wise know God's limits—**
**fools know no bounds.**

# FOR SINNERS ONLY

**READ:**
Ephesians 2:1-10

By grace you have been saved through faith . . . ; it is the gift of God, not of works, lest anyone should boast.
— Ephesians 2:8-9

THE BIBLE IN ONE YEAR:
■ Ezra 3–5
■ John 20

Many non-Christians know the hymn "Amazing Grace" but may not know what *grace* means. One day when evangelist D. L. Moody was studying the meaning of God's grace, he dashed into the street and shouted to the first man he saw, "Do you know grace?" Mystified, the man replied, "Grace who?" No doubt Moody then explained grace—that God has compassion on sin-sick people and freely offers them forgiveness and new life through faith in Christ.

I heard of a man who had lived a troubled life and died without understanding the message of God's grace. A minister had talked to him and encouraged him to come to church, but his response was, "I'm too undeserving." He didn't know that God's grace is for the undeserving.

In Paul's letter to the Ephesians, he bluntly described their pre-Christian lives as being "dead in trespasses and sins" (2:1). Then he used two hope-filled words: *but God* (v.4). They introduce God's mercy and grace that provide forgiveness and new life through Christ. Salvation is through faith, not works, so no one can boast (vv.8-9).

Let's help others to understand that God's salvation is for sinners only—and that includes all of us. That's what makes God's grace so amazing!  —Joanie Yoder

*Amazing grace! How sweet the sound*
*That saved a wretch like me!*
*I once was lost but now am found,*
*Was blind but now I see.* —Newton

---

**The first step to receiving eternal life
is to admit that we don't deserve it.**

# WE NEED ONE ANOTHER

READ:
Hebrews 10:19-25

As His custom was, [Jesus] went into the synagogue on the Sabbath day.
—Luke 4:16

THE BIBLE IN ONE YEAR:
■ Ezra 6–8
■ John 21

If recent polls can be trusted, an upsurge of Lone Ranger spirituality is occurring in the United States. Church attendance is down. Biblical beliefs are being abandoned. More and more of our fellow citizens are looking inward, online, and out-of-doors for the uplift they once sought in church sanctuaries.

How different from Jesus! He made it His practice to join in synagogue services regularly (Luke 4:16). But today, people no longer take Him as an example. They settle for what is loosely called "spirituality" and try to nurture their souls without the timeless traditions of congregational praise, prayer, biblical instruction, and edifying fellowship.

To gather regularly with other worshipers is an uplifting source of comfort, inspiration, and emotional strength. The Bible urges us not to forsake "the assembling of ourselves together" (Hebrews 10:25).

We should, of course, have regular devotional times by ourselves. Just as surely, we need the blessing of uniting with other believers for worship and fellowship. We need to spend time together "in order to stir up love and good works" (v.24). We need to make it our habit to worship with others. We need one another.  —Vernon Grounds

*We each can have sweet fellowship with Jesus*
*As through the Word we learn to trust Him more;*
*But we must also meet with one another*
*As in His name we worship and adore.*  —Hess

**Christians are like coals of fire—together, they glow; apart, they grow cold.**

# ASCENDED!

**READ:**
2 Corinthians 5:1-8

---

We are . . . well pleased rather to be absent from the body and to be present with the Lord.
—2 Corinthians 5:8

---

THE BIBLE IN ONE YEAR:
■ Ezra 9–10
■ Acts 1

Joseph Parker (1830–1902) was a beloved English preacher. When his wife died, he didn't have the customary wording inscribed on her gravestone. Instead of the word *died* followed by the date of her death, he chose the word *ascended*.

Parker found great comfort in being reminded that though his wife's body had been placed in the grave, the "real" Mrs. Parker had been transported to heaven and into the presence of her Savior. When Parker himself died, his friends made sure that his gravestone read:

ASCENDED NOVEMBER 28, 1902

When a believing loved one dies, or when we ourselves face the process of dying, there's great comfort in the fact that "to be absent from the body" is "to be present with the Lord" (2 Corinthians 5:8).

Death for us is not a dark journey into the unknown. It is not a lonely walk into a strange and friendless place. Rather, it is a glorious transition from the trials of earth into the joys of heaven, where we will be reunited with our loved ones in Christ who have gone before. Best of all, we will enjoy the presence of our Lord forever.

Yes, when a believer dies, the body is buried but not the soul. It has ascended! —Richard De Haan

*Oh, how blessed is the promise*
*When our spirit is set free:*
*To be absent from the body*
*Means to live, O Lord, with Thee! —Bosch*

---

**For the Christian, death is the doorway to Glory.**

## PRAYING AND WAITING

READ:
Nehemiah 1:5-11

Rest in the LORD, and
wait patiently for Him.
—Psalm 37:7

THE BIBLE IN ONE YEAR:
■ Nehemiah 1–3
■ Acts 2:1-21

A Christian couple was deeply distressed because their married son and his family had quit going to church and were giving God no place in their lives. As their friend, I advised them to continue showing love, to pray, and to avoid starting arguments. But at the family's annual Christmas gathering, the father gave his son a lecture in the presence of the other siblings. The son and his family left in anger and broke off all contact with his parents.

It's hard to rely on prayer alone when you want something to happen right now. But that is what Nehemiah did. He was distraught by the news that the Israelites in Jerusalem were in grave danger (Nehemiah 1:3-4). He was a man with great leadership ability and in a favorable position to receive help from the king he served, so he was eager to help his people. But he knew that he could be executed for coming into the presence of a Persian king without being invited. Therefore, though he had asked God to give him the opportunity immediately, he trusted God enough to wait. Four months later, the king opened the door for him to make his request (2:1,4).

It's not always easy to be patient, but God can be trusted. Wait patiently for Him. —Herb Vander Lugt

*Praying, resting, waiting, trusting—*
*These are words that tell a story;*
*As we wait for God to lead us,*
*He responds, "Just seek My glory." —Hess*

---

**Delay is not denial—pray on!**

# GROWING IN OLD AGE

**READ:**
Psalm 92:12-15

They shall still bear fruit in old age; they shall be fresh and flourishing.
—Psalm 92:14

THE BIBLE IN ONE YEAR:
■ Nehemiah 4–6
■ Acts 2:22-47

We have a gnarled, ancient plum tree in our backyard that has seen better days. Its bark is dark and creased with age, its limbs are sparse and spindly, and it leans about 45 degrees to the west. Two years ago I had to cut off some branches on one side and the tree lost its symmetry.

I thought we had lost it for sure several winters ago when we had a stretch of sub-zero weather. The man who sprays our trees said he believed it was dead. Yet it came to life that spring and continues to do so every year.

Each April that old tree shrugs off the winter and puts out blossoms— fragrant pink flowers that grow profusely and beautify our yard. As I write this article, I can smell its sweetness in the air.

That plum tree endures because it has roots that tap deep into the soil. It draws its strength and nourishment from hidden subterranean sources.

And so it is with us. Our ability to endure—no, to flourish—is dependent on our being rooted in Christ. Those who read His Word, reflect on it, and pray it into their lives bring forth the fruit of the Spirit (Galatians 5:22-23), even into old age. As Psalm 92:14 says, "They shall be fresh and flourishing." —David Roper

*Our faltering steps and ebbing strength*
*Reveal life as a fading page;*
*Yet holding firm to Christ in faith*
*Keeps hope alive at any age.* —D. De Haan

**Better than counting your years
is making all your years count.**

June 17

## WHAT MOTIVATES US?

READ:
1 Thessalonians 2:3-9

Even so we speak,
not as pleasing men,
but God who tests
our hearts.
—1 Thessalonians 2:4

THE BIBLE IN ONE YEAR:
■ Nehemiah 7–9
■ Acts 3

My wife and I received a notice that we had won a prize of either $1,000 dollars in cash or $250 in vouchers. When we arrived at the collection site, we were told that to be eligible, we would have to sit through a 90-minute presentation.

As we listened, we learned that we could receive vacation accommodations for 25 years at today's prices, which would amount to about $15,000 in savings. But to enjoy this privilege, we had to pay a membership fee of $5,200. We declined the offer but were given some discount vouchers, which we realized we'd probably never use.

Reflecting on that experience, my wife and I wondered why we had endured what had become a 3-hour presentation. What had motivated us? We wanted to be polite, but we also had to admit we were partly motivated by greed.

Wrong motives can even slip into our service for the Lord. Paul wrote to the believers at Thessalonica: "You remember, brethren, our labor and toil; for laboring night and day, that we might not be a burden to any of you" (1 Thessalonians 2:9). He had the right to receive financial help from them, but he didn't want to be accused of unworthy motives.

What motivates us? Let's learn from Paul's example, remembering that God tests our hearts. — Albert Lee

*You know me, O Lord, for who I am,*
*My motives are open to You;*
*Oh, help me to live as Jesus did —*
*With motives both noble and true.* — Sper

**The world sees what we do — God sees why we do it.**

# PAINT SPECKS

**READ:**
1 John 1:5–2:2

---

If we confess our sins, He is faithful and just to forgive us our sins and to cleanse us from all unrighteousness.
—1 John 1:9

---

THE BIBLE IN ONE YEAR:
■ Nehemiah 10–11
■ Acts 4:1-22

Pushing a paint roller high overhead had produced a shower of fine droplets that left tiny white specks on my glasses. Although they were noticeable to others, I was not aware of them. But one morning as I came to work, the angle of the bright sunlight through the lenses of my glasses suddenly made those tiny specks visible and annoying.

So it is with some of our small moral imperfections. Others can see them, but we can't. Then, as we study God's Word, the true light of the Lord Jesus Christ shines on us, and our moral flaws become alarmingly visible. His pure character, genuine love, and unmixed motives reveal specks of sinfulness in everything we do. Little white lies, selfish anger, small hypocrisies, and muddy motives stand out vividly. And they are in all of us to some degree.

How perceptive was the apostle John! He wrote, "If we say that we have no sin, we deceive ourselves" (1 John 1:8). But thank God, "If anyone sins, we have an Advocate with the Father, Jesus Christ the righteous" (2:1). When we confess our sins, He intercedes with the Father on our behalf.

When we confess our shortcomings, God cleanses us — even those tiny specks we don't always see. —Dennis De Haan

*Search out in me all hidden sin,*
*And may Thy purity within*
*So cleanse my life that it may be*
*A temple wholly fit for Thee.* —Swallen

---

**Detecting sin is the first step to deliverance from sin.**

# SHARKS!

**READ:**
**Psalm 3**

---

You, O LORD, are
a shield for me.
—Psalm 3:3

---

THE BIBLE IN ONE YEAR:
■ Nehemiah 12–13
■ Acts 4:23-37

The thought of being surrounded by sharks is not pleasant. I've spent enough time fishing in the Gulf of Mexico, I've read enough articles about their razor-sharp teeth, and I've seen enough films of shark attacks to know how dangerous they can be. But I've also been surrounded by sharks and felt perfectly safe.

Sea World in Florida has an underwater exhibit that allows you to be in a tank with thousands of pounds of living sharks. A plexiglass corridor makes it possible for you to pass through an aquarium housing scores of them. Guided tours allow you to enter the world of these predators, to sense their presence and power, and yet to be safely shielded from attack.

David had the experience of being in "deep water" surrounded by predators. But as a man after God's own heart (1 Samuel 13:14), he had learned to let the Lord be his protection. What was his secret? David brought his fears to the Lord (Psalm 3:1). He refused to listen to those who said that God would not help him (v.2). He even learned to go to sleep (v.5), confident that nothing could touch him without the Lord's permission. David found his refuge in God (v.8).

Father, give us that same confidence. Teach us to trust You as our shield and defender. —Mart De Haan

*Fear not, I am with thee — O be not dismayed,*
*For I am thy God, I will still give thee aid;*
*I'll strengthen thee, help thee, and cause thee to stand,*
*Upheld by My gracious, omnipotent hand.* —Keith

---

**Safety is not the absence of danger**
**but the presence of God.**

# A FATHER'S BLESSING

**READ:**
**1 Peter 3:8-12**

---

Be tenderhearted,
be courteous; not
returning evil for
evil . . . , but on the
contrary blessing.
—1 Peter 3:8-9

---

THE BIBLE IN ONE YEAR:
- Esther 1–2
- Acts 5:1-21

A man who was grieving the death of his father said, "I am crying not only for my father, but for me. His death means that I'll never hear the words I always wanted to hear from him: that he was proud of me, proud of the family I've raised and the life I've lived."

Instead of repeating his father's mistake, the man later gave his own son the words of encouragement he himself had never heard, saying he was proud of him and the life he had made.

Too often, tension between fathers and children are left unresolved. Old wounds remain unhealed. We are unwilling to forgive the angry words and hurts from the past. But for the sake of ourselves and our families, we need to do what we can to dismantle the walls of separation between us.

How can we begin? The Bible's command for all our relationships is: "Love as brothers, be tenderhearted, be courteous, not returning evil for evil or reviling for reviling, but on the contrary blessing . . . . Turn away from evil and do good; . . . seek peace and pursue it" (1 Peter 3:8-9,11).

Let's determine by God's grace to break the cycle of anger and give our children what they long to hear from us—words of blessing and love. — David McCasland

*Our children need to know we care,*
*That when they need us we'll be there;*
*For deep within they need to hear*
*That they are loved by someone dear.* — D. De Haan

---

**The best thing you spend on your children**
**is your time.**

# "APATHEISTS"

**READ:**
**Revelation 3:14-19**

---

Because you are lukewarm, and neither cold nor hot, I will vomit you out of My mouth.
—Revelation 3:16

---

THE BIBLE IN ONE YEAR:
- Esther 3–5
- Acts 5:22-42

Most people profess belief in God, meaning they are theists. True atheism is a rarity.

Recently, however, it has been suggested that we need a new term for the multitude who are theists but are indifferent to God in daily living. They ought to be called *apatheists*. That word is built on the noun *apathy*, which means "indifference," a sort of sluggish unconcern. And sadly, whatever belief an individual professes, he may be living as an apatheist. His faith may make only a minimal difference in his behavior.

The apostle John recorded that Jesus described the church at Laodicea as neither hot nor cold (Revelation 3:16). They were lukewarm or, as we might say, they were apatheists.

What about those of us who profess faith in Jesus? Are we lukewarm? We pray, but is our praying a mere obligation? We attend church and may even engage in some form of Christian service. Yet is all of that a matter of routine, like brushing our teeth or cleaning our house? Have we lost our first love, the zeal we had early in our spiritual journey?

Today, let's make the psalmist's prayer our own: "Will You not revive us again, that Your people may rejoice in You?" (Psalm 85:6). — Vernon Grounds

*Revive us again,*
*Fill each heart with Thy love,*
*May each soul be rekindled*
*With fire from above.* — Mackay

---

**Without a heart aflame for God,**
**we cannot shine for Jesus.**

# "FOLLOW ME"

READ:
Mark 3:13-19

---

Jesus said to them,
"Follow Me . . . . "
They immediately left
their nets and followed
Him. — Mark 1:17-18

---

THE BIBLE IN ONE YEAR:
■ Esther 6–8
■ Acts 6

When the United States launched its space program in 1958, seven men were chosen to become the first astronauts. Imagine the excitement of Scott Carpenter, Gordon Cooper, John Glenn, Gus Grissom, Walter Schirra, Alan Shepard, and Deke Slayton. They were selected to go where no one had ever gone before.

Yet, as astronauts they knew they would face unforeseen dangers, challenges, and trials. Each of them realized that the thrill of being chosen was tempered with the fear of the unknown future.

Imagine another set of men who were chosen for an important mission: the 12 apostles Jesus chose one day on a mountainside near the Sea of Galilee. These men left behind their occupations and families to dedicate themselves to this radical new teacher. They didn't know what kind of political, religious, or financial challenges they would face. Yet they followed Jesus.

Jesus asks the same of His people today. He asks each of us to follow Him, to love Him, to obey Him, and to tell others about Him. Like the apostles, we don't know what our commitment to Jesus might bring.

Lord, help us to follow You faithfully and to trust You completely with our future. — Dave Branon

*I am resolved to follow the Savior,*
*Faithful and true each day;*
*Heed what He sayeth, do what He willeth —*
*He is the living way. —Hartsough*

---

**Following Jesus is always right — but not always easy.**

# WEED CONTROL

**READ:**
Mark 4:13-20

---

The cares of this world, the deceitfulness of riches, and the desires for other things entering in choke the Word.
—Mark 4:19

---

THE BIBLE IN ONE YEAR:
■ Esther 9–10
■ Acts 7:1-21

The Parrotfeather is an attractive aquatic plant that looks like a forest of small fir trees growing on top of the water. In the springtime it produces a blanket of small, white flowers. But it's a noxious weed. It forms a dense mat of vegetation that covers the surface of lakes and ponds, crowding out native plants and destroying fish and wildlife habitat.

Recently I was hiking by a small lake in Washington State that was choked with Parrotfeather plants. It occurred to me that, like that weed, "the cares of this world, the deceitfulness of riches, and the desires for other things entering in choke the Word, and it becomes unfruitful," as Jesus taught in Mark 4:13-20.

Jesus was talking about how unbelievers receive the gospel, but His words can apply to us as well. Sometimes when we read God's Word, our minds are taken up with troubles, worries, and fears. The pressure of things to be done today and concerns about tomorrow's decisions are "weeds" that can choke the Word and make it unprofitable.

To control the weeds, we must ask God to quiet our hearts so we can pay attention to Him (Psalm 46:10). When we turn our worries over to God, we'll be free to enjoy His presence and hear what He has to say. — David Roper

*The weeds will take over and choke out good fruit;*
*But you can control them — just follow this plan:*
*Make sure that the seed of God's Word has deep root,*
*And pull out the weeds just as soon as you can.* — Hess

---

**To uproot the weeds of anxious care,
get down on your knees.**

# THE MAKING OF US

READ:
Hebrews 12:1-11

Whom the LORD loves He chastens, and scourges every son whom He receives.
—Hebrews 12:6

THE BIBLE IN ONE YEAR:
■ Job 1–2
■ Acts 7:22-43

When my husband was a child, his mother sometimes scolded and disciplined him for disobeying her. During one such scolding he said to her imploringly, "You must be nice to your little boy!" His words touched her tender heart. But because she loved him, she continued his discipline and training. Years later as a missionary, Bill was grateful for her tough love, for it was the making of him.

God also disciplines and trains His erring sons and daughters. He may do so directly (1 Corinthians 11:29-32), or He may allow life's hardships to melt us, mold us, and make us more like Jesus. In Hebrews 12:6, we're assured that "whom the LORD loves He chastens." Yet God's chastening doesn't feel very loving. Sometimes we even think it's ruining us. But God's discipline is the very thing that will save us from the ruin of our selfish, stubborn ways.

Although we're unlikely to enjoy God's discipline, we're told that it trains us for right and holy living (vv.7-11). Rather than resisting God's correction, we can yield to Him, confident that His goal is our spiritual growth. Whatever our circumstances, God knows the seriousness of our difficulties and is working powerfully behind the scenes for our good.

His tough love is the making of us. —Joanie Yoder

*God's loving hand of discipline*
*May give us little rest;*
*His only purpose is our good—*
*He wants for us what's best.* —D. De Haan

**God's discipline is designed to make us like His Son.**

# NEVER A QUITTER

READ:
Galatians 6:6-10

---

Be steadfast . . . in the
work of the Lord,
knowing that your
labor is not in vain.
—1 Corinthians 15:58

---

THE BIBLE IN ONE YEAR:
■ Job 3-4
■ Acts 7:44-60

A preacher who was growing weary in the ministry had a dream. He saw himself pounding away at a huge chunk of granite with a pick-axe. It was his job to break it into small pieces. But hard as he tried, he couldn't chip off even a tiny piece. At last, tired and disappointed, he decided to give up.

Just then a stranger appeared and said, "Weren't you given orders to do that work? Your duty is to give your best regardless of what happens." The preacher, with a renewed determination, lifted the pick-axe high in the air and gave the granite a crushing blow. It broke into a thousand pieces. He had almost quit—one blow too soon.

The Lord wants us to keep working at our God-given task no matter how difficult it might be. Even when success seems remote or impossible, we are to remain steadfast, assured that there will be an ample reward for those who persevere.

Have you grown tired in your service for God? Have you become so discouraged that you're tempted to "throw in the towel"? Remember that preacher's dream. Better still, remember God's promise spoken by Paul: "Let us not grow weary while doing good, for in due season we shall reap if we do not lose heart" (Galatians 6:9). —Richard De Haan

*The service that we give to Christ,*
*If steadfast we will be,*
*Is sure to reap a rich reward*
*That someday we will see.* —Sper

---

**Failure is not defeat unless you stop trying.**

# SIGN-SEEKERS

READ:
Luke 11:29-32

This is an evil generation. It seeks a sign, and no sign will be given to it except the sign of Jonah the prophet. —Luke 11:29

THE BIBLE IN ONE YEAR:
■ Job 5–7
■ Acts 8:1-25

A skeptic once said to me, "I'll believe in Jesus if He comes down and appears visibly above my house." Not necessarily!

The Christ-rejecting religious leaders who requested a sign from Jesus had plenty of evidence for believing. They had undoubtedly heard of, if not seen, His miracles of healing, casting out demons, and even raising the dead. What more did they need?

Jesus therefore called them an "evil generation" (Luke 11:29). The only sign they would be given was the sign of Jonah the prophet, who had been thrown into a stormy sea (Jonah 1:2-3). When the Ninevites heard Jonah's message of repentance after he had spent 3 days in the belly of a fish, they believed God had sent him and they repented.

Likewise, the religious leaders who already knew of Jesus' words and works would soon see Him crucified and securely entombed. And in the following weeks they would hear personal testimonies from those who had seen Him alive, and had even touched Him, but they still wouldn't believe.

Today we have in the Gospels a record of what Jesus said and did, written by people who knew Him. If we are open to the truth, we have all the evidence we need to believe. We don't need to be sign-seekers. — Herb Vander Lugt

*If we desire to honor God,*
*We take Him at His Word*
*And ask Him not for special signs,*
*But trust, "Thus saith the Lord."* — D. De Haan

**The sign of genuine faith is
faith that needs no sign.**

# PSALMS, INCENSE, PRAISE

**READ:**
Psalm 150

---

Let everything that has breath praise the LORD.
—Psalm 150:6

---

THE BIBLE IN ONE YEAR:
■ Job 8–10
■ Acts 8:26-40

The well-known English preacher Charles H. Spurgeon (1834–1892) wrote something that would be good to remember at the start of each day: "Let your thoughts be psalms, your prayers incense, and your breath praise." Let's look at each of these phrases.

*Let your thoughts be psalms*. The 150 psalms have a variety of themes, including praise, God's character, and expressions of dependence on the Lord. Throughout the day we can turn our thoughts into psalms by meditating on God's holiness, His worthiness of our worship, and how much we need Him.

*Let your prayers be incense*. In the tabernacle of the Jews, incense was burned continually to offer a sweet savor to the Lord (Exodus 30:7-8). Our prayers are like incense to God (Psalm 141:2), bringing to His nostrils the pleasing scent of our adoration and need for Him.

*Let your breath be praise*. The book of Psalms concludes with the words, "Let everything that has breath praise the LORD. Praise the LORD!" (Psalm 150:6). Talking about God and offering Him words of praise should be as natural to us as breathing.

Keep the Lord in your thoughts, prayers, and speech today. — Dave Egner

> *Worship, praise, and adoration*
> *All belong to Jesus' name;*
> *Freely give your heart's devotion,*
> *Constantly His love proclaim.* — *Anon.*

---

**A heart filled with praise brings pleasure to God.**

**June 28**

# EVER FEEL CONDEMNED?

READ:
1 John 3:16-20

God is greater than our heart, and knows all things.
—1 John 3:20

THE BIBLE IN ONE YEAR:
■ Job 11–13
■ Acts 9:1-21

G od knows us better than we know ourselves. He's aware of our weaknesses, the memories of sins that seem to predispose us to fail again and again. He knows our heredity and upbringing, the past and present influences that push us in the wrong direction. J. I. Packer calls these the "latent forces" of our existence as well as the "patent facts."

At my stage of Christian growth, I struggle with attitudes and actions over which I seem to have little control. I identify with Dostoevsky, who said, "It is nature asserting its rights." Paul called it "sin that dwells in me" (Romans 7:17). It has made me guilty of much, and capable of much more. That's why my heart sometimes condemns me, even though I'm a believer.

God knows all about the forces that drive me. He also knows the intent of my heart—that I want to love others and desire to do right. He knows my shame when I fail and is quick to forgive when I confess (1 John 1:9). This wonderful truth sets my heart at rest when I feel condemned, for "God is greater than my heart, and knows all things" (3:20).

If you have trusted Jesus as your Savior and your heart condemns you at times, remember that He knows all about it and still loves you. — David Roper

*No condemnation now I dread:*
*Jesus, and all in Him, is mine!*
*Alive in Him, my living Head,*
*And clothed in righteousness divine.* — Wesley

**Guilt is a burden God never intended
His children to bear.**

# IT'S A LONG STORY

READ:
2 Chronicles 36:11-17

He who is often rebuked, and hardens his neck, will suddenly be destroyed.
—Proverbs 29:1

THE BIBLE IN ONE YEAR:
■ Job 14–16
■ Acts 9:22-43

In August 1989, a major fire broke out under an elevated section of New Jersey's Interstate 78. The intense heat buckled parts of the highway and forced the closing of the East Coast artery. The governor said it was the worst transportation crisis in years.

An investigation brought to light a longstanding problem. It revealed that the fire broke out in a dump site in which construction debris had been collecting for many years. The owners of the site had been convicted of a multimillion dollar conspiracy to allow the illegal dumping of construction debris. But appeals in federal and state courts frustrated New Jersey's efforts to clean up the area. Not until the day after the fire did a state appeals court finally order the operator of the dump to stop accepting trash and begin clearing the site.

That fire tells a basic story of life. Most of our problems don't just happen. They are the result of a long series of bad decisions. Second Chronicles 36 illustrates this and reminds us that God will not allow His children to continue in sin. Even though He is longsuffering, His patience has a limit. If we don't correct the problem ourselves, we can be sure that He will discipline us.

Let's clean up the trash in our lives today. —Mart De Haan

*Lord, help me see my hidden sin,*
*Those secret wrongs that lurk within;*
*I would confess them all to Thee —*
*Transparent I would always be. —D. De Haan*

---

**The most deadly sins do not leap upon us,**
**they creep up on us.**

**June 30**

## HOME BEFORE DARK

READ:
Acts 20:17-25

---

None of these things move me; nor do I count my life dear to myself, so that I may finish my race with joy.
—Acts 20:24

---

THE BIBLE IN ONE YEAR:
■ Job 17–19
■ Acts 10:1-23

Parents often tell their children, "Be home before dark." And in areas not served by electricity, travelers feel a pressing need to reach their destination while light still lingers in the sky. "Home before dark" means a successful journey and a safe arrival.

Robertson McQuilkin used this phrase to express his desire to remain faithful to the Lord throughout his spiritual journey. His prayer ended with the words "Lord, let me get home before dark." He explained this by first saying, "I fear . . . that I should end before I finish, or finish but not well. That I should stain Your honor, shame Your name, grieve Your loving heart. Few, they tell me, finish well."

McQuilkin's words echo the heartfelt longing of the apostle Paul as he faced danger ahead in Jerusalem: "None of these things move me; nor do I count my life dear to myself, so that I may finish my race with joy, and the ministry which I received from the Lord Jesus, to testify to the gospel of the grace of God" (Acts 20:24).

It is God's word of grace (v.32) that encourages us to continue in faith, for it tells us that He is able to strengthen us until the end of our lives. So let's keep walking and trusting as we pray, "By Your grace, Father, I humbly ask You to help me get home before dark." —David McCasland

*Immortal words of truth we've read,*
*So powerfully penned, so filled with grace,*
*Will follow us through all our days*
*And spur us on to win life's race.* —D. De Haan

**The race of life is run by faith and won by grace.**

# Why Did Jesus Have To Die?

What do people think of the cross? More specifically, what do they think of the cross as it relates to Jesus? That's where the symbol comes from, and that's where the real discussion begins. Why did a beautiful life have to come to such a terrible end? Here are some of the explanations people give for the death of Christ.

### "It's an example of nonresistance."

Some people feel that when Jesus died on the cross He was giving us the ultimate example of how to live in a violent, hostile world. They say that His death shows us how to live successfully by being strong enough to let others have their way.

> **"Father, forgive them, for they do not know what they do."**
>
> —*Jesus, from the cross*

### "It means whatever you want it to mean."

Those who take this approach generally believe that Jesus did not actually accomplish anything when He died on the cross. Since it has become such a part of our awareness, it can be used to symbolize many different things.

### "It has no real meaning."

Some people say that the significance of Christ was in His life not in His death. They believe that He came to live a flawless life on earth so that we could know what God is like. But that was all God sent Him to do. His death, they say, was not related to His mission on earth.

## "It represents failure."

Those who hold this view say that Jesus had a noble and global plan for earth, but that He died before He could carry it out. His mission was aborted when the Roman soldiers nailed Him to the cross like a common criminal.

# The Offensiveness Of The Cross

Some people see so much good in the cross that they fail to see it as a terrible instrument of death. But to others, the cross is so offensive that they fail to see its value. The apostle Paul said it would be that way. Writing to the Christians at Corinth, he said:

> We preach Christ crucified, to the Jews a stumbling block and to the Greeks foolishness (1 Corinthians 1:23).

And what about people today? Does the cross still offend? Do people still stumble over its simple message?

- If their philosophical point of view does not include the reality of sin and the need of a Savior, the answer is yes!
- If by their godly living and high morals they expect to win God's approval, yes!
- If they expect His favor because of their national heritage or family name, yes!
- If they think God is too loving to punish people for their wrongs, yes!

The message of the cross, a first-century implement of execution, will offend them.

We must realize, however, that the cross is not just something hard to live with. It actually makes life possible. In fact, the cross resolved the greatest dilemma of all time.

# The Dilemma Of The Cross

The cross resolves two great dilemmas—one from God's perspective and one from man's. Parents can understand the dilemma of not wanting to correct a disobedient child with painful discipline, while at the same time realizing that they can't ignore his bad behavior.

> **"The message of the cross is foolishness to those who are perishing."**
>
> —1 Corinthians 1:18

What do you do? You love that little one. But he has disobeyed you, and now he is lying in an attempt to cover it up. He has to be punished and you've got to do it.

The situation caused by our sin is infinitely more complex, but there are parallels. Because God is a holy God, He cannot ignore our sin. Yet because He is a loving God, He is not merely willing to let us get what we deserve.

Another illustration might help us to see the dilemma from man's perspective. Imagine a group of people trapped on the roof of a high-rise building engulfed in flames. The only way to safety is to jump to the roof of an adjoining building 30 feet away! In desperation, people begin to attempt the impossible leap. Some jump farther out than others, but all fall to their death.

So it is with man's condition before God. Our sin caused a separation between us and a holy God that cannot be bridged by anything we do. We are helpless to save ourselves. But the love of God provided a way: the cross of Christ.

The necessity for Calvary's tree can be traced back to a much earlier tree. All our problems began when our first parents willfully and disobediently ate of the tree of the knowledge of good and evil. God had said that Adam and

> Because God is a holy God, He cannot ignore our sin.

his wife would die if they ate the fruit of that tree. And they did. From that time on, no man was the man he was created to be. From that time on, the children of Adam were born physically alive but spiritually dead. Not only was the garden paradise lost, but so was the inno-

> Because God is a loving God, He is not merely willing to let us get what we deserve.

cence man was created with.

Every child born from Eden until today has proven that innocence was lost. Once created to walk with God, man has inherited a nature that causes him to forget God, to hate his fellowmen, and to live a life of self-destruction. Because of this, David the king of Israel said, "Behold, I was brought forth in iniquity, and in sin my mother conceived me" (Psalm 51:5).

And the apostle Paul wrote, "Through one man sin entered the world, and death through sin" (Romans 5:12) and "the wages of sin is death" (6:23). In another letter he wrote, "In Adam all die" (1 Corinthians 15:22).

This is our condition. When Adam followed the way of the serpent, he didn't just hurt himself. When he defied his Maker, spiritual and physical death fell upon all men. And so it has come now to us. The proof is, all of us sinned against God the first chance we got.

Furthermore, we can't do anything to help ourselves. No amount of self-improvement or good deeds can win back what Adam lost. The prophet Isaiah saw this clearly, for he said that our best efforts are nothing better than dirty rags (Isaiah 64:6). The apostle Paul expressed the same awareness (Ephesians 2:8-9). His words remind us that no man can pull himself up to God by yanking on his own bootstraps.

> **All of us sinned against God the first chance we got.**

This is bad news. But the Bible, the most reliable book in the world, claims to be true. We are born into this world spiritually dead. We are born separated from God. We are born into a world of physical and spiritual death, and unless something happens, we will live out our lives in rebellion against God. Unless something happens, we are destined for the judgment of God—the second death, the lake of fire created for the devil and all of his demons.

> **Unless something happens, we are destined for the judgment of God.**

And if that were not enough, the Bible tells us that there's not a thing in the world we can do on our own to merit a rescue. Without a doubt, we need help. We need rescue. We need to be delivered from our guilt and bondage—before it is everlastingly too late.

# The Resolution Of The Cross

When Adam and Eve sinned, God could have struck them dead instantly. And He would have been just in doing so, because His holy nature demands that disobedience be punished by death.

Yet, because God is love, He did not strike our first parents dead. Instead, He sought them out, provided them with a covering of animal skins, and gave to them a wonderful promise (Genesis 3:15).

> God Himself resolved the dilemma. Love found a way.

God announced the good news that He Himself resolved the dilemma. His holiness is counter-balanced by His love! Love found a way. Love found another tree, the cross (Romans 5:6).

The tree in the Garden of Eden has given way to the cross. On that tree of humiliation, goodness triumphed over evil. Mercy triumphed over justice. The rescue was completed. The mission was accomplished. The dilemma was resolved.

# The Call Of The Cross

Look at the cross. Look at the One dying there. He never sinned, yet He is on the cross to bear the penalty for the sins of the whole world. He's dying there on your behalf. That should be you on that cross.

It's an ugly scene, isn't it? It shows us how terrible sin really is, and what a horrible price had to be paid to set us free from it. If you are a Christian, looking at the cross should fill your heart with gratitude for what Christ did for you there. As your sacrifice and substitute, He made it possible for you to be forgiven and to be saved from your sin. Why don't you give Him your thanks right now? Then determine to walk in obedience to God.

If you are not a Christian, won't you trust Him as your Savior? Your sin is real. You cannot do anything about it—except to trust in Jesus Christ. Don't wait. Tell Him that you believe in Him as your personal Savior. Ask Him to save you. He will, because it was for you that He died on that excruciating cross. He was your sacrifice. He paid the penalty for your sin. Trust Him now!

> God so loved the world that He gave His only begotten Son, that whoever believes in Him should not perish but have everlasting life. —John 3:16

Excerpted from the booklet *Why Did Christ Have To Die?* © 1999 RBC Ministries. Read it on the Web at **www.discoveryseries.org/q0202**

## RESERVED FOR YOU

READ:
1 Peter 1:3-9

You greatly rejoice, though now for a little while, if need be, you have been grieved by various trials.
—1 Peter 1:6

THE BIBLE IN ONE YEAR:
■ Job 20–21
■ Acts 10:24-48

Have you ever taken one of *those* vacations? You planned to arrive at a distant location where you knew you'd have a great time, but on the way you had so many traveling difficulties that you wondered if the journey was worth it.

Car problems. Traffic delays. Getting lost. Sick kids. Irritable fellow travelers. You knew the destination would be great, but the trip was anything but smooth. Yet you kept pressing on because you knew it would be worth the trouble.

That's a picture of the Christian life. Those who have trusted Jesus as Savior are on a journey filled with difficulties, setbacks, tragedies, and obstacles. Trouble always seems to be present or just around the corner. But we know that an indescribably great destination is in our future (1 Peter 1:4). And sometimes the assurance of what's reserved for us in heaven is all that keeps us going.

Peter understood. He said that as we make our way through life, we will suffer grief as a result of our troubles. Yet we can actually rejoice through our difficulties, because God has reserved something special for us at the end of the journey.

Troubled today? Look ahead. Heaven will be worth the trip. — Dave Branon

*It will be worth it all when we see Jesus,*
*Life's trials will seem so small when we see Christ;*
*One glimpse of His dear face all sorrow will erase,*
*So bravely run the race till we see Christ.* —Rusthoi

**The gains of heaven will more than compensate us for the losses of earth.**

# LOVE IS VULNERABLE

**READ:**
**Hosea 11:1-11**

How can I give you up,
Ephraim? . . . My heart
churns within Me; My
sympathy is stirred.
—Hosea 11:8

THE BIBLE IN ONE YEAR:
■ Job 22–24
■ Acts 11

The experience of a heartbroken Christian woman (I'll call her Mary) illustrates how love makes the lover vulnerable. Mary was a devoted wife who deeply loved her husband, but after 8 years and two children he left her for another woman. Her faith in God and her love for her children kept her going.

Today, her son is living a sinful lifestyle, and her daughter has abandoned her husband and children. Neither of them will have anything to do with their mother.

The prophet Hosea suffered a similar heartbreak because of his adulterous wife Gomer. What he experienced mirrors how God must have felt when His people turned to pagan idolatry and all the wickedness associated with it. God had been a loving husband and father to them, but they had spurned His love. Although His holy character demanded that He chasten them, He also felt deep anguish.

Centuries later, God came to earth in the person of Jesus, who endured the agony of Calvary to bear the sins of the whole world. Yet many people still reject Him.

Yes, love is vulnerable, and there are no guarantees that it will be returned! But God continues to love, and in His strength we can do the same.  — Herb Vander Lugt

*Your love, O God, would spare no pain*
*To conquer death and win;*
*You sent Your only Son to die*
*To rescue us from sin.* — Gustafson

**Nothing costs as much as loving—except not loving.**

# GOOD MEDICINE

READ:
Proverbs 17:17-22

---

A merry heart does
good, like medicine.
—Proverbs 17:22

---

THE BIBLE IN ONE YEAR:
■ Job 25–27
■ Acts 12

In a *Better Homes and Gardens* article titled "Laugh Your Way to Good Health," Nick Gallo made an observation that echoes what Solomon wrote thousands of years ago: "A merry heart does good, like medicine" (Proverbs 17:22). Gallo said, "Humor is good medicine — and can actually help keep you in good health." He quoted William F. Fry, M.D., who describes laughter as "inner jogging" and says that it's good for a person's cardiovascular system.

Comparing laughter to exercise, Gallo pointed out that when a person laughs heartily several physical benefits occur. There's a temporary lowering of blood pressure, a decreased rate of breathing, and a reduction in muscle tension. He said that many people experience a "relaxed afterglow." He concluded, "An enduring sense of humor, especially combined with other inner resources such as faith and optimism, appears to be a potent force for better health."

Christians, above all others, should benefit from laughter because we have the greatest reason to be joyful. Our faith is firmly rooted in God, and our optimism is based on the assurance that our lives are under His wise control.

Don't be afraid to enjoy a good laugh — it's good medicine. — Richard De Haan

*Laughter is a remedy*
*For sorrow and for care;*
*It brings joy to troubled souls,*
*To damaged hearts, repair.* — Sper

---

**He who laughs, lasts.**

# A STRONG CONSTITUTION

**READ:**
1 Peter 2:1-10

You are a chosen
generation, a royal
priesthood, a holy
nation, His own
special people.
—1 Peter 2:9

THE BIBLE IN ONE YEAR:
■ Job 28–29
■ Acts 13:1-25

The Declaration of Independence of the United States speaks of all people being "created equal" and that we are endowed with certain "unalienable rights." The Constitution guarantees that the government will protect those rights for all its citizens. These two documents clearly reveal that the nation's freedom depends largely on a strong constitution.

The Bible is a more far-reaching "bill of rights" than either of these documents. It originated with God, who backs it with His justice, His concern for all people, and His sovereignty. And it is the only charter that guarantees freedom from sin's penalty and power.

A man went to a clergyman to get some advice about religious virtue and the freedom it brings. "What must I do to attain holiness?" he asked. The pastor replied, "Follow your heart." Then he added, "To follow your heart you are going to need a strong constitution." "Which constitution?" asked the man. "The Bible!" said the pastor.

Peter said that Christians, as "a holy nation," are to "proclaim the praises of Him who called [us] out of darkness into His marvelous light" (1 Peter 2:9). There we find true freedom. When we live by our "constitution," we will be able to enjoy our rights and fulfill our calling. — Dennis De Haan

*God's changeless Word will change our lives,*
*But we must do our part;*
*When we live out its principles,*
*We'll keep it in our heart.* — Sper

**The best constitution in the world is the Bible.**

# FROZEN SNOWBALL

READ:
**Hebrews 12:25–13:6**

---

We are receiving a kingdom which cannot be shaken.
—Hebrews 12:28

---

THE BIBLE IN ONE YEAR:
■ Job 30–31
■ Acts 13:26-52

Baseball pitcher Tug McGraw had a wonderful philosophy of pitching. He called it his "frozen snowball" theory. "If I come in to pitch with the bases loaded," Tug explained, "and heavy hitter Willie Stargell is at bat, there's no reason I want to throw the ball. But eventually I have to pitch. So I remind myself that in a few billion years the earth will become a frozen snowball hurtling through space, and nobody's going to care what Willie Stargell did with the bases loaded!"

The Bible tells us the earth will someday "melt with fervent heat; both the earth and the works that are in it will be burned up" (2 Peter 3:10). Yet McGraw's point is valid: We need to keep life in perspective. Most of the things we worry about have no eternal significance.

The writer of Hebrews was concerned about our perspective. Throughout the book, he keeps our eyes focused on heaven and away from earth. Unless our minds are on heaven, we will have little eternal influence on earth.

There will come a time when the earth will be shaken, and things that once seemed permanent will be gone (Hebrews 12:27). What you fear most today will be forgotten like yesterday's headlines. What really matters is what you do today that has a touch of eternity about it. — Haddon Robinson

*O for a heart that is willing to serve,*
*Laboring while it is day!*
*Nothing is lost that is done for the Lord,*
*He will reward and repay.* — Anon.

---

**The one who lives for this life only**
**will have eternity to regret it.**

# THE "WHAT THEN?" TEST

READ:
Matthew 6:19-24

Riches are not forever.
—Proverbs 27:24

THE BIBLE IN ONE YEAR:
■ Job 32–33
■ Acts 14

From the 16th century comes a story of a probing conversation between an ambitious young man and a devout Christian named St. Philip Neri. The youth said to him excitedly, "My parents finally agreed to my studying law!" Philip asked simply, "What then?"

He replied, "Then I shall become a lawyer!" "And then?" pursued Philip. "Then I shall earn lots of money, buy a country house, get a carriage and horses, marry a beautiful woman, and lead a delightful life!" he responded.

Again Philip asked, "And then?" "Then . . ." The young man began reflecting for the first time on death and eternity. He realized that he had not acknowledged God in his plans and was building his life on temporal values.

The point of this story is not that riches are wrong. But if they become our central goal, we are ignoring eternity and trusting money, not God. Jesus said it's impossible to love both money and God (Matthew 6:24), and He warned, "Do not lay up for yourselves treasures on earth, . . . but lay up for yourselves treasures in heaven" (vv.19-20).

Young and old alike must make important life-plans. But let's keep eternity in mind by always subjecting them to the "what then?" test. — Joanie Yoder

*Shall the great Judge say, when my task is through,*
*That my soul had gathered some riches too?*
*Or shall at the last it be mine to find*
*That all I had worked for I had left behind?* — *Anon.*

**The true measure of our wealth
is the treasure we have in heaven.**

# MAKE A DIFFERENCE

**READ:**
Luke 3:1-20

While Annas and Caiaphas were high priests, the word of God came to John the son of Zacharias in the wilderness. —Luke 3:2

THE BIBLE IN ONE YEAR:
■ Job 34–35
■ Acts 15:1-21

Seven men are mentioned in Luke 3, who had political, economic, and religious control over Israel: Roman Emperor Tiberias Caesar, Governor Pontius Pilate, the tetrarchs Herod, Philip, and Lysanias, along with high priests Annas and Caiaphas. While they were in power, "The word of God came to John the son of Zacharias in the wilderness. And he went into all the region around the Jordan, preaching a baptism of repentance for the remission of sins" (vv.2-3).

What possible difference could it make for a person with no money and power to respond to God's word when it seemed that others were so firmly in control? How could the actions of one insignificant person change anything? The answer is revealed in John the Baptist's message of repentance, his announcement of the coming Messiah (vv.16-17), and his bold confronting of Herod (v.19). John's role was to prepare the way for Jesus the Messiah, and the world was blessed by his obedience.

Today our task as Christians is to reflect the crucified and risen Savior in everything we do, and to tell others about Him. God calls each of us to live according to His instructions in the Bible. Our response will make all the difference in the world. — David McCasland

*The laws of God are true and right;*
*They stand as firm today*
*As when He put them in His Word*
*And told us to obey.* — Fasick

**Obedience to God is the key to a lasting influence.**

# INNER STRENGTH

**READ:**
Ephesians 3:14-21

*[I pray] that He would grant you, according to the riches of His glory, to be strengthened with might through His Spirit in the inner man.*
**—Ephesians 3:16**

THE BIBLE IN ONE YEAR:
■ Job 36–37
■ Acts 15:22-41

A large company uses suction to extract contaminating substances from steel drums. Powerful pumps draw the materials out of the barrels, but the workers must carefully regulate the force of these pumps. If they take out too much air, the drums will collapse like paper cups, because the outer pressure will exceed the inner pressure.

Likewise, when adversity and hardship come into our lives, God must empower us from within or we will be unable to withstand the pressures from without. True, we get solid support from loved ones and Christian friends, but it is our spiritual inner man, "strengthened with might through His Spirit" (Ephesians 3:16), that sustains us and keeps us from crumpling.

The Holy Spirit works to strengthen us and renew our minds as we read the Bible and pray. If we neglect the Scriptures, seldom talk with the Lord, and stop fellowshiping with other believers, we'll grow weak and vulnerable. Then we will be unable to withstand the pressures of temptation or trouble.

Let's ask the Lord to develop our inner strength so that when life's blows and burdens press upon us we will not cave in. — Dave Egner

*Help us, O Lord, when troubles come*
*To trust Your Word and not succumb,*
*And help us not to turn aside*
*But in Your strength and love abide.* — D. De Haan

**The power of Christ within you is greater than the pressure of troubles around you.**

# "PIGGIES"

**READ:**
1 Peter 5:5-7

---

[Cast] all your care upon Him, for He cares for you. —1 Peter 5:7

---

THE BIBLE IN ONE YEAR:
- Job 38–40
- Acts 16:1-21

I recall walking along a Texas creek many years ago with my brother-in-law Ed and his 3-year-old son David. David had been collecting smooth, round stones from the stream while we walked. He called them "piggies," because their rounded shape reminded him of little pigs.

David had stuffed a number of "piggies" in his pockets, and after running out of pockets he began carrying them in his arms. After a while he began to stagger under the load and lag behind. It was obvious he would never make it back to the house without help, so Ed said, "Here, David, let me carry your piggies."

Reluctance clouded David's face for a moment, and then it lit up. "I know," he said. "You carry me and I'll carry my piggies!"

I've often thought of that incident and my own childish insistence that I must carry my own load. Jesus offers to take all of my burdens but I resist out of stubbornness and pride. "You carry me," I say, "but I'll carry my 'piggies.'"

How foolish it is to try to carry all your burdens on your own when Jesus asks you to cast "all your care upon Him, for He cares for you" (1 Peter 5:7).

Have you put all of your "piggies" in Jesus' strong arms today? — David Roper

*I would tell the Lord my longings,*
*Roll on Him my every care,*
*Cast upon Him all my burdens,*
*Burdens that I cannot bear.* —Weigle

---

**God cares.**

## MARRIAGE IN HEAVEN

READ:
Mark 12:18-27

When they rise from the dead, they neither marry nor are given in marriage, but are like angels in heaven. —Mark 12:25

THE BIBLE IN ONE YEAR:
■ Job 41-42
■ Acts 16:22-40

When I was a student at Moody Bible Institute, I knew a professor whose wife had died. Later he married the widow of his best friend. One day a student asked him, "Will your first wife know about your second marriage when you see her in heaven, and if so, how do you think she'll react?" The professor smiled and said, "Of course she will, and because she will be perfect she will not be jealous. Even though we will not live as marriage partners, I believe we will know each other. We will all be the best of friends forever."

In Mark 12, we read about some enemies of Jesus who invented a story about a woman whose husband died and left no son. Under Jewish law, the brother of the deceased had to marry the widow for the purpose of having a son (Deuteronomy 25:5). According to their story, this happened with seven brothers. Jesus' detractors asked, "When they rise, whose wife will she be?" He said they neither understood the Scriptures nor God's power to raise the dead to a glorious new existence without marriage.

I believe that in heaven we will have special feelings for one another. We will love perfectly and enjoy complete healing from all the hurts of our earthly relationships. That will be more fulfilling than any marriage. — Herb Vander Lugt

*The love we've known while here below*
*In heaven will find its highest joy,*
*For we will know Christ's perfect love*
*That memories cannot destroy.* — D. De Haan

---

**The pleasures of earth cannot compare
to the joys of heaven.**

# THE TREE

READ:
Matthew 27:27-35

[Jesus] bore our sins in His own body on the tree.
—1 Peter 2:24

THE BIBLE IN ONE YEAR:
■ Psalms 1–3
■ Acts 17:1-15

The corkscrew willow tree stood vigil over our backyard for more than 20 years. It shaded all four of our children as they played in the yard, and it provided shelter for the neighborhood squirrels. But when springtime came and the tree didn't awaken from its winter slumber, it was time to bring it down.

Every day for a week I worked on that tree — first to fell it and then to chop two decades of growth into manageable pieces. It gave me a lot of time to think about trees.

I thought about the first tree — the one on which hung the forbidden fruit that Adam and Eve just couldn't resist (Genesis 3:6). God used that tree to test their loyalty and trust. Then there's the tree in Psalm 1 that reminds us of the fruitfulness of godly living. And in Proverbs 3:18, wisdom is personified as a tree of life.

But it is a transplanted tree that is most important — the crude cross of Calvary that was hewn from a sturdy tree. There our Savior hung between heaven and earth to bear every sin of every generation on His shoulders. It stands above all trees as a symbol of love, sacrifice, and salvation.

At Calvary, God's only Son suffered a horrible death on a cross. That's the tree of life for us. — Dave Branon

*On a hill far away stood an old rugged cross,*
*The emblem of suffering and shame;*
*And I love that old cross where the dearest and best*
*For a world of lost sinners was slain.* — Bennard

**The cross of Christ reveals man's sin at its worst and God's love at its best.**

# OVERCOMING GREED

**READ:**
1 Timothy 6:6-19

---

Let them do good, that they be rich in good works, ready to give, willing to share.
—1 Timothy 6:18

---

THE BIBLE IN ONE YEAR:
- Psalms 4–6
- Acts 17:16-34

Greed — it has toppled highly paid executives, brought down giant corporations, and cost thousands of workers their jobs and retirement funds. One columnist has written that unrestrained corporate greed is a greater threat than terrorism.

Greed whispers in our ear that we would be happier if we had more money, more things, and more power. It creates discontent and a growing desire to do whatever it takes to gain position and possessions. But the Bible commands us to trust in God, not in "uncertain riches" (1 Timothy 6:17).

Paul told Timothy that the way to overcome greed is to flee from it and to "pursue righteousness, godliness, faith, love, patience, gentleness" (1 Timothy 6:11). And those "who are rich in this present age," who have more than is needed, should "be rich in good works, ready to give, willing to share" (vv.17-18).

Contentment and generosity are the opposite of greed (vv.6-8). As we learn to thank God for what we have and freely share it with others, we stop trying to fill the spiritual vacuum in our heart with things. And when we love Jesus more than money and possessions, we find that He is the greatest treasure of our lives. We discover that knowing Him is the source of genuine satisfaction. — David McCasland

*God's riches fill up our supply,*
*Whatever we may need,*
*So we can then be generous*
*And not controlled by greed.* —Sper

---

**The best remedy for greed is generosity.**

# NO GREATER LOVE

READ:
1 John 4:7-11

In this is love, not that
we loved God, but that
He loved us and sent
His Son to be the pro-
pitiation for our sins.
—1 John 4:10

THE BIBLE IN ONE YEAR:
■ Psalms 7–9
■ Acts 18

On our family-room wall, in a small shadowbox, hangs a "treasure" that belongs to my wife Carolyn. Oh, we have things more intrinsically valuable on the walls of our home — a handmade quilt from the Blue Ridge Mountains of Kentucky, antique mirrors, oil paintings, and a magnificent dulcimer from an artisan in the backcountry of Idaho.

Carolyn's treasure, though, is far more valuable to her than any other possession, for it contains a gift from our granddaughter Julia. It was a present to her "Nana" on Valentine's Day several years ago when Julia was only 6 years old — a small, red, clay heart. Inscribed on it in childish scrawl are the words "I Luv U."

The little heart is crudely made, ragged on the edges, and bears a number of thumbprints and smudges, but Carolyn has enshrined it in a frame made especially for that heart. Each day it reminds her of Julia's love.

Is God's love more valuable to you than silver or gold or any other possession? He "sent His only begotten Son into the world, that [you] might live through Him" (1 John 4:9). He did that because He loves you, not because you loved Him. And because of His love, one day you will be with Him in heaven. There is no greater love! — David Roper

*Love sent my Savior to die in my stead,*
*Why should He love me so?*
*Meekly to Calvary's cross He was led,*
*Why should He love me so?* — Harkness

**God's eternal love is the source of our eternal life.**

# THE CLUE
# OF SILENCE

READ:
Isaiah 53

---

The chief priests
accused Him of
many things, but He
answered nothing.
—Mark 15:3

---

THE BIBLE IN ONE YEAR:
■ Psalms 10–12
■ Acts 19:1-20

The story *Silver Blaze* by Sir Arthur Conan Doyle centers around a clue of silence. Detective Sherlock Holmes investigates the theft of a prized racehorse, which had been guarded by a watchdog. In gathering evidence, Holmes learns that the dog didn't bark during the intrusion. The detective deduces that the dog knew the culprit, and this leads to solving the crime.

For anyone investigating the identity of Jesus, the Bible holds many clues. One of them is His silence. Centuries before Jesus lived, the prophet Isaiah wrote of Him: "As a sheep before its shearers is silent, so He opened not His mouth" (53:7). The significance of this remained obscure until Jesus was brought before His accusers and "answered nothing" (Mark 15:3).

It's a small but important piece of evidence, especially when combined with other clues: His birth in Bethlehem (Micah 5:2; Luke 2:4), His Davidic lineage (Isaiah 11:10; Luke 3:31), and the casting of lots for His clothes (Psalm 22:18; John 19:23-24). These and more than 200 other fulfilled prophecies provide overwhelming evidence of the identity of Jesus.

He is the Messiah, the Son of God, the Savior of all who put their faith in Him. — Dave Egner

*THINK ABOUT IT*
*Are you convinced that Jesus is the promised Savior?*
*Have you accepted the forgiveness and eternal life He*
*offers? If you have doubts, read the gospel of John.*

---

**Believing Christ died — that's history;**
**believing Christ died for me — that's salvation.**

# THE TRUTH ABOUT TRUTH

READ:
1 Corinthians 1:18-25

. . . always learning and never able to come to the knowledge of the truth. —2 Timothy 3:7

THE BIBLE IN ONE YEAR:
■ Psalms 13–15
■ Acts 19:21-41

In 1692, Harvard College adopted as its motto *Veritas Christo et Ecclesiae* — "Truth for Christ and the Church." Its crest showed three books, one face down to symbolize the limitation of human knowledge. But in recent decades that book has been turned face up to represent the unlimited capacity of the human mind. And the motto has been changed to *Veritas* — "Truth."

The pursuit of knowledge is praiseworthy, yet learning can quickly lead to pride and a refusal to acknowledge any limits on our mental abilities. When that happens, biblical truth is ignored or rejected.

What, then, is the truth about truth? A wise king wrote centuries ago, "The fear of the LORD is the beginning of knowledge" (Proverbs 1:7). We must recognize the relationship between God and truth. Without the help of the Holy Spirit and the instruction of God's Word, man will be ever "learning and never able to come to the knowledge of the truth" (2 Timothy 3:7). When we acknowledge and obey His truth, however, we will be set free from spiritual ignorance and error (John 8:32; 17:17).

That's why we must be diligent in our study of the Bible (2 Timothy 2:15). It is the only book that tells us the truth about truth. — Vernon Grounds

*For Your holy Book we thank You;*
*May its message be our guide,*
*May we understand the wisdom*
*Of the truth Your laws provide.* —Carter

**Study God's written Word to know**
**Christ the living Word.**

# WITHOUT A BUMPER STICKER

**READ:**
Acts 4:5-22

---

They saw the boldness of Peter and John . . . . And they realized that they had been with Jesus. —Acts 4:13

---

THE BIBLE IN ONE YEAR:
■ Psalms 16–17
■ Acts 20:1-16

While driving in rush-hour traffic one day, I found myself behind a car with a bumper sticker. It had a yellow smiley face on it with these words: SMILE — JESUS LOVES YOU.

Suddenly another car squeezed in front of the "smiley" car, forcing the driver to hit the brakes. With that, he shook his fist angrily, displaying anything but a smiley face. I felt ashamed, until I remembered my own impatience as a driver. The incident reminded me that our actions and reactions, more than the display of a sticker on our car, show whether we really know the Lord Jesus.

Acts 4 tells us that Peter and John faced opposition from local rulers, elders, and scribes as they proclaimed the good news of Christ. But their reaction caused their opponents to start thinking. Even though Peter and John were not highly educated, the people marveled at their bold witness and realized that these two men had been with Jesus. There was no need for a bumper sticker on the apostles' donkey. Their words and actions said it all.

Do you feel too untrained or timid to be a witness for God? If you'll spend time getting to know Jesus, He will empower you to impress others with Himself. You'll have boldness — without a bumper sticker. —Joanie Yoder

> For me 'twas not the truth you taught,
> To you so clear, to me so dim;
> But when you came to me, you brought
> A deeper sense of Him. —Clelland

---

**Actions speak louder than bumper stickers.**

# THE ADAM LEGACY

**READ:**
**Romans 5:12-21**

---

By one Man's obedience many will be made righteous.
—Romans 5:19

---

THE BIBLE IN ONE YEAR:
■ Psalms 18–19
■ Acts 20:17-38

Our new grandson Jackson had fine features, soft blemish-free skin, and ten tiny fingers and toes on two little hands and feet. How could any proud Grampa not see him as a "perfect" baby? He certainly was a miracle of divine formation (Psalm 139:13-14).

The apostle Paul gave us a broader view of such "perfect" little infants when he wrote, "Through one man sin entered the world, and death through sin . . . . Nevertheless death reigned from Adam to Moses, even over those who had not sinned according to the likeness of the transgression of Adam" (Romans 5:12-14). In other words, every child is born with a tendency to sin. But that's not Paul's final word. He also wrote about Jesus, the "last Adam," who became a "life-giving spirit" (1 Corinthians 15:45).

Long after man's first sin, a baby was born who was God incarnate (John 1:14). God made Christ, "who knew no sin to be sin for us" (2 Corinthians 5:21). When we trust Jesus as our Savior, the Holy Spirit creates within us a new desire to do what is pleasing to God. The flesh still has its pull, but the pull of the Spirit is stronger.

In the "first Adam" we're all sinners. But let's concentrate on who we are in the "last Adam." — Dennis De Haan

*One with Adam are we all,*
*One with Adam in his fall;*
*But another Adam came —*
*Fallen sinners to reclaim.* — D. De Haan

---

**If anyone is in Christ, he is a new creation;**
**old things have passed away. —2 Corinthians 5:17**

# New Songs

**READ:**
Psalm 40:1-10

---

He has put a new song in my mouth—praise to our God.
—Psalm 40:3

---

THE BIBLE IN ONE YEAR:
■ Psalms 20–22
■ Acts 21:1-17

The song of the humpback whale is one of the strangest in nature. It is a weird combination of high- and low-pitched groanings. Those who have studied the humpback whale say their songs are noteworthy because these giants of the deep are continually changing them. New patterns are added and old ones eliminated so that over a period of time the whale actually sings a whole new song.

There's a sense in which a Christian should be continually composing new songs of praise around the fresh mercies of God. Unfortunately, many of us just keep singing "the same old song."

We must repeatedly affirm the fundamentals of our faith. But as the psalmist tells us, the works of God's deliverance in the lives of His people are many. His works, which are more than we can count, give us reasons to express our praise to Him in numerous ways (Psalm 40:5).

So why do we express our testimony of God's saving grace in the same old way year after year? A fresh experience of the mercies of the cross and of Christ's resurrection power should continually fill our hearts and minds with new songs.

The gospel story never changes — thank God for that. But our songs of praise should be ever new. —Mart De Haan

*God's blessings are too numerous*
*To count them all at night;*
*That's why we can give praise to Him*
*As fresh as morning's light.* —Sper

---

**Seeing God's work in our lives**
**puts a new song on our lips.**

# FAMILY TIE

READ:
Ephesians 2:11-22

The whole building,
being fitted together,
grows into a holy
temple in the Lord.
—Ephesians 2:21

THE BIBLE IN ONE YEAR:
■ Psalms 23–25
■ Acts 21:18-40

An elderly man who visited an art gallery was deeply moved by a painting that portrayed Christ on the cross. It was so realistic in depicting the suffering of the Savior that his heart was filled with gratitude for the great price the Lord Jesus paid for his redemption. With tears trickling down his cheeks, he exclaimed, "Bless Him! I love Him! I love Him!"

Other visitors standing nearby wondered what the man was talking about. One person walked over and looked at the painting. Soon he too felt deep emotion welling up in his heart. Turning to the old man, he gave him a firm handshake and said, "So do I! I love Him too!" The scene was repeated as a third man and then a fourth walked over, gazed at the painting, and exclaimed, "I love Him too!" Although these men were from different churches, they felt a common bond because of their faith in Christ.

As believers, we need an awareness of our spiritual unity with other Christians. We need to focus on the fundamentals on which we agree — such as our love for the Savior who died for us — rather than bicker about lesser issues.

Regardless of sincere disagreements, we as blood-bought believers should recognize that we have a strong family tie in Christ. — Richard De Haan

*Blest be the tie that binds*
*Our hearts in Christian love!*
*The fellowship of kindred minds*
*Is like to that above.* —Fawcett

---

**As we draw near to Christ
we are drawn near to each other.**

# DOES GOD LOVE ME?

**READ:**
**Romans 5:6-11**

---

We love Him because
He first loved us.
—1 John 4:19

---

THE BIBLE IN ONE YEAR:
■ Psalms 26–28
■ Acts 22

It's not easy to understand the depth of God's love for us. Because of our pride and fear, we fail to grasp how undeserving we are and how free His love is.

At times I struggle with pride, so I tend to believe that I have earned any love I receive. Pride tells me that I am loved only when I am lovable, respectable, and worthy.

At other times I feel the tug of fear. Deep down inside, I know that I don't deserve the love I get. My motives are never pure, and I fear I will be rejected if they are exposed. So even while I am basking in acceptance, I live with the fear of being unmasked, revealing that I am much less than what others think me to be.

When I consider my relationship with God, therefore, I tend to feel that His affection for me is based on my performance. When I do well, He loves me; but if I foul up, then I expect only His scorn.

Yet God does not love us because we deserve it. He loves us in spite of what we are. In 1 John 4:10 we read, "In this is love, not that we loved God, but that He loved us and sent His Son." Because of what Jesus Christ has done for us, we know we are always loved by God. That simple truth shatters our pride and dispels our fear. — Haddon Robinson

*Oh, such love, my soul, still ponder —*
*Love so great, so rich, so free!*
*Say, while lost in holy wonder,*
*"Why, O Lord, such love to me?"* — Kent

---

**No one is beyond the reach of God's love.**

# TRUTH SEEKERS

**READ:**
Psalm 119:89-96

I will never forget Your
precepts, for by them
You have given me life.
—Psalm 119:93

THE BIBLE IN ONE YEAR:
■ Psalms 29–30
■ Acts 23:1-15

The young woman's quest for God began when she was 11 years old, living under atheistic communism in the former Soviet Union. That's when she saw some artwork that depicted the baby Jesus. When she heard that this represented what authorities called a "myth" about God sending His Son to earth, she began to seek the truth.

She also heard that God had written a book of His truth, and she searched for a copy. It wasn't until she was almost 30 that she finally found a Bible she was permitted to read. At last she had the information she needed to trust Jesus as Savior.

From 1971 to 1989, this young woman risked her own safety to search for the truth of God's Word. Today she is a lawyer who works to protect her fellow Russian citizens from religious persecution. The message of God's love in Christ is spreading because this one woman was a truth seeker.

God's truth can have an impact on us and on the people with whom we interact. The psalmist wrote, "Unless Your law had been my delight, I would then have perished in my affliction. . . . By them You have given me life" (Psalm 119:92-93).

Let's make the Bible our delight. God will give us passion for His eternal Word if we are truth seekers.  — Dave Branon

*The Word of God is truth;*
*So when my faith grows dim,*
*I look into His Word*
*And trust my life to Him.* —Hess

---

**If you're searching for nuggets of truth,
the Bible is a gold mine.**

# NO SALE

**READ:**
Acts 8:9-25

---

Peter said to him, "Your money perish with you, because you thought that the gift of God could be purchased with money!" —Acts 8:20

---

THE BIBLE IN ONE YEAR:
■ Psalms 31–32
■ Acts 23:16-35

**P**olice officers in St. Louis have had at least one easy arrest. It occurred at the back door of the police station when a drunk driver pulled his car right up to the booking window, thinking he was at Burger King. After attempting to place his order at what he thought was a drive-up window, the surprised driver was arrested by the booking officer and charged with drunk driving.

A man named Simon also got the surprise of his life. According to Acts 8, he was a former sorcerer in Samaria before becoming a follower of Christ. His surprise came when he walked up to the apostles and offered them money. He wanted them to give him the power to lay hands on people and impart to them the Holy Spirit. The apostle Peter emphatically refused, and accused him of being under the influence of something worse than alcohol.

Peter wasn't overreacting. It's dangerous to think that the power of the Holy Spirit is like a product that can be bought and sold. The Spirit's work is a gift of God that is freely given on the basis of faith, and faith alone. He has given us His Spirit to accomplish His purposes, not ours. The Spirit cannot be bought or bargained for.

Thank You, Lord, for the gift of Your Spirit. — Mart De Haan

*Holy Spirit, all divine,*
*Dwell within this heart of mine;*
*Cast down every idol throne,*
*Reign supreme and reign alone.* —Reed

---

**We don't need more of the Spirit;**
**the Spirit needs more of us.**

# DYING DAILY

**READ:**
2 Corinthians 4:7-12

We are hard-pressed on every side, . . . always carrying about in the body the dying of the Lord Jesus.
—2 Corinthians 4:8,10

THE BIBLE IN ONE YEAR:
■ Psalms 33–34
■ Acts 24

Are you in a situation where you are often misunderstood for your faith in Christ? Are you surrounded by people with a carping, critical spirit? Do you get little or no credit for the work you do in your church or for your family?

The proper response is a willingness to have a humble and submissive spirit — to die as Jesus did throughout His life. Yes, our Lord died once on the cross; but in another sense He also died every day. The cross was the culmination of an entire lifetime of dying. He was willing to be misunderstood and maligned, to give up home and comforts, to take the role of a servant. That was His "death." We must be willing to die in that way as well.

When we die with Him, God's gift to us is "the life of Jesus" (2 Corinthians 4:10), the most attractive life ever lived. His beauty will gradually grow in us and become our beauty as well.

Remember this saying: "A picture is worth a thousand words." The portrait you draw of Jesus with your humble, tranquil presence in the face of grievous wrong is worth many words on the subject. Some may see the life of Jesus revealed in you and long to enter into that life. That's how dying daily can help bring life to another. — David Roper

*Dear Jesus, take my heart and hand,*
*And grant me this, I pray:*
*That I through Your sweet love may grow*
*More like You day by day.* — Garrison

---

**Living daily for Christ requires dying daily to self.**

# GOD FORGIVES DISOBEDIENCE

**READ:**
Hosea 14

---

I will heal their backsliding. I will love them freely. —Hosea 14:4

---

THE BIBLE IN ONE YEAR:
■ Psalms 35–36
■ Acts 25

I'll never forget the painful lesson I learned in early childhood about disobedience. My father, who had been mowing our lawn, interrupted his work to go shopping. He left the push mower standing near some flowers and ordered me not to touch it while he was gone. But I disobeyed him and gave it a push. To my shock, the mower veered and knocked over several flowers.

When Dad returned, I blubbered, "I didn't mean to do it!" Wisely, he replied, "Why did you do it then?" I knew the truth—I did mean to push the mower. My sin wasn't that I mowed the flowers down, it was that I disobeyed my father.

This childhood lesson is a reminder to be sorry for disobedience and not just the consequences. Rather than blubber to God, "I didn't mean to do it," I do what Hosea told wayward Israel to do: "Take words [of repentance] with you, and return to the LORD" (Hosea 14:2). I tell the Lord honestly that I knew His will but chose to disobey, and I cry out for His mercy. Praise God, He forgives!

Are you grieved that you chose to disobey, and not merely sorry about the consequences? Then "take words with you, and return to the LORD" today. He promises to forgive you of your sin, for He loves you freely (v.4). —Joanie Yoder

*I've strayed, O Lord, and turned aside,*
*I've disobeyed Your voice;*
*But now with contrite heart I turn*
*And make Your will my choice.* —D. De Haan

---

**Repentance keeps the way clear
in our walk with God.**

# SAVING DYLAN

**READ:**
**John 9:1-12**

---

Neither this man nor his parents sinned, but that the works of God should be revealed in him. —John 9:3

---

THE BIBLE IN ONE YEAR:
■ Psalms 37–39
■ Acts 26

The baby lay critically ill in the hospital, fighting to breathe. He had pneumonia, which made staying alive a struggle for his 8-month-old body. Doctors, nurses, and his family fought to save this weak baby boy.

Some people say he should never have made it to 8 months of age. Others say this precious child should not have been allowed to be born, or that he should have been left to die after he was born.

Why would anyone say this? For one simple reason: Dylan has Down syndrome. Through no fault of his own or of his parents, my great-nephew has an extra chromosome, and he will face some added struggles in his life.

But isn't his life worth as much as the life of a sick baby without an extra chromosome? Are we not all of equal value in the eyes of our Creator? Aren't we all deficient in some way? Our lack of perfection should remind us that no one has the right to judge another's worth.

Our imperfections are opportunities for God to work in our lives. That's what Jesus told His disciples when they asked why a man had been born blind. He said it happened so that "the works of God should be revealed in him" (John 9:3).

We're seeing God work in Dylan's life. That's what he's here for — just like the rest of us. — Dave Branon

*People in whom the world sees no value,*
*But only as burdens to bear,*
*Teach us great lessons of God's sovereign power —*
*He loves them as treasures so rare.* —Carbaugh

---

**If God didn't have a purpose for us,**
**we wouldn't be here.**

# THE PURSUIT OF HAPPINESS

READ:
Psalm 34

---

Oh, taste and see that
the LORD is good;
blessed is the man who
trusts in Him!
—Psalm 34:8

---

THE BIBLE IN ONE YEAR:
■ Psalms 40–42
■ Acts 27:1–26

In 1948, *Life* magazine brought together a group of labor-union representatives, industrial leaders, university scholars, and clergy to discuss what the framers of the United States Constitution had in mind when they referred to "the pursuit of happiness." They agreed that steady work under good conditions at a living wage was absolutely essential. Some included the values of racial fairness, unselfishness, and integrity.

This led one participant, a brilliant young woman who had been crippled by polio, to say, "It is my experience that suffering and pain are, unfortunately, great character builders — not that suffering is good in itself, but because it often helps to shift our expectation of happiness from without to a search for it from within." True, but we can find inner happiness only by knowing God personally and walking the path of trust and obedience.

Happiness isn't found by pursuing it. It's a by-product of seeking an ever-closer walk with God. When we do, we will find a depth of happiness no person or thing can give. That's what David referred to when he said, "Oh, taste and see that the LORD is good; blessed is the man who trusts in Him!" (Psalm 34:8). — Herb Vander Lugt

*Happiness is never found*
*When happiness is sought;*
*It's found instead in Jesus*
*And what His blood has bought.* —D. De Haan

---

**To know happiness, know God.**

# BOTH GLAD AND SAD

READ:
Luke 12:16-21

Do not lay up for yourselves treasures on earth, . . . but lay up for yourselves treasures in heaven.
—Matthew 6:19-20

THE BIBLE IN ONE YEAR:
■ Psalms 43–45
■ Acts 27:27-44

There's an old legend about three men who were crossing a desert on horseback at night. As they approached a dry creek bed, they heard a voice commanding them to dismount, pick up some pebbles, put them in their pockets, and not look at them till the next morning. The men were promised that if they obeyed they would be both glad and sad. After they did as they were told, the three mounted their horses and went on their way.

As the first streaks of dawn began to spread across the sky, the men reached into their pockets to pull out the pebbles. To their great surprise, they had been transformed into diamonds, rubies, and other precious gems. It was then that they realized the significance of the promise that they would be both glad and sad. They were happy that they had picked up as many pebbles as they did, but sorry — so sorry — that they had not collected more.

I wonder if we will have a similar feeling when we get to heaven. We will be happy for the treasure we laid up in heaven while on earth, and joyful for the rewards Christ will give us. But we will also experience regret for not having done more to serve Him.

Let's make the most of our opportunities so that we'll be more glad than sad. — Richard De Haan

*The day will come when we will stand*
*Before our Judge, God's Son;*
*Have we so lived that He will say,*
*"Well done, My child, well done"?* —Sper

**The crowns we wear in heaven
must be won on earth.**

# A Matter Of Taste

**READ:**
2 Corinthians 6:1–7:1

---

Let us cleanse ourselves from all filthiness of the flesh and spirit.
—2 Corinthians 7:1

---

THE BIBLE IN ONE YEAR:
■ Psalms 46–48
■ Acts 28

Two cockroaches decided to visit their favorite restaurant. While the larger of the two was enjoying his meal, the smaller one said, "You wouldn't believe the house I just left. It was spotless. The lady had to be a cleanaholic. Everything was immaculate — the sink, the counter, the floors. You couldn't find a crumb anywhere." The other cockroach stopped his munching, looked with some annoyance at his companion, and said, "Do you have to talk like that while I'm eating?"

This story about roaches can apply to human nature as well. The second letter to the Corinthians shows that Paul's readers had much to learn about clean living. They needed to develop a stronger hunger and thirst for righteousness. So the apostle pleaded with them to turn away from all filthiness (7:1). He reminded them that God wants His people to separate themselves from spiritual garbage.

If "cleanness" of heart sounds unappealing, perhaps we've been satisfied with the crumbs of our earthly desires. We need to learn to savor the flavor of godliness.

Father, forgive us for feeding the cravings of our sinful flesh. Help us to cultivate instead the tastes that Your Holy Spirit wants to produce in us. — Mart De Haan

*If we desire to taste what's good*
*And lose our taste for sin,*
*We must with ruthless honesty*
*Expose the dirt within.* — D. De Haan

---

**Sin cannot flourish where godliness is cultivated.**

# POWER OUTAGE

**READ:**
2 Timothy 1:6-12

---

God has not given us a spirit of fear, but of power and of love and of a sound mind.
—2 Timothy 1:7

---

THE BIBLE IN ONE YEAR:
■ Psalms 49–50
■ Romans 1

The silence awakened me at 5:30 one morning. There was no gentle whir of fan blades, no reassuring hum from the refrigerator downstairs. A glance out the window confirmed that a power outage had left everyone in our neighborhood without electricity just as they would be preparing for work.

I realized that alarm clocks would not sound, and there would be no TV news. Coffee makers, toasters, hair dryers, and many telephones would be useless. Beginning a day without power was simply an inconvenience and a disruption of routine—but it felt like a disaster.

Then I thought of how often I rush into the day without spiritual power. I spend more time reading the newspaper than the Bible. Talk radio replaces listening to the Spirit. I react to difficult people and circumstances in a spirit of fear rather than the spirit of "power and of love and of a sound mind" that God has given us (2 Timothy 1:7). I must appear as spiritually unkempt as a person who dressed and groomed in the dark.

Our power outage was short-lived, but the lesson remains of my need to begin each day by seeking the Lord. His strength is not for my success or well-being, but so that I will glorify Christ by living in His power. — David McCasland

*There's never a lack of God's power*
*In prayer and reading His Word,*
*For Jesus in heaven is listening —*
*Your prayer will always be heard.* — Hess

---

**The human spirit fails us
unless the Holy Spirit fills us.**

# KEEP AT IT!

**READ:**
Isaiah 55:6-13

---

My word . . . shall not return to Me void, but it shall accomplish what I please.
—Isaiah 55:11

---

THE BIBLE IN ONE YEAR:
- Psalms 51–53
- Romans 2

They know Tom Dotson pretty well in the prisons of Michigan. They ought to. He spent more than a decade behind bars.

Tom gave his testimony at the annual banquet for prison chaplains in Muskegon, Michigan. He said he had grown up in a Christian home but had rebelled and rejected the gospel. His wife, who sang at the banquet, stayed with him in spite of his repeated failures. A prison chaplain faithfully worked with him, Tom genuinely surrendered to Jesus Christ, and his life was changed.

Dotson urged Christian workers, "Continue on in your ministry with people like me, no matter how frustrating. We may have lots of setbacks. But don't give up. There's power for change in even the most frustrating person through the sacrifice of Christ, the One who really sets us free." Then, looking right at the chaplain who had patiently witnessed to him, Tom said tenderly, "Thank you for not giving up on me."

God will "abundantly pardon" all who come to Him (Isaiah 55:7). His powerful Word can bring change (v.11), freeing men and women from the prison of sin (John 8:32).

Are you about to give up on someone you think will never change? Don't! Keep at it! — Dave Egner

*Be not weary in well-doing,*
*Though your labors cause you pain —*
*There could never be a harvest*
*Without sowing of the grain.* — Anon.

---

**Instead of giving up on a person,
give that person to God.**

# ALREADY, BUT NOT YET

READ:
Luke 10:1-12; 17-20

[Jesus] said to them, "I saw Satan fall like lightning from heaven." —Luke 10:18

THE BIBLE IN ONE YEAR:
■ Psalms 54–56
■ Romans 3

If Jesus has won the victory over sin, suffering, and death, why is it that we still sin, suffer, and die? To understand this seeming contradiction, we must recognize the "already, but not yet" tension of the gospel.

On the one hand, God's kingdom has already come in the person of Jesus. As the incarnate God-man, He died on the cross so that through His death and resurrection He might destroy the devil (Hebrews 2:14).

On the other hand, the perfect kingdom toward which He pointed awaits His personal return to earth. We experience the tension of living between the "already, but not yet" aspects of God's kingdom.

Luke 10 illustrates this tension. Upon returning from preaching, the disciples were jubilant. "Even the demons are subject to us in Your name," they told Jesus (Luke 10:17). He replied that He had seen Satan "fall like lightning from heaven" (v.18). He also assured them that nothing would hurt them (v.19). Yet many of them suffered and died as martyrs, and evil is still rampant today.

Even so, we can face whatever comes, for someday we'll enter fully into the victory Jesus has won. In the meantime, we can take comfort in knowing that nothing shall separate us from God's love (Romans 8:35-39). — Herb Vander Lugt

*God's kingdom has come in Jesus the king,*
*He died and He rose, redemption to bring;*
*Yet still we await the glorious day*
*When Satan and sin no longer hold sway.* —D. De Haan

---

**Satan may win some battles,
but he has already lost the war.**

# A MASSIVE CELEBRATION

**READ:**
**Revelation 5:6-14**

Oh, worship the LORD in the beauty of holiness! Tremble before Him, all the earth. —Psalm 96:9

THE BIBLE IN ONE YEAR:
■ Psalms 57–59
■ Romans 4

We all love to have someone tell us, "Hey, great job. I appreciate you." And if several people tell us we are doing something right, that's even better.

God loves the praise of His people too, and He truly deserves it. Our most important work on earth is to exalt Him (Psalm 96:9), "that in all things God may be glorified" (1 Peter 4:11). It's our responsibility and privilege to worship, love, exalt, and serve the Lord.

Revelation 5:9-13 tells of a future day in heaven when believers from "every tribe and tongue and people and nation" who have been redeemed by Jesus' blood will surround His throne with praises. All of those individuals — multiplied over the millennia — add up to a mind-boggling congregation of God-glorifying people.

God's greatness is so overwhelming, so unfathomable, and so indescribable that millions and millions of people — all praising Him and bowing before Him in worship — will give Him the glory He deserves.

Even now, each of us can participate in celebrating God's majesty by glorifying Him with our lives. And one day we will join with people from every nation in that massive heavenly celebration. — Dave Branon

*Sing praise to God who reigns above,*
*The God of all creation,*
*The God of power, the God of love,*
*The God of our salvation.* — Schütz

---

**We have all eternity to praise God—**
**begin today.**

# THE OIL OF HELPFULNESS

READ:
Isaiah 61:1-3

---

The LORD has anointed Me . . . to give them beauty for ashes, the oil of joy for mourning.
—Isaiah 61:1,3

---

THE BIBLE IN ONE YEAR:
■ Psalms 60–62
■ Romans 5

There's a story of an eccentric old man who carried an oil can with him everywhere he went. If he passed through a squeaky door or a stiff gate, he applied oil to the hinges. His practice of lubricating made life easier for those who followed after him.

Nearly every day we encounter people whose lives creak and grate harshly with problems. In such situations we face two choices — either to aggravate their problems with a spirit of criticism or to lubricate their lives in the Spirit of Christ.

Some people we meet carry unbearable burdens and long for the oil of a sympathetic word. Others are defeated and feel like giving up. Just one drop of encouragement could restore their hope. Still others are mean and sin-hardened. Such people can become pliable toward the saving grace of Christ through regular applications of the oil of kindness.

When we receive Christ as our Savior and Lord, the Holy Spirit indwells us and equips us to bless others. If we're prepared to pour out God's oil of helpfulness every day and everywhere, beginning at home, we'll minister Christ's beauty and the oil of joy to many hurting people.

Perhaps the old man with the oil can wasn't so eccentric after all. — Joanie Yoder

*PUTTING IT INTO PRACTICE*
- *Lend a listening ear.*
- *Pause to pray specifically.*
- *Speak a word of encouragement.*

---

**The human spirit can gain new hope
from an encouraging word.**

# OUT OF THE THORNS

**READ:**
Hebrews 12:7-11

---

No chastening seems to be joyful for the present, but painful.
—Hebrews 12:11

---

THE BIBLE IN ONE YEAR:
- Psalms 63–65
- Romans 6

The gorse bush is a shrub that was imported from Europe and now grows wild in the Pacific Northwest. It has dense, dark green shoots, and in springtime it provides a dazzling display of fragrant, vibrant yellow flowers. But it's best known by hikers and fishermen for its vicious spines.

Remarkably, the flowers grow right out of the thorns.

Missionary and artist Lilias Trotter wrote, "The whole year round the thorn has been hardening and sharpening. Spring comes — the thorn does not drop off, it does not soften. There it is as uncompromising as ever, but halfway up appear two brown fuzzy balls, mere specks at first, that break at last — straight out of last year's thorn — into a blaze of golden glory."

So it is with the suffering that accompanies God's chastening. Just when our situation seems hopeless and hardest to bear, tiny signs of life appear that will soon burst into bloom. Take the toughest issue, the most difficult place. There, God in His grace can cause His beauty to be seen in you.

No chastening seems pleasant at the time, "Yet when it is all over we can see that it has quietly produced the fruit of real goodness in the characters of those who have accepted it in the right spirit" (Hebrews 12:11 PHILLIPS). — David Roper

*For all the heartaches and the tears,*
*For gloomy days and fruitless years*
*I do give thanks, for now I know*
*These were the things that helped me grow!* — Crandlemire

---

**God's hand of discipline**
**is a hand of love.**

# MORNING, NOON, NIGHT

**READ:**
Psalm 55:16-23

---

Evening and morning and at noon I will pray, and cry aloud, and He shall hear my voice.
—Psalm 55:17

---

THE BIBLE IN ONE YEAR:
■ Psalms 66–67
■ Romans 7

In May 2003, a powerful earthquake struck northern Algeria. TV news images showed distraught people searching the rubble for survivors, while others numbly visited hospitals and morgues to see if their loved ones were alive or dead. Families stood together weeping and crying out for help. Their burden of uncertainty and grief could be seen, heard, and felt.

If you've experienced an intense feeling of loss, you'll appreciate the words of David in Psalm 55, penned during a painful time in his life. Oppressed by the wicked, hated by his enemies, and betrayed by a friend, David spoke of the anxiety and anguish that threatened to crush his spirit: "Fearfulness and trembling have come upon me, and horror has overwhelmed me" (v.5).

But instead of caving in to fear, David poured out his heart to God: "As for me, I will call upon God, and the LORD shall save me. Evening and morning and at noon I will pray, and cry aloud, and He shall hear my voice" (vv.16-17).

Prayer lifts our eyes from personal tragedy to the compassion of God. It enables us to cast our burdens on the Lord instead of breaking under their weight. When our hearts are filled with pain, it's good to call on God in prayer — morning, noon, and night.  — David McCasland

*What a Friend we have in Jesus,*
*All our sins and griefs to bear!*
*What a privilege to carry*
*Everything to God in prayer.*  — Scriven

---

**In prayer, God hears more than words;**
**He listens to your heart.**

# IS LOVE
# A NAME
# FOR GOD?

**READ:**
1 John 4:11-21

God is love, and he who
abides in love abides in
God, and God in him.
—1 John 4:16

THE BIBLE IN ONE YEAR:
■ Psalms 68–69
■ Romans 8:1-21

Wilferd Peterson visited a mosque where a religious leader said, "There is no God save Allah, and Muhammad is his prophet."

Peterson considered that people have many names for God. Among the Hindus, it is Brahma. Jews and Christians call Him Jehovah. Ancient Greeks worshiped Zeus. But is there a universal name for God that will bring all people together?

Approaching the religious leader, he asked, "Would you agree that all men everywhere should think of God as love?" The man's face lit up. "That's it! That's what the whole world needs." Peterson wrote, "Give God the universal name of *Love* and we will create a golden cord to tie together the truths of all the religions of the world." Was he right? Absolutely not!

John wrote that God is love (1 John 4:16). But he also recorded Jesus' words that God must be worshiped in spirit and in truth (John 4:24) and that He is "the way, the truth, and the life" (14:6). That sets Him above all other gods.

Love is not a name for God; love is God's nature. He expressed it to the fullest extent when He sent His Son to die for our sins (John 3:16). Only when we accept Christ's sacrifice for us will we know the love of the one true God that can bind people together. — Dennis De Haan

*When Jesus gave His life for me,*
*Enduring all the agony*
*Upon the cross of Calvary,*
*He showed the love of God.* — Sper

**God is love—but love is not God.**

# AFRAID OF THE DENTIST?

READ:
1 Samuel 12:6-25

---

Do not fear. You have done all this wickedness; yet do not turn aside from following the LORD.
—1 Samuel 12:20

---

THE BIBLE IN ONE YEAR:
■ Psalms 70–71
■ Romans 8:22-39

Why are so many people afraid of going to the dentist? It may be the result of a bad experience. One woman said of her childhood dentist, "I started getting upset and crying and he said, 'If you don't shut up, I'm going to slap you.'" She now drives 70 miles to The Dental Fears Clinic in Kansas City.

People who are afraid to go to God have a similar problem. Some may have been mistreated by spiritual leaders. Others may have learned unhealthy fear of God as children. Still others, overwhelmed by their sin, see only God's righteous demand for justice and miss the loving provision of His Son's sacrifice for sin.

The people in today's Bible reading (1 Samuel 12) were afraid because Samuel exposed their sin. But he also told them that God longed to forgive them.

We need to replace irrational fears with healthy ones. God's Word repeatedly assures us that the pain of going to Him is far less than the pain of avoiding Him. It also assures us that because of Jesus we can "come boldly to the throne of grace, that we may obtain mercy" (Hebrews 4:16).

A dentist fills the holes in your teeth, but God wants to fill the holes in your heart — with Himself. Don't let your unhealthy fear stop Him. — Mart De Haan

*The love of God is my pillow,*
*Soft and healing and wide;*
*I rest my soul in its comfort,*
*And in its calm I abide. — Long*

---

**Only God can fill the emptiness of an aching heart.**

# AN UNBROKEN CHAIN

READ:
2 Tim. 1:1-7; 2:1-2

---

The things that you
have heard from me
. . . commit these
to faithful men.
—2 Timothy 2:2

---

THE BIBLE IN ONE YEAR:
■ Psalms 72–73
■ Romans 9:1-15

Whenever I meet a Christian for the first time, I'm interested in learning how he came to trust Jesus as his Savior. Each person has a different story to tell, but they all testify that they learned the truth because of the efforts of others — their parents, pastors, Sunday school teachers, Bible club leaders, friends, writers. Someone has rightly observed that the body of Christ grows through "an unbroken chain of teachers."

In today's Scripture we learn that Timothy became a believer through the influence of his grandmother Lois, his mother Eunice, and the teaching of Paul (2 Timothy 1:5; 2:2). The apostle told Timothy to become part of that chain and "commit these truths to faithful men who will be able to teach others also" (v.2).

The "faithful men" Paul had in mind were probably church elders, yet he was expressing a principle that applies to every believer. We had to receive the truth from someone; now it is our gracious privilege and solemn duty to transmit that truth to others.

Think of yourself as a link in the living chain that extends from the time Jesus lived on earth to the present. We must keep that chain strong by telling others about Him so that the gospel will reach to future generations. — Herb Vander Lugt

*Give me a passion for souls, dear Lord,*
*A passion to save the lost;*
*O that Thy love were by all adored,*
*And welcomed at any cost.* — Tovey

---

**The good news is meant to be shared.**

August 8

## "WE CUT THE COAL"

READ:
Romans 16:1-16

I commend to you Phoebe . . . ; for indeed she has been a helper of many and of myself also. —Romans 16:1-2

THE BIBLE IN ONE YEAR:
- Psalms 74–76
- Romans 9:16-33

Winston Churchill knew that people who work behind the scenes don't always get the credit they deserve. During World War II, many of England's coal miners wanted to enlist and fight on the front lines. Churchill acknowledged their patriotism but reminded them of how valuable their work was to the cause of the war. "Some must stay in the pits," he said, "and others must stay in the army. Both are equally needed, and for both there is equal credit."

Looking ahead to when children would ask their parents what they did in the war, Churchill said, "One will say, 'I was a fighter pilot'; another will say, 'I was in the submarine service'; . . . and you in your turn will say with equal pride and with equal right, 'We cut the coal.'"

Paul too recognized the vital importance of those who worked behind the scenes. Much of Romans 16 is dedicated to honoring some of his fellow workers in the faith — people such as Phoebe, Andronicus, and Urbanus — whom we would otherwise never know about. Their service was valuable to Paul and to the cause of reaching people for Christ.

Your labor for the Lord may be unseen and unheralded, but it is essential. Continue to "cut the coal." You are valuable to the Lord. —Dave Egner

*Use now what God has given you,*
*Count not its worth as small;*
*God does not ask of you great things,*
*Just faithfulness — that's all!* —Bosch

**Your little is a lot when you give your all.**

# STAY HOME
# AND KEEP THEM

**READ:**
James 1:21-27

Be doers of the Word,
and not hearers only.
—James 1:22

THE BIBLE IN ONE YEAR:
■ Psalms 77–78
■ Romans 10

A church member told his pastor that he was going to the Holy Land. He said that it was his intention to visit Mount Sinai. "In fact," he told the minister, "I plan to climb to the top of that mountain, and read the Ten Commandments aloud when I get there."

Thinking this would please the pastor, he was surprised to hear, "You know, I can think of something even better than that." The man responded, "You can, Pastor? And what might that be?"

He replied rather bluntly, "Instead of traveling thousands of miles to read the Ten Commandments on Mount Sinai, why not stay right here at home and keep them?"

God wants us to read His Word, of course. But more important, He wants us to obey it. So, as we open the Bible each day, we should pray not only for illumination to understand it but also for a willingness to obey it. Hearing and doing must go hand-in-hand (James 1:22).

When Saul heard Jesus speaking to him on the road to Damascus, he asked, "Lord, what do You want me to do?" (Acts 9:6). That's a good question for us to ask whenever we read the Bible or hear it read.

Let's be "doers of the Word." — Richard De Haan

*We take delight to read God's Word,*
*We say, "Ah, yes, it's true!"*
*But we must go beyond mere words*
*And seek His will to do.* — D. De Haan

**The Spirit of God enables us
to obey the Word of God.**

# COUNTLESS WONDERS

**READ:**
Job 9:1-10

---

[God] does great things past finding out, yes, wonders without number. —Job 9:10

---

THE BIBLE IN ONE YEAR:
■ Psalms 79–80
■ Romans 11:1-18

When writer Aletha Lindstrom needs a lift for her spirits, she thinks of her favorite poetry book called *Who Tells The Crocuses It's Spring?* That prompts her to ask other questions like, "Who makes the trees turn all those beautiful colors in the autumn? Who splashes rain in shining puddles? Who makes the stars shimmer in the night?"

Such questions ought to stimulate our own grateful meditation. Centuries ago, Job exclaimed that it is God who "does great things past finding out, yes, wonders without number" (Job 9:10).

It is God who reminds the sun to rise at its appointed time every morning. It is God who keeps the earth steadily rotating at tremendous speed. It is God who feeds the sparrow and dresses the lilies in their splendor. It is God who guides the feathered flocks southward in the autumn and then brings them north again in the spring.

Argue if you like that all these wonders are simply the operation of the laws of nature. But just as civil law is the expression of human will, so also natural law is the expression of God's will and wisdom.

As we see the wonders of creation all around us, let's worship the One who designed them. — Vernon Grounds

> *This is my Father's world —*
> *The birds their carols raise;*
> *The morning light, the lily white*
> *Declare their Maker's praise.* —Babcock

---

**In the wonders of creation**
**we see God at work.**

# WHAT'S YOUR IDENTITY?

READ:
Galatians 3:26–4:7

You are all sons of
God through faith in
Christ Jesus.
—Galatians 3:26

THE BIBLE IN ONE YEAR:
■ Psalms 81–83
■ Romans 11:19-36

How do people identify you? Do they say, "Hey, there's the guy who sells cars." Or "That woman is a school teacher."

When our oldest daughter was little, she sang on a national children's radio program, and I liked being known as "Lisa Sue's dad." Since 1990, I've enjoyed being "The *Sports Spectrum* guy" because of my work with that magazine. We all have little titles that others use to identify us.

Jesus asked His disciples, "Who do men say that I am?" (Mark 8:27). Some thought He was Elijah or another prophet. But those who knew Him best said, "You are the Christ" (v.29). That was the right label for the Savior of the world.

What are you called by those who know you best? Do they say, "He's a follower of Jesus — you can just tell"? It may depend on how you talk with people, how you treat your family, and the way you live.

The apostle Paul said we are all "sons of God through faith in Christ Jesus" (Galatians 3:26). That intimate identification with God the Father should naturally express itself to our friends and acquaintances.

Those closest to Jesus knew He was the Savior. Do those close to us know that we belong to Him? — Dave Branon

*Show me the way, Lord, let my light shine*
*As an example of good to mankind;*
*Help them to see the patterns of Thee*
*Shining in beauty, lived out in me.* —Neuer

**Do those who know you
know you are a Christian?**

# THE POWER OF LOVE

READ:
Matthew 5:43-48

---

Love your enemies, . . . and pray for those who spitefully use you and persecute you.
—Matthew 5:44

---

THE BIBLE IN ONE YEAR:
■ Psalms 84–86
■ Romans 12

Fyodor Dostoevsky tells the story of brothers Ivan and Alyosha Karamazov. Alyosha is a devoted follower of Jesus; Ivan is a skeptic.

As the story unfolds, Ivan meets his brother at a café. In an effort to undermine the faith of Alyosha, he recites a lengthy poem he has written about the Grand Inquisitor. In it the Inquisitor rails at Jesus for His decision to grant free will to human beings and thus bring so much pain and suffering into the world.

As the Grand Inquisitor finishes his argument, Ivan portrays Jesus as having no answer. Instead, Jesus walks up to the Inquisitor and kisses him. Ivan hopes Alyosha will see this as an irrational act. But as he finishes speaking, Alyosha, imitating Jesus, leans forward and kisses Ivan.

Alyosha's profound gesture completely changes the tenor of the scene, for it represents the triumph of love over doubt and skepticism. Love overrides every objection. No logical argument can overthrow it.

That's why Jesus calls us to love our enemies, and to do good to those who spitefully use us and persecute us (Matthew 5:44). Love, not rational argument, overcomes hatred. The goodness of God revealed in our love draws people to repentance. — David Roper

*Open my eyes, Lord, to people around me,*
*Help me to see them as You do above;*
*Give me the wisdom and strength to take action,*
*So I may show them Your wonderful love.* — K. De Haan

---

**It's better to give others a piece of your heart
than a piece of your mind.**

# APPRECIATED

**READ:**
Matthew 26:6-13

Wherever this gospel
is preached in the
whole world, what this
woman has done will
also be told as a
memorial to her.
—Matthew 26:13

THE BIBLE IN ONE YEAR:
■ Psalms 87–88
■ Romans 13

The heroes and heroines of the Bible often take us by surprise. The woman in today's Scripture reading is a prime example. (John 12:3 tells us her name was Mary.) She was singled out by Jesus to be mentioned wherever the gospel is preached. Mary had scandalized some of those dining with Jesus by her lavish devotion as she anointed Him with perfume worth more than a year's wages. I believe Mary did this in anticipation of Jesus' death.

"Why this waste?" asked those at the table who expressed a concern for the poor (Matthew 26:8-9). If they had been attending Jesus' funeral rather than a dinner with Him, they may have reacted quite differently. Yet, when Mary showed Him her extravagant love while He was alive, she was severely criticized for such waste.

We can learn a valuable lesson from Mary's devotion. We need to break out our best perfumes for the living. Yet all too often we wait until someone we know has died to show the appreciation that we fail to show in life.

Is there someone who comes to your mind, a friend or family member, who would be honored and encouraged by an expression of your love and appreciation? Then do something to show it — while the person is still alive. —Haddon Robinson

*Show love to others young and old,*
*Encourage them while they are near;*
*For when they've gone to their reward,*
*Your loudest praise they will not hear.* —D. De Haan

---

**Give praise to others while they are here;**
**they won't need it in the hereafter.**

# THE BIBLE STANDS!

**READ:**
Joshua 6:1-5,20

---

By faith the walls of
Jericho fell down after
they were encircled
for seven days.
—Hebrews 11:30

---

THE BIBLE IN ONE YEAR:
■ Psalms 89–90
■ Romans 14

Unbelievers have long scoffed at the biblical story of the fall of the ancient city of Jericho. That's why I was delighted to see this headline on the front page of the newspaper:

NEW STUDY BACKS BIBLICAL
VERSION OF JERICHO'S DEMISE

The Associated Press article began, "The walls of Jericho did come tumbling down as recounted in the Bible, according to an archaeological study." Archaeologist Bryant G. Wood of the University of Toronto said, "When we compare the archaeological evidence at Jericho with the biblical narrative describing the Israelite destruction of Jericho, we find remarkable agreement." Wood noted that the Bible places the event after spring harvest and indicates that the Israelites burned the city — both facts confirmed by the archaeological remains. Once again, archaeology bears testimony to the truthfulness of Scripture.

Our belief in the authenticity of the Bible does not depend on scientific research but on its claim to be God's Word. As 2 Timothy 3:16 tells us, "All Scripture is given by inspiration of God." We can therefore have complete confidence in what it says.

It's a fact — the walls of Jericho did indeed fall. The Bible stands! — Richard De Haan

*The Bible stands like a mountain towering*
*Far above the works of men;*
*Its truth by none ever was refuted,*
*And destroy it they never can.* — Lillenas

---

**To the wise, God's Word is sufficient.**

**August 15**

# THE TOTAL PACKAGE

**READ:**
**Colossians 1:19-23**

---

You were bought at a price; therefore glorify God in your body and in your spirit.
—1 Corinthians 6:20

---

THE BIBLE IN ONE YEAR:
■ Psalms 91–93
■ Romans 15:1-13

Our family had lived in the same house for many years, and it was time for a change of scenery. When we finally discovered a house we liked, we began negotiating for its purchase.

We had to find out if the refrigerator stayed. And the stove. But we knew some things were not going to stay. The furniture didn't come with the house. And I jokingly wondered if we could keep the cars in the garage.

When you buy a house, you may not get the total package. The owner takes his belongings with him, although you may have the option to buy some of them.

Many things in life have purchase options. But that's not how it is with our faith in Jesus Christ. When Jesus purchased us with His blood on the cross, He didn't get only a portion of us. He's not just the Lord of the religious stuff; He owns everything. So why do we sometimes live as if parts of us don't belong to Jesus? That's not fair to the buyer.

"You were bought at a price," Paul wrote. "Therefore glorify God in your body and in your spirit, which are God's" (1 Corinthians 6:20).

Christ bought us — body, soul, and spirit. Let's make sure we let Him use the total package for His glory. — Dave Branon

*You have bought us, and no longer*
*Can we claim to be our own;*
*Giving freely, naught withholding,*
*We shall serve You, Lord, alone.* — Murray

---

**Jesus gave His all;**
**He deserves our all.**

# THINK YOUNG

**READ:**
Isaiah 40:25-31

Those who wait on the LORD shall renew their strength.
—Isaiah 40:31

THE BIBLE IN ONE YEAR:
■ Psalms 94–96
■ Romans 15:14-33

In the book *Geeks and Geezers,* authors Warren Bennis and Robert Thomas present a fascinating look at "how era, values, and defining moments shape leaders" of two very different generations — the geeks (those 21-35) and the geezers (those over 70).

One of their findings is that among the older group of "geezers," every person who was able to continue to play a leadership role retained the qualities of curiosity, playfulness, eagerness, fearlessness, warmth, and energy. Instead of being defeated by time and age, they were "open, willing to take risks, hungry for knowledge and experience, courageous, eager to see what the new day brings."

That's a great attitude to have, but how can a Christian get it and keep it? The Bible says that our strength comes from a trusting relationship with God: "Those who wait on the LORD shall renew their strength; they shall mount up with wings like eagles, they shall run and not be weary, they shall walk and not faint" (Isaiah 40:31).

Our minds more than our bodies cause us to lose heart and give up. The young are not immune, because "even the youths shall faint and be weary" (v.30). God gives power to young and old who place their hope in Him. He stirs our spirits to run, walk, and soar for Him. — David McCasland

*We're often weary in life's race,*
*Driven by its hurried pace,*
*But when we wait upon the Lord,*
*His strength becomes our sure reward.* — D. De Haan

---

**No one is old
who is young at heart.**

# A ROCK-SOLID FOUNDATION

READ:
Matthew 7:21-27

---

No other foundation can anyone lay than that which is laid, which is Jesus Christ.
—1 Corinthians 3:11

---

THE BIBLE IN ONE YEAR:
- Psalms 97–99
- Romans 16

As Christians we can become so preoccupied with our earthly affairs that we shift our confidence from Jesus Christ to faith in our own intellect. Then something happens to shake the foundation on which we had been building.

Phillip E. Johnson, a gifted lawyer and primary spokesman for the Intelligent Design movement, suffered a stroke and was likely to have another. Plagued by frightening thoughts during those first few days after his stroke, he was profoundly touched when a friend came and sang, "On Christ, the solid rock, I stand—all other ground is sinking sand."

Johnson writes, "What was the solid rock on which I stood? I had always prided myself on being self-reliant, and my brain was what I had relied on. Now the self with its brain was exposed as the shaky instrument it had always been. I was a Christian, even an ardent one in my worldly fashion, but now all the smoke was blown away, and I saw Truth close up." He resolved to keep Jesus at the center of his life and is now a different man.

How quickly we rely on our intellect and reasoning, only to find that it is a "shaky instrument." Let's never forget that Jesus is the only rock-solid foundation of truth on which we can always depend. — Herb Vander Lugt

*My hope is built on nothing less*
*Than Jesus' blood and righteousness;*
*I dare not trust the sweetest frame,*
*But wholly lean on Jesus' name.* —Mote

---

**Build your life on the solid foundation—
Jesus Christ.**

**August 18**

# MEET THE TATES

**READ:**
1 Corinthians 12:12-27

---

The eye cannot say to
the hand, "I have no
need of you"; nor again
the head to the feet, "I
have no need of you."
—1 Corinthians 12:21

---

THE BIBLE IN ONE YEAR:
- Psalms 100–102
- 1 Corinthians 1

Teamwork is essential in business and industry. To underscore this point, *Co-op Magazine* included this item: "You've heard of the corny Tate family. They pervade every organization. There is Dick Tate, who wants to run everything. Ro Tate tries to change everything. Agi Tate stirs up trouble whenever possible, and Irri Tate always lends him a hand.

"Whenever new ideas are suggested, Hesi Tate and Vegi Tate pour cold water on them. Imi Tate tries to mimic everyone, Devas Tate loves to be disruptive, and Poten Tate wants to be a big shot. But it's Facili Tate, Cogi Tate, and Medi Tate who always save the day and get everyone pulling together."

A one-man show doesn't get very far. But nowhere is this truth brought to a higher and more powerful fulfillment than in the body of Christ. The Scriptures teach that by God's design all who are in Christ have been made dependent on one another. We may think we can go it on our own, but we can't. We can't fulfill our high calling as members of the body of Christ until we begin to realize that we all have a vital part to play. We are family. We need one another.

Lord, help us to overcome our stubborn pride. Teach us to cooperate — for our sake and for Yours. — Mart De Haan

*If great and small work side by side*
*When it comes time to lend a hand,*
*And if they turn their backs on pride,*
*Christ's servant-heart they'll understand.* — Branon

---

**Coming together is a start; keeping together**
**is progress; working together is success.**

# GRACE AND GLORY

**READ:**
Psalm 84:5-12

---

The LORD will give grace and glory; no good thing will He withhold from those who walk uprightly.
—Psalm 84:11

---

THE BIBLE IN ONE YEAR:
■ Psalms 103–104
■ 1 Corinthians 2

There's a circular path in the park where I walk behind our home in Boise, Idaho. When I've walked three times around, I've gone 1 mile.

It's easy to lose count of the laps on my 3-mile walk. So each morning I pick up nine small stones and put them in my pocket, discarding one each time I finish a lap.

I always feel good when there's one stone left in my pocket. It puts spring in my step. I pick up the pace.

It occurs to me that my walk through life is a lot like those daily walks. I've completed three-score and ten years and don't have far to go. That too puts spring in my step.

I'm in no hurry to leave this life, but my times are in God's hands. As the body is breaking down under the weight of the years, there is a grace within that sustains me. I go now "from strength to strength," and in good time I will appear "before God in Zion" (Psalm 84:7,11). That will be glory for me.

Our Lord gives "grace and glory," the psalmist says — grace for our earthly walk and glory when we have finished it. "No good thing will He withhold from those who walk uprightly" (v.11).

Do you need grace today? God gives it with both hands. All you have to do is take it. — David Roper

*When all my labors and trials are o'er,*
*And I am safe on that beautiful shore,*
*Just to be near the dear Lord I adore*
*Will through the ages be glory for me. — Gabriel*

---

**God gives grace for this life
and glory in the life to come.**

# TWICE IS ONCE TOO MANY

**READ:**
James 3:1-12

---

With [our tongue] we bless our God and Father, and with it we curse men.
—James 3:9

---

THE BIBLE IN ONE YEAR:
- Psalms 105–106
- 1 Corinthians 3

When I begin to grade the papers from the students in my college freshman writing class, I'm rather lenient about correcting their mistakes, hoping I won't see the same errors again.

But when the next paper contains the identical mistakes, I begin to get a little irritated. I expect the students to learn from their errors and avoid them the next time. Usually, though, it doesn't quite work that way.

Sounds like our Christian life. The Lord patiently reminds us through the Holy Spirit's presence, for example, that we shouldn't say negative things about others. He tells us to be kind and compassionate instead of fault-finding and vindictive (Ephesians 4:31-32). But we sometimes slip back into our old habit of letting both "fresh" and "bitter" words come from our lips in our conversations about others (James 3:8-12).

With my students, I go back to the basics to erase old habits. We train. We review. We practice. We eliminate the errors.

The Lord patiently continues to work with us about the way we speak of other people. As we listen to His training, learn from our mistakes, and depend on His power, we'll grow and change. — Dave Branon

*To be like Jesus — that's our goal,*
*Though it doesn't happen fast;*
*We trust the Spirit — He's our Guide,*
*Till we're glorified at last.* — Branon

---

**To put failure behind you,
face up to it.**

# A NEW SONG

Make melody to Him
with an instrument of
ten strings. Sing to Him
a new song.
—Psalm 33:2-3

THE BIBLE IN ONE YEAR:
■ Psalms 107–109
■ 1 Corinthians 4

I was walking in the park one morning, listening to a tape by the Brooklyn Tabernacle Choir. I had my ancient Walkman clipped to my belt and my headphones clamped over my ears, tuned in to another world. The music was joyous! Oblivious to my surroundings, I began to sing and dance.

Then I spied my neighbor, leaning against a tree with a bemused look on her face. She couldn't hear my music, but she was delighted by my behavior. I wish she could have heard my song.

I thought afterward of the new song God has placed in our hearts, a song we hear from another world. It tells us that God loves us and always will, and that He has "delivered us from the power of darkness" (Colossians 1:13) and "made us sit together in the heavenly places in Christ Jesus" (Ephesians 2:6). And someday He'll take us to be with Him forever.

In the meantime He has given us eternally useful things to do. Grace now and glory ahead! Is this not a reason to sing?

Next time you're down in the dumps, think about God's goodness. Tune in to the music of heaven and sing a new song with the angels. It may set your feet to dancing and cause great wonderment in those around you. Perhaps they'll want to hear the music too. — David Roper

*I'll sing with the ransomed a new song on high,*
*And all because Jesus my Savior is nigh;*
*The earth with its heartaches is all of the past,*
*For now I am home with my Savior at last.* —Johnson

**God's work in our life
puts a new song in our heart.**

# THE HUMANITY OF JESUS

**READ:**
Hebrews 2:9-18

---

We do not have a
High Priest who
cannot sympathize
with our weaknesses.
—Hebrews 4:15

---

THE BIBLE IN ONE YEAR:
■ Psalms 110–112
■ 1 Corinthians 5

I once overheard this comment about a person who was always critical: "The trouble with him is that he's forgotten what it's like to be human!" How easily we forget our past struggles and become unsympathetic toward those who are struggling today. But there's one who hasn't forgotten what it's like to be human — Jesus.

In Hebrews 2:9-18, we "see" Jesus' humanity more fully. As a man, He was able by God's grace to experience death in our place. And during His earthly life Jesus was made perfect through His sufferings (v.10). But there's more. "Both [Jesus] who sanctifies and [we] who are being sanctified are all of one." Because of this oneness, Jesus is not ashamed to call us brothers and sisters (v.11).

In a body like ours, Jesus lived, worked, and overcame every obstacle, so He knows what it's like to be one of us. Having passed through all these experiences without sinning, He then went to heaven and is now our approachable High Priest at the throne of grace (vv.17-18; 4:14-16).

We all need someone who knows what it's like to be human yet has limitless power to help us overcome our human weaknesses. Jesus is that one. He longs to hear us speak His name and ask for His help. — Joanie Yoder

*God lived as man, as one of us,*
*And understands our need for grace;*
*He is not distant nor detached*
*From all the trials that we face.* — Sper

---

**No one understands like Jesus.**

# TRAIN TO FINISH STRONG

**READ:**
1 Corinthians 9:19-27

I discipline my body and bring it into subjection, lest, when I have preached to others, I myself should become disqualified.
—1 Corinthians 9:27

THE BIBLE IN ONE YEAR:
■ Psalms 113–115
■ 1 Corinthians 6

Eighty years ago, Eric Liddell electrified the world by capturing an Olympic gold medal in the 400 meters — a race he was not expected to win. Liddell was the favorite at 100 meters, but he had withdrawn from that race after learning the qualifying heats would be on Sunday, a day he observed as one of worship and rest. Instead of lamenting his lost chance in the 100, he spent the next 6 months training for the 400 — and set a new Olympic record.

Paul used a sports metaphor to emphasize the Christian's need for spiritual discipline. "Everyone who competes for the prize is temperate in all things" (1 Corinthians 9:25), that is, goes into strict training. "Now they do it to obtain a perishable crown, but we for an imperishable crown." Paul longed to remain faithful to Christ because he wanted to bring the message of salvation to others (vv.19,27).

Throughout Liddell's life, he disciplined himself spiritually each day by spending time in God's Word and in prayer. He remained faithful until he died of a brain tumor in a Japanese internment camp during World War II.

Strengthened by the grace and power of God, Eric Liddell ran well and finished strong in the race of life. And so can we. — David McCasland

*To win the race of life in Christ,*
*This must become our daily goal:*
*To trust in God for grace and strength,*
*For discipline and self-control.* —Sper

**In the race of life,
it takes discipline to finish strong.**

# LONELY, BUT NOT ALONE

READ:
John 16:25-33

You will be scattered, each to his own, and will leave Me alone. And yet I am not alone, because the Father is with Me. —John 16:32

THE BIBLE IN ONE YEAR:
■ Psalms 116–118
■ 1 Corinthians 7:1-19

Her brief note to me spoke volumes. "I am a handicapped person in a wheelchair," she wrote. "I am very lonely even though I know I'm never alone. God is always there. I don't have a lot of people to talk to."

*Loneliness* has been termed the most desolate word in the English language. It is no respecter of age, race, economic status, or intelligence. Albert Einstein said, "It is strange to be known so universally, and yet to be so lonely."

God made us for intimacy and companionship with others. Even before sin entered the world, He declared that it is not good for man to be alone (Genesis 2:18). That's why many people often feel so empty inside.

Jesus knew loneliness too. He surely must have felt it when His disciples deserted Him (Mark 14:50). The Father's presence more than compensated for this, however. He said, "I am not alone, because the Father is with Me" (John 16:32). That intimacy with the Lord is available to all who put their trust in Him and His Word (14:16-23).

We can lessen our feelings of loneliness by reaching out to others. But even more important, we must reach out to the Lord. He is always with us, and He wants us to fellowship with Him throughout the day. — Dennis De Haan

*When we are feeling all alone*
*And no one seems to care,*
*We must remember: Jesus said*
*That He is always there.* — Sper

**Those who know Jesus
are never alone.**

# HALF-BAKED CHRISTIANS

READ:
Hosea 7

___

Ephraim is a cake unturned. . . . But they do not return to the LORD their God.
—Hosea 7:8,10

___

THE BIBLE IN ONE YEAR:
■ Psalm 119:1-88
■ 1 Corinthians 7:20-40

The prophet Hosea used the tribe of Ephraim as a poetic representation of the northern kingdom of Israel. In a colorful admonition, he wrote that Ephraim had become "a cake unturned" (Hosea 7:8).

In today's terminology, the prophet might have said that Ephraim was "half-baked." The people were like a pancake burned on one side but raw on the other. Although they took advantage of the Lord's goodness, they did not seek Him with their heart. When they needed help, they turned to other sources (vv.10-11,14-16). They had become tasteless and useless to God, so He was forced to judge them.

Jesus echoed the words of the prophet. Although He had gentle words for penitent sinners, He gave a scathing rebuke to the haughty and self-righteous who wanted to live as they pleased. He was furious at two-faced religious leaders who talked a good talk but turned around and exploited their followers (Matthew 23:13-30).

God is never soft on sin. He sent His only Son to redeem us from sin's penalty (John 3:16). Let's not be half-baked Christians, claiming God's forgiveness but still living as we please. The only fitting response to God's mercy and grace is to serve Him in humility and love. —Haddon Robinson

*THINKING IT THROUGH*

*What is the basis of our salvation? (Ephesians 2:8-9).*

*How are we to respond to God's grace? (v.10).*

*How does God correct His children? (Hebrews 12:5-11).*

---

**God's grace is not license to live as we please—
it's liberty to please God.**

# A Faithful Friend

**READ:**
2 Timothy 1:15-18

---

A friend loves at all
times, and a brother
is born for adversity.
—Proverbs 17:17

---

THE BIBLE IN ONE YEAR:
■ Psalm 119:89-176
■ 1 Corinthians 8

After one of my relatives had a stroke, she needed help to get around and could no longer remember recent events. One day, my wife Ginny suggested that we take her out to dinner. I wondered if we should, because afterward she wouldn't even remember what we had done. Ginny responded, "While we are with her she will know we love her." How true!

All of us need to know we are loved. I recall the answer I received when I asked a 90-year-old shut-in how his grandchildren were doing. He said, "I don't know. I never see them."

The apostle Paul was locked in a damp Roman dungeon, awaiting execution. He couldn't help but feel hurt that many former friends had deserted him. How grateful he was for the friendship of Onesiphorus!

This man left his family and an active ministry in Ephesus to befriend Paul. When he arrived in Rome, he searched diligently to find where Paul was imprisoned (2 Timothy 1:17). And he courageously visited the apostle again and again. Paul said of Onesiphorus, "He often refreshed me, and was not ashamed of my chain" (v.16).

Remember, "A friend loves at all times," especially in adversity (Proverbs 17:17). Like Onesiphorus, let's commit ourselves to being faithful to our friends. — Herb Vander Lugt

*Someday I hope with you to stand*
*Before the throne, at God's right hand,*
*And say to you at journey's end,*
*"Praise God, you've been to me a friend."* —Clark

---

**Adversity is the test of true friendship.**

# A Sure Thing

READ:
Genesis 2:8-17

It is appointed for men to die once, but after this the judgment.
—Hebrews 9:27

THE BIBLE IN ONE YEAR:
■ Psalms 120–122
■ 1 Corinthians 9

A man who was suffering from poor health decided to move to a warmer climate. Wanting to make sure he would choose the area best suited to his needs, he visited several locations. While in Arizona, he asked, "What's the average temperature?" "What about the humidity?" "How many days of sunshine are there?" When he asked, "What's the death rate?" he received this answer: "Same as where you come from, friend — one death for every birth."

In spite of medical progress in prolonging life and improving its quality, the death rate remains unchanged. "It is appointed for men to die once" (Hebrews 9:27), because "all have sinned" (Romans 3:23) and "the wages of sin is death" (6:23).

It is therefore essential to live with the right perspective — that death follows life, and that after death comes the judgment. Everyone who trusts Christ for salvation will come forth from the grave "to the resurrection of life," but everyone who rejects Him will "come forth . . . to the resurrection of condemnation" (John 5:29). For unbelievers, death seals their doom. But for believers, death leads to glory.

Wise is the person who faces up to the certainty of death. And wiser still is the one who prepares for it. — Richard De Haan

*As sure as setting of the sun*
*In evening's western sky,*
*This life's brief day will soon be done*
*And we will have to die.* — D. De Haan

**Dying is the last page of time
and the first page of eternity.**

# A TIME TO CRY

READ:
John 11:1-7,32-36

---

Jesus wept.
—John 11:35

---

THE BIBLE IN ONE YEAR:
■ Psalms 123–125
■ 1 Corinthians 10:1-18

My father (Richard De Haan) had been battling a debilitating disease for many years. We asked the Lord to take him home. But as I knelt by his bed and watched him take that last breath, the tears I had choked back on other occasions came out like a flood. As my brothers and my mother hugged and prayed, the finality was overwhelming.

That event helped me understand the significance of the shortest verse in the Bible: "Jesus wept" (John 11:35). God the Son wept! He knew the reality of heaven. He was the source of all hope of a future day of resurrection. And yet, Jesus cried. He loved His friends Mary and Martha and Lazarus so much that "He groaned in the spirit and was troubled" (v.33). Jesus truly felt their heartache.

When someone we love dies, we struggle with a wide range of emotions. If a young person dies, we ask "Why?" When death comes after long-term suffering, we struggle to understand why the Lord waited so long to bring relief. We begin to think of God as distant, untouched by our sorrow. We may question His wisdom or His goodness. Then we read, "Jesus wept." God is deeply touched by our anguish.

When a painful situation invades your life, remember the Bible's shortest verse. Jesus shed tears too. — Kurt De Haan

*Two years ago today, Kurt De Haan,*
*managing editor of* Our Daily Bread *for 13 years,*
*was reunited with his father when God called him Home.*
*(March 29, 1953–August 28, 2003)*

---

**If you doubt that Jesus cares,
remember His tears.**

# DAILY BREAD

READ:
Leviticus 24:1-9

I am the living bread
which came down from
heaven. If anyone eats
of this bread, he will
live forever.
—John 6:51

THE BIBLE IN ONE YEAR:
■ Psalms 126–128
■ 1 Corinthians 10:19-33

Bread has come to be regarded as something less than what it was in Bible times. We don't usually think of it as a symbol of life's necessities. In Jesus' day, however, bread represented nourishment in all its many forms.

This helps us understand why the Lord told Israel to put bread in the Holy Place of the tabernacle—His "house of symbols." There in that first room, 12 loaves were to be displayed on a golden table "before the LORD" (Leviticus 24:6). Those loaves reminded Israel that God always provides for His own when they come to Him on His terms. The bread reflected God's promise to provide for all who hunger and thirst for righteousness (Matthew 5:6; 6:31-34).

For the believer in Christ, bread may represent the Bible, Jesus, Christian fellowship, or any of the provisions God has made for our spiritual needs. He cares for us and He's ready to feed us, but His offer is not unconditional. He promised to provide daily "bread" for those who in obedience have separated themselves to live and to eat from the hand of God.

The Lord cares for all who willingly and humbly receive their physical and spiritual food from Him. — Mart De Haan

*In You, O Lord, we take delight,*
*Our every need You can supply;*
*We long to do what's true and right,*
*So, Lord, on You we will rely.* — D. De Haan

**Only Christ the Living Bread**
**can satisfy our spiritual hunger.**

# GROUND SQUIRRELS

READ:
Romans 8:27-39

---

I was at ease, but
He has shattered me.
—Job 16:12

---

THE BIBLE IN ONE YEAR:
■ Psalms 129–131
■ 1 Corinthians 11:1-16

Ground squirrels hibernate near our home during the winter, and they reappear when the snow melts in the spring. My wife Carolyn and I enjoy watching them scurry back and forth from one hole to another, while others stand like tiny sentries watching for predators.

In mid-May, a man from a nearby golf course arrives on a little green tractor with a tank loaded with lethal gas. The groundskeeper tells us that these little critters have to be eliminated because they dig holes in the fairways. Some survive, but most do not. It always makes us a little sad to see the tractor arrive.

If I could, I'd chase the little animals away. I'd destroy their holes and force them to settle someplace else. I'm sure they would resent my interference, but my actions would be solely for their good.

So it is with God. He may break up our comfortable nests now and then, but behind every difficult change lies His love and eternal purpose. He is not cruel or capricious; He is working for our ultimate good (Romans 8:28). He wants us to be "conformed to the image of His Son" (v.29) and to give us glorious enjoyment in heaven forever. How then can we fear change when it comes from Someone whose love for us never changes? (vv.38-39).  — David Roper

*What tenderness the Father shows*
*To sinners in their pain!*
*He grants to them His strength to bear*
*The hurt that brings them gain.*  — D. De Haan

---

**God's love can seem harsh
until we view it with hindsight.**

# BE GLAD FOR TODAY

**READ:**
Psalm 118:14-24

---

This is the day the LORD has made; we will rejoice and be glad in it.
—Psalm 118:24

---

THE BIBLE IN ONE YEAR:
■ Psalms 132–134
■ 1 Corinthians 11:17-34

In Edith Schaeffer's book called *The Tapestry,* she describes a summer when her husband Francis was away in Europe for 3 months. During that time of missing him greatly, Edith and her sister Janet took their children to live in a former schoolhouse on Cape Cod. On a shoestring budget they shared the rent, lived without a car, and created daily adventures for the five young children.

Looking back years later, Edith said of that summer: "Never again have I spent time of that sort with my own children or my sister and nephews. The sudden precious moments in life need to be recognized for the unique periods they are, not wasted by wishing for something else."

Edith's perspective offers us a key to applying the words of Psalm 118:24, "This is the day the LORD has made; we will rejoice and be glad in it." During difficult times, we are tempted to become passive while waiting for a storm of life to pass. But God invites us to actively pursue the opportunities at hand instead of lamenting over what we don't have.

Because the Lord has made this day, we can look past the closed doors to see people and opportunities we had previously overlooked. In celebrating their value, we will discover joy and gladness from God. — David McCasland

*The God who put us here on earth*
*Knows life is tinged with sadness,*
*And so He gives us many things*
*To fill our hearts with gladness.* —Hess

---

**You don't have to worry about eyestrain from looking on the brighter side of life.**

September 1

# A FRIEND OF SINNERS

READ:
Matthew 9:9-13

I have not come to call the righteous, but sinners, to repentance.
—Luke 5:32

THE BIBLE IN ONE YEAR:
■ Psalms 135–136
■ 1 Corinthians 12

Jesus was having dinner one evening when "many tax collectors and sinners came and sat down with Him" (Matthew 9:10). The religious leaders of that day were outraged by His behavior. Their conclusion was that Jesus was a friend of sinners, and as it turns out, He was. "The Son of Man has come to seek and to save that which was lost" (Luke 19:10).

Jesus was morally separate from sinners and never took part in their lifestyle. Yet He did not separate Himself physically from sinful people. He spent time with them and became their friend.

Just like Jesus, you and I can't help but rub shoulders with all kinds of people in our daily activities. Tertullian, an early Roman writer, described the relationships between the Christians and non-Christians of his day this way: "We live among you, eat the same food, wear the same clothes . . . . We sojourn with you in the world, renouncing neither forum, nor market, nor bath, nor booth, nor workshop, nor inn . . . . We till the ground with you, we join with you in business ventures."

We too must seek the lost, as Jesus did—and it doesn't take much effort. It's good to ask ourselves from time to time, "How many friends do I have who are lost?" — David Roper

*Lead me to some soul today,*
*O teach me, Lord, just what to say;*
*Friends of mine are lost in sin*
*And cannot find their way.* — Houghton

**To be a friend of Jesus is to be a friend of sinners.**

# FAITH MIXED WITH DOUBT

READ:
Psalm 42

Why are you cast down, O my soul? . . . Hope in God; for I shall yet praise Him.
—Psalm 42:11

THE BIBLE IN ONE YEAR:
■ Psalms 137–139
■ 1 Corinthians 13

When my close friend Sharon was killed in a car accident, my heart broke. I'm ashamed to admit it, but when life's circumstances hurt so much, my faith is often mixed with doubt. When Sharon died, I cried out to God with these questions:

*Lord, I sure don't understand You. Why did You allow this death?*

"Have you not heard? The everlasting God . . . neither faints nor is weary. His understanding is unsearchable" (Isaiah 40:28). "My thoughts are not Your thoughts, nor are your ways My ways" (Isaiah 55:8).

*Lord, You are beyond my understanding. But I still wonder, have You turned Your back on the world?*

"God sits on His holy throne" (Psalm 47:8) and "rules by His power forever" (66:7).

*Lord, I do believe You are ruling this world, but do You care about the pain? Have You forgotten to be good?*

I am "good and ready to forgive, and abundant in mercy to all those who call upon [Me]" (Psalm 86:5).

*Yes, Lord, You have been good to me in countless ways, including listening to my doubts and questions about You.*

The answers God gives us in His Word may not take away our sadness, but we can always rest in the truth that He is wise, sovereign, and good. —Anne Cetas

*God understands your heartache,*
*He knows the bitter pain;*
*O trust Him in the darkness,*
*You cannot trust in vain.* —Smith

**Every loss leaves an empty space
that only God's presence can fill.**

# SHALLOW FRIENDLINESS

READ:
John 15:9-17

A man who has friends must himself be friendly.
—Proverbs 18:24

THE BIBLE IN ONE YEAR:
■ Psalms 140–142
■ 1 Corinthians 14:1-20

Recently I received a phone call from a friendly-sounding person who told me she wanted to make my life easier. She called me by my first name and warmly asked how my day was going. Then she informed me that she could help me save thousands of dollars a year if I would simply refinance my home with a particular mortgage company. But once she understood that I really wasn't interested, her friendliness evaporated.

Such insincere friendliness is often just a culturally correct attitude that some people use to impress others or to get something from them.

Contrast that self-serving attitude with the genuine friendship Jesus showed us. He said, "Greater love has no one than this, than to lay down one's life for his friends" (John 15:13). Then He demonstrated self-sacrificing love for us by dying on the cross to forgive our sins.

When we trust Jesus as our Savior and learn to obey Him, we experience a deep friendship that gives reality and sincerity to the friendliness we show to others.

Lord, help us to avoid the shallow friendliness that uses others to get what we want. Teach us instead to radiate the warmth of genuine Christlike friendliness to everyone we meet. — Dave Egner

*If friendliness is genuine,*
*It surely will convey*
*A warm and caring attitude*
*In all we do and say.* — D. De Haan

---

**True friendliness can be a magnet that draws people to Christ.**

# LET'S GET GROWING!

**READ:**
**Psalm 1**

---

Grow in the grace and
knowledge of our Lord
and Savior Jesus Christ.
—2 Peter 3:18

---

THE BIBLE IN ONE YEAR:
■ Psalms 143–145
■ 1 Corinthians 14:21-40

Several years ago my interest in flowers had our home resembling a nursery. There's something about the presence of growing plants that I find very enjoyable. As I daily inspected their progress, I gained from my little green friends a new appreciation of the joy and necessity of the wonderful process of growth.

As Christians, we too are like plants. We should put down our roots, break up through the earth, spread out our branches, and burst into blossom. Such a thriving condition, however, isn't always evident in our lives. It's so easy to become bored and listless in the bland routine of our daily activities. Often we just hang on and merely exist without moving steadily toward maturity and fruitfulness.

At such times we are at a spiritual standstill and must allow Jesus the "Sun of Righteousness" (Malachi 4:2) to warm our hearts anew with His love. We must send our roots deep into the Word of God by meditating on it day and night (Psalm 1:2). Then we will be like a fruitful tree planted by rivers of living water, and our branches will extend outward in an ever-increasing influence and witness. They will be filled with blossoms that reflect the beauty of righteous living.

If we've become dormant, let's get growing! — Mart De Haan

> *If God can make a tiny seed*
> *Into a bloom so fair,*
> *What can He make, O soul, of you*
> *Through study, faith, and prayer?* — Anon.

---

**Decay starts when growth stops.**

# WHO'S WHO IN "WHOEVER"?

**READ:**
John 3:14-21

For God so loved the world that He gave His only begotten Son, that whoever believes in Him should not perish but have everlasting life. —John 3:16

THE BIBLE IN ONE YEAR:
■ Psalms 146–147
■ 1 Corinthians 15:1-28

Henry Moorhouse always enjoyed preaching on John 3:16. When he came to the word *whoever,* he emphasized its all-inclusiveness. That term, he pointed out, makes it clear that everyone and anyone who trusts Christ will be saved.

He was glad that the word *whoever* appeared in John 3:16 instead of the name Henry Moorhouse. If that name were there, he couldn't be sure it meant him. He explained how he came to that conclusion:

"I once bought a typewriter that was shipped mistakenly to another man named Henry Moorhouse at a different address. If John 3:16 had said that God loved Henry Moorhouse, I could have thought it meant the other Henry Moorhouse. But since it says 'whoever,' there can be no mistake!" He could be sure it included him.

Yes, *whoever* covers everyone. If you already believe in Christ, thank Him for your salvation. If not, place your trust in Christ right now and receive His gift of eternal life and all the blessings that accompany it — deliverance from condemnation, forgiveness of sin, peace with God, and the promise of heaven.

Who's the who in "whoever"? It's you. It's me. It's everyone and anyone. That's who! — Richard De Haan

*When Jesus said "whoever,"*
*He included you and me;*
*For no one is excluded*
*From His offer full and free.* — Hess

**Salvation is a gift that anyone can open.**

# MISTER ROGERS

**READ:**
Colossians 3:22–4:1

Whatever you do, do it
heartily, as to the Lord
and not to men.
—Colossians 3:23

THE BIBLE IN ONE YEAR:
■ Psalms 148–150
■ 1 Corinthians 15:29-58

The late Fred Rogers, creator and host of the much-loved children's television program *Mister Rogers' Neighborhood*, had a special understanding of his ministry and his work. His widow, Joanne, told a journalist: "I always remind people that he was an ordained Presbyterian minister and this was his ministry. His work was his ministry, and he loved his work; my, did he love his work. That's what makes me sad about losing him. Because I think he would have worked for a long time more if he could have, yet he accepted that with all of his heart and was ready to go to heaven."

We may feel that work is secular, but view leading a Bible study as spiritual. The Bible draws no such distinction, however. Paul instructed Christians to work "not with eyeservice, as men-pleasers, but in sincerity of heart, fearing God. And whatever you do, do it heartily, as to the Lord and not to men, knowing that from the Lord you will receive the reward of the inheritance; for you serve the Lord Christ" (Colossians 3:22-24).

When we honor God and help people, then our work and ministry blend together in pleasing service to the Lord. Mister Rogers showed us how we can do that in our own neighborhood. — David McCasland

*No matter what my daily chores might be*
*To earn my livelihood, still may I see*
*My job, the real position that I hold,*
*Is bringing others to the Master's fold.* —Stalter

**Daily work done for God**
**takes on eternal value.**

# MIRROR IMAGE

READ:
2 Corinthians 3:7-18

We all, with unveiled face, beholding as in a mirror the glory of the Lord, are being transformed into the same image.
—2 Corinthians 3:18

THE BIBLE IN ONE YEAR:
■ Proverbs 1–2
■ 1 Corinthians 16

Years ago, an elderly businessman asked me, "What is your biggest problem?"

I pondered this for a while before replying: "When I look in the mirror every morning, I see my biggest problem staring at me."

Today's Scripture reading teaches me that Christians are to be like mirrors. Paul said that our faces are not to be veiled. This is logical. No one installs a mirror and then places a curtain over it. A covered mirror will not fulfill the purpose of reflecting the objects before it.

In 2 Corinthians 3:18, we are described as "beholding as in a mirror the glory of the Lord." When we behold His glory, we will be "transformed into the same image"—that is, the likeness of Christ.

We may wonder why we are still so far from being like Christ in our thinking and behavior. Perhaps this question will help: "Whose life do we mirror?"

God's people must reflect God's glory. To do that we must make it our habit to behold His glory. We must read and meditate on His Word. We must pray and trust God's Holy Spirit to work in our hearts. Only then can we obey His commands and depend on His promises.

Whose glory are you reflecting today?  — Albert Lee

*Lord, may our walk and service be*
*An image bright of things above,*
*As we reflect the unity*
*Of Father, Son, and Spirit's love.*  —Anon.

---

**The face is a mirror of the heart—**
**do people see Jesus in yours?**

# WHO'S TO BLAME?

**READ:**
Luke 13:1-5

Do you suppose that
these Galileans were
worse sinners?
—Luke 13:2

THE BIBLE IN ONE YEAR:
■ Proverbs 3–5
■ 2 Corinthians 1

A husband and wife were killed when their car was struck by a drunk driver. Why did this happen? They were good people, active in their church, and dearly loved. They were in no way at fault, and we can't blame God for the other driver getting drunk.

Some people would blame the devil. Yet we must recognize the fact that an intoxicated driver who loses control of his car is likely to kill someone.

Jesus referred to two tragedies that occurred in His day. In one, Pilate had killed some Galileans and mixed their blood with their sacrifices (Luke 13:1). In the other, 18 Israelites died when a tower fell on them (v.4). The idea was that people who died like that must have been guilty of horrendous sins.

Jesus rejected that kind of thinking. He told His hearers that instead of trying to find someone to blame, they should see such events as a call to repentance. If they willfully rejected Him as their Messiah and persisted in that sin, they would face a fearful end.

When we hear of inexplicable tragedies, let's be content to leave the "why" question unanswered. Assured of God's love (Romans 8:39), let's look at these events as a time for self-examination and repentance. —Herb Vander Lugt

*As members of a fallen race,*
*The question that we all must face*
*Is "Have we chosen to repent*
*And trusted Christ whom God has sent?"* —D. De Haan

**Life's tragedies are a call
to reflect and repent.**

# UNFAMILIAR ROADS

READ:
**Psalm 119:105-112**

Teach me Your way,
O LORD, and lead me
in a smooth path.
—Psalm 27:11

THE BIBLE IN ONE YEAR:
■ Proverbs 6–7
■ 2 Corinthians 2

Trouble often lies ahead when we go down unfamiliar roads.

I know a teenager who decided to take a different way to work one morning. As he tried to navigate unfamiliar city streets, he went through an intersection without seeing the red octagonal sign that said STOP.

Within a few seconds, he did stop, but not for a stop sign. He was pulled over by a helpful gentleman in a police car, who reminded him that he should have stopped. It cost him $80 to learn about unfamiliar roads.

What would have happened if a guide had accompanied this young driver? What if someone had been next to him to tell him which way to go and to alert him to danger ahead? He wouldn't be out the $80, that's for sure.

In life, we often have to walk down unfamiliar paths— paths that may feel threatening. So how do we do that without making costly mistakes?

We take Someone along who knows the way. The psalmist recognized that Guide when he wrote, "Lead me, O LORD, in Your righteousness . . . make Your way straight before my face" (Psalm 5:8).

Does your path today seem unfamiliar? Ask your Father to travel the road with you. —Dave Branon

*Take Jesus with you as your faithful guide,*
*You cannot fail when He is at your side;*
*You may encounter trouble on life's road,*
*But He will help to lift your heavy load.* —Hess

---

**The Spirit within us**
**will faithfully guide us.**

# A WAY OF LIFE

**READ:**
Colossians 3:5-9

Do not let the sun go down on your wrath.
—Ephesians 4:26

THE BIBLE IN ONE YEAR:
■ Proverbs 8–9
■ 2 Corinthians 3

"How did everything get so dirty so fast?" I grumbled as I dusted the glass tabletop. "I had the whole house clean a month ago."

"Cleaning is a way of life, not an event," my husband responded.

I know he's right, but I hate to admit it. I want to clean the house once and have it stay that way. But dirt doesn't surrender that easily. Speck by speck, the dust returns. Piece by piece, the clutter piles up.

Sin is like the dust and clutter in my house. I want to eliminate all of it with one prayer of confession and repentance. But sin doesn't surrender that easily. Thought by thought, bad attitudes return. Choice by choice, unpleasant consequences pile up.

The apostle Paul told the believers in Colosse to get rid of "anger, wrath, malice, blasphemy, filthy language" (Colossians 3:8). And he told the church at Ephesus, "Be angry, and do not sin: do not let the sun go down on your wrath" (Ephesians 4:26).

Christ's death and resurrection eliminated the need for daily sacrifice. But confession and repentance are still essential to the Christian's daily life. Getting rid of such things as anger, rage, and malice is a way of life, not a one-time event. — Julie Ackerman Link

*We're thankful, Lord, that when we fall*
*We can begin anew*
*If humbly we confess our sin,*
*Then turn and follow You.* —Sper

**The best eraser in the world**
**is an honest confession to God.**

## PRECIOUS NAMES

**READ:**
Luke 10:1,17-24

---

Rejoice because your names are written in heaven. —Luke 10:20

---

THE BIBLE IN ONE YEAR:
■ Proverbs 10–12
■ 2 Corinthians 4

No one expected the second anniversary of the 9/11 terrorist attacks to be as emotionally charged as the first. But that changed at Ground Zero in New York City when a group of 200 young people began reading the names of those who had died at the World Trade Center. The readers were the sons, daughters, brothers, sisters, nieces, and nephews of the victims. The 2,792 names, precious to those who read them, brought a fresh reminder of those they had loved and lost.

A person's name represents his identity, accomplishments, and relationships. Someday our name may appear on a memorial plaque or gravestone as a mark of remembrance and honor.

But there is a heavenly ledger that is the most important of all. When Jesus' followers reported their successful service to Him, He replied: "Do not rejoice in this, . . . but rather rejoice because your names are written in heaven" (Luke 10:20). Then He thanked the Father for making the way to Him simple enough for even a child to understand (v.21).

A child values a loving relationship. In that spirit, we should rejoice that through faith in Christ we belong to God and are secure in His love for all eternity. Our names are precious to Him. —David McCasland

*Our names are recorded in heaven,*
*Christ's death this high honor secured;*
*Believers have now a new standing*
*That nothing can change—we're assured.* —D. De Haan

---

**When you trust Jesus here on earth**
**He writes your name in heaven.**

# THE BAD SAMARITAN

READ:
**Matthew 23:1-15**

Woe to you, scribes
and Pharisees,
hypocrites! For you
pay tithe . . . and have
neglected . . . justice
and mercy and faith.
—Matthew 23:23

THE BIBLE IN ONE YEAR:
■ Proverbs 13–15
■ 2 Corinthians 5

A good-Samaritan-turned-bad saved a woman's life and then stole her purse. Police in Los Angeles said that a passerby had noticed a distressed woman getting ready to jump off a bridge. The man struggled with the woman until she broke free and then fell back onto the concrete and was knocked unconscious. That's when the surprise came. According to witnesses, the suspect then grabbed the woman's purse and ran off.

That man's outrageous behavior illustrates the pattern of the Pharisees. They too seemed ready to go to the rescue of others (Matthew 23:15). They were advertised as men of prayer, men of the Scriptures, champions of the faith, and helpers of the needy. But the intentions of their hearts revealed that they were actually thieves and exploiters of people.

None of us is above such behavior. We too can reach out to others with an honest desire to help them, yet underneath we may become more interested and concerned about our own welfare than about theirs.

Lord, we don't want to be like that. We long to be as real and loving as Your Son. Help us not to succumb to selfishness. As we express Your love to others, don't let our motives turn into a desire for self-advantage. — Mart De Haan

*There is a power of selfishness,*
*The proud and willful I,*
*And if my life would helpful be,*
*That proud old self must die.* — Anon.

**A good motive turns bad on the hinge of selfishness.**

# A LIFE-LONG ISSUE

READ:
Psalm 90

The days of our lives are seventy years; and if . . . they are eighty years, yet their boast is only labor and sorrow.
—Psalm 90:10

THE BIBLE IN ONE YEAR:
■ Proverbs 16–18
■ 2 Corinthians 6

Scientists predict that the average lifespan in the United States may reach 100 by the end of the 21st century. They say the genetics that control aging could be altered to extend life beyond the 70 to 80 years referred to in Psalm 90:10. Life's final chapter, however, will still read, "It is soon cut off, and we fly away."

Moses, who wrote those words, likened our existence to grass that flourishes in the morning and is cut down and withers in the evening (vv.5-6). Although he lived to be 120 (Deuteronomy 34:7), life's brevity was never far from his mind. That's why he prayed, "Teach us to number our days, that we may gain a heart of wisdom (Psalm 90:12).

D. J. De Pree, a longtime member of the RBC Board of Directors, took those words literally. He calculated the number of days from the date of his birth until he would turn 70. At the end of each day he'd reduce his total by one. To see that figure decline reminded him to make each day count for the Lord.

We are all part of a rapidly passing scene. That should sober us, but not discourage us. Moses affirmed God as his "dwelling place" (v.1). That's the way to face the life-long issue of our fleeting earthly existence. — Dennis De Haan

*To gain a heart of wisdom takes a lifetime,*
*And we are told to seek it all our days;*
*But whether life is long or too soon ended,*
*God's lovingkindness fills our heart with praise.* — Hess

**A life lived for God will count for eternity.**

# JESUS' VERY OWN PEACE

READ:
Matthew 16:21-23

---

My peace I give you.
—John 14:27

---

THE BIBLE IN ONE YEAR:
■ Proverbs 19–21
■ 2 Corinthians 7

On the eve of the execution of Christian martyr Nicholas Ridley (1500–1555), his brother offered to stay with him in the prison to be of comfort. Ridley declined, saying that he planned to sleep as soundly as usual. Because he knew the peace of Jesus, he could rest in his Lord.

The next morning, Ridley told a fellow Christian who was also being executed, "Be of good heart, brother, for God will either assuage the fury of the flame, or else strengthen us to abide it." Then they knelt and prayed by the stake and, after a brief conversation, were burned to death for their faith.

Jesus had given Nicholas Ridley *His* peace (John 14:27). But what kind of peace did Jesus have? In Matthew 16:21-23, we see His peace in His determination to go to Jerusalem even though He knew He would suffer and die (see Luke 9:51). Peter rebuked Him, but Jesus trusted His Father and went to the cross. His purpose for living was to die.

Amy Carmichael said, "The peace of Jesus stood every sort of test, every strain, and it never broke. It is this, His very own peace, which He says 'I give.'"

No matter how big or small our trials may be, we can trust Jesus to give us His very own peace in the midst of them. — Anne Cetas

*FOR FURTHER THOUGHT*
*How can we be at peace with God? (Romans 5:1-2).*
*How do we find peace in our trials? (Philippians 4:6-7).*
*Have you experienced Jesus' peace?*

---

**When Jesus rules the heart, peace reigns.**

# LED BY
# THE SPIRIT

READ:
Romans 8:5-17

_____

As many as are led by
the Spirit of God, these
are sons of God.
—Romans 8:14

_____

THE BIBLE IN ONE YEAR:
■ Proverbs 22–24
■ 2 Corinthians 8

As a young pastor during the 1940s, Francis Schaeffer was known for his organizational skill. A summer Bible school at his St. Louis church drew 700 children from all over the city and sparked a full-page story in the local newspaper. But when he and his wife began L'Abri Fellowship in Switzerland, Schaeffer intentionally set no organizational goals.

He described this unusual approach as God's specific leading for them and said it was the hardest thing he had ever done. But he wanted God's hand to be seen and not the success of well-organized programs.

Schaeffer said, "It's a very hard thing in our own generation, it seems to me, to find anything that can't be explained on the basis of public relations. We'll look to the personal God to see what He wants to do with this work."

Paul said, "As many as are led by the Spirit of God, these are sons of God" (Romans 8:14). This may apply to specific decisions, but it also speaks of a general approach to life. God's children should not attempt anything without the leadership of the Holy Spirit.

Being led by the Spirit and following His direction is a walk of faith that brings honor to God and leads to life and peace (vv.6,13). — David McCasland

*Led by the Spirit means yielding to Him*
*In all of the facets of life;*
*Trying to do all the work on your own*
*Leads to disorder and strife. — Hess*

_____

**A man's heart plans his way,**
**but the LORD directs his steps.** ——Proverbs 16:9

# HOW TO BE A FRIEND

READ:
**Proverbs 27:6-17**

A man who has
friends must himself
be friendly.
—Proverbs 18:24

THE BIBLE IN ONE YEAR:
■ Proverbs 25–26
■ 2 Corinthians 9

Our daughter Melissa had many friends during her high school days. One of her best friends was Katie. After Melissa's death in a car accident, Katie told us how they had become friends.

Katie was the new girl in school in fifth grade, having transferred from California. She felt alone and awkward and out of place — until one day early in her first year. That's when Melissa noticed her sitting alone on the bus.

Mell got up from her seat, sat down next to Katie, and started asking questions. They sat next to each other every day from then on and became inseparable friends for the next 7 years.

Our world has so many people who need just one act of love to change their lives. These people may not think they fit in, or they may be facing turmoil that makes them feel all alone. Sometimes all we need to do is extend a hand, offer a smile, or speak a word of encouragement. As believers, we know and experience the love of God (1 John 3:16), so we are especially able to reach out to people and share that love.

There are enough people to go around so that everyone can have friends. Let's take the initiative to make sure no one is left out. — Dave Branon

*I went outside to find a friend*
*But could not find one there;*
*I went outside to be a friend,*
*And friends were everywhere!* —Payne

**When you see someone in need,
be a friend in deed.**

# NOTHING HIDDEN

**READ:**
1 Timothy 5:24-25

---

Some men's sins are
clearly evident . . . .
Likewise, the good
works of some . . . and
those that are other-
wise cannot be hidden.
—1 Timothy 5:24-25

---

THE BIBLE IN ONE YEAR:
■ Proverbs 27—29
■ 2 Corinthians 10

A woman had been maligned and misrepresented by an envious co-worker. She was frustrated because her attempts to confront her in private had only made matters worse. So she decided to swallow her pride and let the matter go. She said, "I'm glad the Lord knows the true situation." She expressed a profound truth that both warns and comforts.

Paul pointed out that nothing can be concealed forever (1 Timothy 5:24-25). This serves as a solemn warning. For example, a news report told about a highly respected person who was arrested for crimes he had been secretly committing for years.

Yet the fact that nothing can be hidden can also be a great consolation. I have known people who never held a position of honor, nor were they recognized for their service. After they died, however, I learned that in their own quiet way they had touched many lives with their kind words and helpful deeds. Their good works could not remain hidden.

We can hide nothing from God—that's a solemn warning! But it's also a great comfort, for our heavenly Father knows about every encouraging smile, every kind word, and every loving deed done in Jesus' name. And someday He will reward us. —Herb Vander Lugt

*Be strong and to the will of God be true,*
*For though your book of life be sealed,*
*God knows what lies ahead awaiting you,*
*He knows when it should be revealed.* —Anon.

---

**Neither vice nor virtue
can remain a secret forever.**

# FEEDING THE WOLF

**READ:**
Romans 6:15-23

---

Make no provision for the flesh, to fulfill its lusts. —Romans 13:14

---

THE BIBLE IN ONE YEAR:
■ Proverbs 30–31
■ 2 Corinthians 11:1-15

There's a story about an old Cherokee chief sitting before a flickering fire with his grandson. The boy had broken a tribal taboo, and his grandpa wanted to help him understand what made him do it. "It's like we have two wolves inside us," said the chief. "One is good, the other is bad. Both demand our obedience."

"Which one wins?" asked the boy.

"The one we feed!" said the wise old chief.

Every follower of Jesus Christ can identify with that struggle. We fight an ongoing battle with selfish and sinful desires. They rise up within us and put incredible pressure on us to satisfy them. They are like ravenous hungers and unquenchable thirsts. First they are small "harmless" desires, but they grow stronger and can ultimately control us (Romans 6:16).

To resist we must believe what the Bible tells us about temptation's power. We must also believe that the Holy Spirit will help us to resist or to break free from its power.

But then comes the hard part. When an evil desire demands to be fed, we must say no—perhaps again and again and again. Paul said, "Make no provision for the flesh" (13:14).

Remember, what we feed will control us. —Dave Egner

*Lord, grant me strength from day to day—*
*How prone I am to go astray!*
*The passions of my flesh are strong;*
*O God, please shield me from all wrong.* —D. De Haan

---

**It is easier to resist the first evil desire
than to satisfy all the ones that follow.**

# INFORMING GOD

**READ:**
Psalm 139:1-6

Can anyone teach
God knowledge?
—Job 21:22

THE BIBLE IN ONE YEAR:
- Ecclesiastes 1–3
- 2 Corinthians 11:16-33

We cannot tell God anything He doesn't already know. When we pray, we simply put into words what He's been aware of all along.

That doesn't make prayer unnecessary; rather, it encourages us to pray. We find relief in talking to Someone who knows us and our situation fully. It's a comfort to know that God's response arises not from information we give Him, but from His perfect knowledge of our circumstances. He knows all conditions — past, present, future — that bear on our well-being.

"Your Father knows," Jesus said in Matthew 6:8. He knows our thoughts, our intentions, our desires; He is intimately acquainted with all our ways (Psalm 139:3). He knows the anguish of our heart, the strain of continual frustration, the enemies inside and outside that war against our souls.

So, can we presume to dictate the time and terms of our deliverance from trials or adversity? Can we say our way is better, more likely to develop our soul? No, we cannot teach God anything. He alone knows the way to bring us to glory. Out of all possible paths, He has chosen the best, the route most adapted to who we are and what He has in store for us.

We cannot teach God knowledge, but we can love and trust Him. That's all He asks of us. — David Roper

*The answer God may choose for me*
*Is sure to be the best,*
*So may I always thankful be,*
*And in His goodness rest.* —D. De Haan

**God knows the end from the beginning,
so we can trust Him with everything between.**

# IF DOUBTFUL, DON'T!

**READ:**
Romans 14:14-23

---

He who doubts is condemned if he eats, because he does not eat from faith; for whatever is not from faith is sin.
—Romans 14:23

THE BIBLE IN ONE YEAR:
■ Ecclesiastes 4–6
■ 2 Corinthians 12

In his book *Illustrations of Bible Truth,* H. A. Ironside tells about a man who was getting ready to attend a banquet. He wanted to put on a white shirt he had worn on a previous occasion, so he was inspecting it carefully to see if it was too dirty. His wife noticed what he was doing and called out, "Remember, dear, if it's doubtful, don't." The issue was settled. The man threw the shirt into the laundry hamper.

That wife's advice reminds me of the principle in today's text. It's a principle that can be applied to questionable matters of conscience. If doubtful, don't.

The doubtful things the apostle Paul wrote about in Romans 14 had to do with meat and wine considered to be "unclean" by some but not by others (vv.14,21). He indicated that if we have doubts about whether an action is right or wrong and we do it anyway, our action is not from faith and is therefore a sin (v.23). He also pointed out that it is wrong to do anything by which a brother in Christ "stumbles or is offended or is made weak" (v.21). We must never give another Christian a reason to violate his or her conscience.

When faced with questionable practices and a troubled conscience, we would do well to make this our guideline: If it's doubtful, don't! — Richard De Haan

*There is a treasure you can own*
*That's greater than a crown or throne;*
*This treasure is a conscience clear*
*That brings the sweetest peace and cheer.* — Isenhour

---

**One little word can spare us a lot of trouble.**
**It's NO.**

# SENT DOWN

READ:
**Philippians 2:5-11**

Humble yourselves
under the mighty hand
of God, that He may
exalt you in due time.
—1 Peter 5:6

THE BIBLE IN ONE YEAR:
■ Ecclesiastes 7–9
■ 2 Corinthians 13

A sportswriter described former major league baseball player and manager Don Baylor as a person who always remembered how it felt to be "sent down" to the minor leagues. When one of his players had to be demoted, he would always meet with him to explain the decision. A team owner said of Baylor, "He has been through a lot of life lessons he can share with the players." It makes a big difference when the manager knows how a player feels.

It's always humbling to be reduced in rank, privilege, or responsibility. But these things may come as part of God's training in our lives. The apostle Peter wrote, " 'God resists the proud but gives grace to the humble.' Therefore humble yourselves under the mighty hand of God, that He may exalt you in due time" (1 Peter 5:5-6).

The apostle Paul described Jesus as our example of humble submission to God. He was sent down from heaven to become a man—a "bondservant" who was obedient to the point of dying on the cross for our sins (Philippians 2:6-8).

Humility and submission to God are not signs of weakness but evidence of Christlike power and character. We can receive courage and strength from Jesus Himself, who knows how it feels to be "sent down." —David McCasland

*Teach me to do the humble task*
*The very best I can,*
*And not to look for greater calls,*
*Which may oppose Thy plan.* —Bernheisel

**The mighty Architect of the universe**
**became the humble Carpenter of Nazareth.**

# THE RIGHT SIGNAL

**READ:**
Matthew 14:14-21

When Jesus went out He saw a great multitude; and He was moved with compassion for them.
—Matthew 14:14

THE BIBLE IN ONE YEAR:
■ Ecclesiastes 10–12
■ Galatians 1

It was a tragic mistake. On July 3, 1988, the guided-missile cruiser *USS Vincennes* shot down an Iranian airliner with 290 souls aboard. All were lost. The ship's captain mistakenly thought they were under attack by an F-14 Iranian fighter.

Public opinion polls showed that most Americans opposed paying compensation to the victims' families. The cruel treatment of American hostages in Iran was still fresh in many minds. But President Reagan approved compensation. Asked by reporters if such payment would send the wrong signal, he replied, "I don't ever find compassion a bad precedent."

The principle of revenge is so much simpler to practice. Yet compassion is Christ's way — a deep caring for the physical, emotional, and spiritual needs of the whole person. It reveals the heart of God for sinful people — for you and for me.

The feeding of the 5,000 was a miracle born out of compassion. Jesus was moved by the physical and spiritual needs of the people (Matthew 14:14; Mark 6:34). He was not content just to teach them and then send them on their way.

As Christians, we must look at the whole person through the eyes of Jesus. Being moved by compassion always sends the right signal. —Dennis De Haan

*Give me a heart sympathetic and tender,*
*Jesus, like Thine, Jesus, like Thine;*
*Touched by the needs that are surging around me,*
*And filled with compassion divine.* —Anon.

---

**Compassion is love in action.**

# WHO GETS THE LOVE?

**READ:**
Luke 15:11-32

---

Son, you are always with me, and all that I have is yours.
—Luke 15:31

---

THE BIBLE IN ONE YEAR:
- Song of Solomon 1–3
- Galatians 2

A sociologist was writing a book about the difficulties of growing up in a large family, so he interviewed the mother of 13 children. After several questions, he asked, "Do you think all children deserve the full, impartial love and attention of a mother?"

"Of course," said the mother.

"Well, which of your children do you love the most?" he asked, hoping to catch her in a contradiction.

She answered, "The one who is sick until he gets well, and the one who is away until he gets home."

That mother's response reminds me of the shepherd who left 99 sheep to seek the one that was lost (Luke 15:4), the woman who searched for the one coin (v.8), and the father who threw a party when his wayward son returned (vv.22-24).

The religious leaders of Jesus' day resented the way He gave so much attention to sinners (vv.1-2). So He told those stories to emphasize God's love for people who are lost in sin. God has more than enough love to go around. Besides, those who are "well" and are not "lost" experience the Father's love as fully as those to whom He gives special attention (v.31).

Father, forgive us for feeling slighted when You shower Your love on needy sinners. Help us to see how needy we are and to abide in Your boundless love. — Mart De Haan

*The One who made the heavens,*
*Who died on Calvary,*
*Rejoices with His angels*
*When sinners are set free.* — Fasick

---

**God loves every one of us as if there were but one of us to love.** —Augustine

# GOD'S APPOINTMENTS

**READ:**
**Proverbs 16:1-9**

A man's heart plans
his way, but the LORD
directs his steps.
—Proverbs 16:9

THE BIBLE IN ONE YEAR:
■ Song of Solomon 4–5
■ Galatians 3

Life-changing events do not happen by accident. They are not determined by the stars. They are not by chance. There is no such thing as chance. The Lord uses every situation in life to accomplish His purposes.

Frank W. Boreham (1871-1959), British pastor and essayist, said, "It was not by chance that Elijah and Ahab met on the grassy slopes of Carmel. It was not by chance that Herod and John met on the highways in Galilee. It was not by chance that Pilate and Jesus met in the judgment hall at Jerusalem. It was not by chance that Peter and Cornelius met on the Syrian seaboard. It was not by chance that Philip and the Ethiopian met on the sandy road to Gaza. It was not by chance that Nero and Paul met amid the antique splendors of ancient Rome. . . . No, our meetings are no more by chance than the meeting of Stanley and Livingstone in Central Africa."

We should begin each day with a sincere desire to please the Lord, gladly anticipating His appointments for us. They may be circumstances that are unplanned, or the people we meet unexpectedly. But we should welcome them as opportunities to witnesss, to serve others, and to grow spiritually.

Recognizing God's sovereign leading, let us rejoice in His appointments. — Richard De Haan

*All things work out for good, we know —*
*Such is God's great design;*
*He orders all our steps below*
*For purposes divine. —Peterson*

---

**The stops of a good man are ordered by the Lord**
**as well as his steps.** —Müller

# "HE'S IN HEAVEN"

**READ:**
2 Corinthians 5:1-8

For to me, to live is
Christ, and to die is
gain.
—Philippians 1:21

THE BIBLE IN ONE YEAR:
■ Song of Solomon 6–8
■ Galatians 4

On August 28, 2003, my good friend Kurt De Haan, the former managing editor of *Our Daily Bread*, died of a heart attack while on his lunchtime run. When I learned the news, I said to myself, "He's in heaven," which brought me great comfort.

A few days later I was talking with my former pastor Roy Williamson, now in his eighties. I asked him about a man from our congregation. "He's in heaven," he said. I also inquired about another person. "She's in heaven too," he replied. Then, eyes twinkling, he said, "I know more people in heaven than I do on earth."

Later I was thinking about Pastor Williamson's words. He could have simply said, "He died," or "She died." But how reassuring to hear that those dear saints of God are in heaven. What joy to know that when believers in Christ die, they are instantly with Jesus! The apostle Paul put it like this: "We are confident, yes, well pleased rather to be absent from the body and to be present with the Lord" (2 Corinthians 5:8). No more pain. No more sadness. No more sin. Only peace. Only joy. Only glory.

We still grieve when a believing loved one dies. Grief is love's expression. But beneath it all is an unshakable joy, because we know our loved one is in heaven. — Dave Egner

*Friends will be there I have loved long ago,*
*Joy like a river around me will flow;*
*Yet, just a smile from my Savior, I know*
*Will through the ages be glory for me. —Gabriel*

---

**God's children never say goodbye**
**for the last time.**

# A LESSON IN PRAISE

**READ:**
Psalm 150

---

Praise the LORD!
—Psalm 150:1

---

THE BIBLE IN ONE YEAR:
■ Isaiah 1–2
■ Galatians 5

Psalm 150 is not only a beautiful expression of praise, it's also a lesson in praising the Lord. It tells us where to praise, why we're to praise, how we're to praise, and who should offer praise.

*Where do we praise?* In God's "sanctuary" and "mighty firmament" (v.1). Wherever we are in the world is a proper place to praise the One who created all things.

*Why do we praise?* First, because of what God does. He performs "mighty acts." Second, because of who God is. The psalmist praised Him for "His excellent greatness" (v.2). The all-powerful Creator is the Sustainer of the universe.

*How should we praise?* Loudly. Softly. Soothingly. Enthusiastically. Rhythmically. Boldly. Unexpectedly. Fearlessly. In other words, we can praise God in many ways and on many occasions (vv.3-5).

*Who should praise?* "Everything that has breath" (v.6). Young and old. Rich and poor. Weak and strong. Every living creature. God's will is for everyone to whom He gave the breath of life to use that breath to acknowledge His power and greatness.

Praise is our enthusiastic expression of gratitude to God for reigning in glory forever. — Julie Ackerman Link

> *Let every creature rise and bring*
> *Peculiar honors to our King;*
> *Angels descend with songs again,*
> *And earth repeat the loud amen!* — Watts

---

**Praise is the overflow of a joyful heart.**

# GOD'S TENDER CARE

**READ:**
**Psalm 31:1-14**

You have considered my trouble; You have known my soul in adversities.
—Psalm 31:7

THE BIBLE IN ONE YEAR:
■ Isaiah 3–4
■ Galatians 6

During a time of grief, C. S. Lewis observed that his neighbors walked across the street to avoid him when they saw him approaching.

David too knew a time of grief when he said, "I am a reproach among all my enemies, but especially among my neighbors . . . . I am forgotten like a dead man" (Psalm 31:11-12).

Perhaps you've known times when friends seem to forget you in your sorrow. They fail to call, or write, or promise to pray.

But those are the times when we can sense God's tenderness most deeply. When the days are long and lonely and no one seems to care, He seeks us out and surrounds us with lovingkindness. Our sorrow, far from burdening Him, draws out His tender compassion. He knows the troubles of our soul (v.7). And He cares. Thus we can commit our spirit into His hand (v.5), as our Lord Jesus did when all forsook Him and fled.

Poet Frank Graeff asks, "Does Jesus care when my heart is pained too deeply for mirth and song; as the burdens press, and the cares distress, and the way grows weary and long?" The answer? Yes! He invites us to give our burdens and cares to Him, because He cares for us (1 Peter 5:7).

Trust God to care for you today. — David Roper

*O yes, He cares — I know He cares!*
*His heart is touched with my grief;*
*When the days are weary, the long nights dreary,*
*I know my Savior cares!* — Graeff

---

**We can never get beyond the circle of God's care.**

# THINK TOGETHER

READ:
Philippians 4:4-13

---

If there is any virtue and if there is anything praiseworthy—meditate on these things.
—Philippians 4:8

---

THE BIBLE IN ONE YEAR:
■ Isaiah 5–6
■ Ephesians 1

An executive of the world's largest toymaker said, "We are such a machine in terms of what we deliver on an annual basis that it doesn't allow time to think."

In an effort to stimulate creativity, this company is taking selected employees out of corporate headquarters and encouraging them to think together in new ways. For instance, when asked to devise a method to prevent an egg from breaking if dropped from 14 feet, one group went beyond the conventional approach of trying to cushion its fall and created an egg bungee cord.

What about us? Are our lives so focused on activity and production that we don't take time to think? In Paul's letter to the Philippians, he told them to meditate on things that are true, noble, just, pure, lovely, and of good report (4:8). What would happen if we began this kind of thinking together in our churches and homes? Might we discover creative, God-given approaches to problems that seem to defy solution? Would our perspective on life undergo a radical change?

"Meditate on these things" is a great command. Obeying it with our families and other believers could open doors of discovery for helping others, serving God, and living for Him. Now that's something to think about!  —David McCasland

*Lord, help us to think of the right and the true,*
*The pure and the noble — it all points to You;*
*For if we consider what's worthy of praise,*
*We'll then want to live for You all of our days.* —Fitzhugh

---

**Right thinking leads to right living.**

# A WEB OF RELATIONSHIPS

**READ:**
John 15:1-14

You shall love the LORD your God with all your heart, with all your soul, with all your mind, and with all your strength.
—Mark 12:30

THE BIBLE IN ONE YEAR:
■ Isaiah 7–8
■ Ephesians 2

A Harvard Business School professor wrote an open letter to the nation's graduates. He told them that in one sense they needed to forget what they had learned in school. He said that schools tend to put too much emphasis on the idea that success comes as a result of passing tests. The professor pointed out that in the workplace doing well depends largely on learning to succeed in what he called a "web of relationships"—the ability to cooperate with others and function as an effective team.

This truth also applies to living the Christian life. We often think that spiritual maturity and success result from how much we know about biblical facts and principles.

Jesus showed us, however, that real success comes from something else—from loving one another in the same way He loved us. He made it clear that we can do this only if we "abide" in Him (John 15:7). This means that we must stay close to Him through prayer and willingly obey His commands (v.10). Our web of relationships must extend first to God and then to others.

The secret of spiritual success is not just in acquiring individual knowledge—it's in combining that knowledge with love in all our relationships. — Mart De Haan

> Lord, help us learn from what You did
> When You lived on this earth;
> You spread Your love to all You met—
> You gave each one true worth. — Branon

**As Christians draw close to Christ,
they draw closer to one another.**

# FOLLOW THE INSTRUCTIONS

**READ:**
Psalm 119:129-136

---

The entrance of Your words gives light; it gives understanding to the simple.
—Psalm 119:130

---

THE BIBLE IN ONE YEAR:
■ Isaiah 9–10
■ Ephesians 3

After a woman sued a fast-food restaurant for being burned by coffee, companies started changing their manuals and warning labels. Check out these instructions:

• On a frozen dinner: DEFROST BEFORE EATING
• On an iron: CAUTION! DO NOT IRON CLOTHES ON BODY
• On a peanut butter jar: MAY CONTAIN PEANUTS
• On a milk bottlecap: AFTER OPENING, KEEP UPRIGHT

If some people need these obvious guidelines on household items, think about how much more we need God's direction. Psalm 119 tells of the importance of His instruction manual — the Bible. On the pages of Scripture we find what God wants us *to believe, to be,* and *to do.*

"*Believe* on the Lord Jesus Christ, and you will be saved" (Acts 16:31).

"*Be* kind to one another, tenderhearted, forgiving one another, even as God in Christ forgave you" (Ephesians 4:32).

"*Go* into all the world and *preach* the gospel to every creature" (Mark 16:15).

Ask the Lord to teach you His statutes and to direct your steps according to His Word (Psalm 119:133,135). Then read it often and follow the instructions. — Anne Cetas

*Give us, O Lord, a strong desire*
*To look within Your Word each day;*
*Help us to hide it in our heart,*
*Lest from its truth our feet would stray.* —Branon

---

**Scripture is meant to give us protection,
correction, and direction.**

# LIFTING A BURDEN

READ:
**Genesis 45:1-15**

---

Do not therefore be grieved or angry with yourselves because you sold me.
—Genesis 45:5

---

THE BIBLE IN ONE YEAR:
■ Isaiah 11–13
■ Ephesians 4

It was the last weekend of the 1964 baseball season. Bill Valentine was umpiring a game between the Detroit Tigers and the New York Yankees.

Dave Wickersham was pitching for Detroit, and he had 19 victories for the season. One more would be a sign of stardom. But it wasn't to be.

After a close play, Wickersham tapped the umpire on the shoulder to ask for a time-out. Touching an umpire is against the rules, so Valentine tossed Wickersham from the game—depriving him of his chance for a 20-win season.

For the next 39 years, Valentine lived with a gnawing regret for booting the pitcher in that split-second decision. But he doesn't carry that regret anymore. Last year, Wickersham wrote the umpire a note, telling him he was right in his decision and that he held no hard feelings. That note lifted a weight from Valentine's shoulders.

In Genesis 45, Joseph lifted a burden of guilt from his brothers, who had sold him into slavery—something far more serious than a simple misunderstanding. Yet he was willing to forgive them.

Is there someone who needs to hear a forgiving word from you that would lift a burden of regret?  —Dave Branon

*Let me forget the hurt and pain*
*Found along life's way;*
*Let me remember kindnesses*
*Given day by day.*  —Berry

---

**Ground filled with the roots of bitterness
needs to be plowed by the grace of God.**

# "WRECK" A BIBLE

**READ:**
2 Timothy 3:10-17

All Scripture is given by inspiration of God, and is profitable for doctrine, for reproof, for correction, for instruction.
—2 Timothy 3:16

THE BIBLE IN ONE YEAR:
■ Isaiah 14–16
■ Ephesians 5:1-16

The Bible is a remarkable book. Millions of copies are bought each year. It has been the number-one bestseller for decades. But tragically, the Bible is said to be the least-read bestseller of all time.

The apostle Paul taught that the Scriptures are given to us by God and are capable of bringing about transformation in those who take it seriously (2 Timothy 3:16). Evangelist and preacher D. L. Moody said, "The Scriptures were not given to increase our knowledge but to change our lives."

So why do we often neglect this source of transforming power? Writer and professor J. I. Packer said, "If I were the devil, one of my first aims would be to stop folk from digging into the Bible."

Do you use your Bible every day until it eventually falls apart? Bible teacher Alan Redpath advised believers to "wreck" a Bible every 10 years. Here's why: God wants to speak to us through the Bible, telling us how to live for Him and answering crucial questions. Through it He warns us about the dangers of sin and provides us with nourishing spiritual food.

Don't neglect your Bible. If you do, you will neglect your own spiritual health. — Joanie Yoder

> *The treasures of the Word of God*
> *Are great beyond compare;*
> *But if we do not search them out,*
> *We cannot use what's there.* — Sper

**A well-worn Bible is a sign of a well-fed soul.**

# DON'T DESPAIR, SHARE

READ:
2 Peter 3

Be diligent to be found by Him in peace, without spot and blameless.
—2 Peter 3:14

THE BIBLE IN ONE YEAR:
■ Isaiah 17–19
■ Ephesians 5:17-33

During these days of horrific world events, Christians should be appalled but not taken by surprise. Jesus forewarned us of terrible times to come (Luke 21:25-28). In today's reading, Peter reassured believers by reminding them of God's unfolding purposes and final victory.

The apostle described ungodly scoffers, who in the last days will say, "Where is the promise of His coming?" (2 Peter 3:4). We too may wonder why Christ doesn't come back and change things now. Peter affirmed that the Lord "is not slack concerning His promise," but delays His return to give people everywhere more time to repent (v.9).

We mustn't forget that "with the Lord one day is as a thousand years, and a thousand years as one day" (v.8). Eventually the day of the Lord will come, bringing a judgment of consuming fire. This will be followed by a new heaven and a new earth, the home of righteousness and of God's forgiven people (v.13).

As we anticipate that triumphant day, we must live consistent, holy lives (v.14), resist all evil influences (v.17), and grow in the grace and knowledge of Christ (v.18). Then, instead of despairing over evil, we will be able to share the good news of Jesus with the world. — Joanie Yoder

*We know not when the Lord may come*
*To right the wrongs of this old earth,*
*But this we know—He's left us here*
*To share good news of second birth.* —Hess

**We don't know what this world is coming to,**
**but we know the One who is coming to this world.**

# BUT IF NOT . . .

**READ:**
Daniel 3:1-18

We do not serve
your gods, nor will we
worship the gold image
which you have set up.
—Daniel 3:18

THE BIBLE IN ONE YEAR:
■ Isaiah 20–22
■ Ephesians 6

I recall a Sunday school lesson from nearly 40 years ago in which we were taught to love God in spite of our circumstances. Loving God is easy when He grants our requests and provides what we desire. Loving Him in difficult circumstances tests our faith.

In Daniel 3, we read of the life-and-death decision Shadrach, Meshach, and Abed-Nego had to make. If they chose to worship the golden image, they would live; if they refused, death was certain. They answered King Nebuchadnezzar: "Our God whom we serve is able to deliver us from the burning fiery furnace . . . . But if not, . . . we do not serve your gods, nor will we worship the gold image which you have set up" (vv.17-18).

Were Shadrach, Meshach, and Abed-Nego lacking in faith when they said "but if not"? No. They knew God was fully capable of delivering them from the fiery furnace.

There's a lesson in this for all of us. Is God all-powerful? Yes. Is He able to deliver us from all our problems? Yes. Does God always deliver us from our difficulties? No.

We may not fully comprehend God's purpose in our difficulty and suffering, but we must not cease to love Him. We must trust Him and hope in Him in spite of the trials that threaten to overwhelm us. — Albert Lee

*I have learned to love my Savior,*
*And I trust Him more each day;*
*For no matter what the trial,*
*He will always be my stay.* — Hess

**Genuine faith stays strong
when deliverance seems distant.**

# WATCHING THE WIND

READ:
Acts 8:26-34

---

He who observes the wind will not sow, and he who regards the clouds will not reap.
—Ecclesiastes 11:4

---

THE BIBLE IN ONE YEAR:
■ Isaiah 23-25
■ Philippians 1

When it comes to telling others about Jesus, I'm sometimes like a cautious farmer who keeps his eye on the weather, looking for the perfect day to plant his crops. The season passes and he sows nothing. The opportunity is gone; the harvest is lost (Ecclesiastes 11:4).

I hesitate and wonder, "Is this person ready to listen to the gospel? Is this the time to speak?" You can never tell what's going on in the depths of another person's heart. Some may be dwelling in darkness yet longing for someone to lead them into the light.

The Ethiopian eunuch in his royal chariot seemed to have it all together (Acts 8:27). He enjoyed prestige, wealth, and power, yet inwardly he was empty and searching. He was reading Isaiah's promise of the suffering Savior and trying to come to grips with his words. Right at that moment, Philip took the opportunity to tell the eunuch about Jesus (v.35).

I have a friend who often leads people to Jesus. I asked him once how he knew they were ready to receive the gospel. "It's easy," he replied. "I ask them."

So I must stop worrying about the wind and the clouds and get on with it—scattering the seed wherever I go, regardless of the weather. You just never know. — David Roper

> Toiling through the changing seasons
> In the sunshine and the rain,
> Zealous sowing with compassion
> Yields a wealth of golden grain. — Anon.

---

**Sowing the seed of God's Word is never out of season.**

# GOD OF THE HILLS & STREETS

READ:
Psalm 121

The LORD shall preserve your going out and your coming in from this time forth, and even forevermore.
—Psalm 121:8

THE BIBLE IN ONE YEAR:
■ Isaiah 26–27
■ Philippians 2

The 121st Psalm was a favorite of my father. The Scottish people called it "The Traveler's Psalm." Whenever a family member, a guest, or a friend was leaving on a journey, this psalm was read—or more often sung—at family prayers. When my father left the "old country" alone as a teenager to come to the United States, he was bidden farewell with this psalm.

Over the years, my father enjoyed many hearty days and endured others that were dark and grim. He carried this psalm's words with him into battle during World War I, and then out of it as he lay in a hospital for almost a year recovering from shrapnel wounds.

In verse 1, the psalmist looked beyond the hills to the God who made them. My father lived in the toughest section of New York City. Although he seldom saw hills, he held to the assurance that the God of the hills was the God of the dangerous streets as well.

How many "goings out" and "comings in" my father made in his 87 years! And when he went out for the last time, I believe he was singing Psalm 121 as he descended into the valley and traveled home to the other side.

How reassuring that the God of the hills and the streets goes before every believer in Christ! — Haddon Robinson

*He will ever keep thy soul,*
*What would harm He will control;*
*In the home and by the way*
*He will keep thee day by day.* — Psalter

**Because God is with us,
we need not fear what lies ahead.**

# BECOMING WHAT WE ARE

READ:
Philippians 3:1-11

---

The Lord is the Spirit;
and where the Spirit
of the Lord is, there is
liberty.
—2 Corinthians 3:17

---

THE BIBLE IN ONE YEAR:
■ Isaiah 28–29
■ Philippians 3

At a British university, a group of students had raised the question, "What do you want to be?" Different answers were given—a champion athlete, an influential politician, a noted scholar. Shyly, yet clearly, one student said something that caused thoughtful silence: "You may laugh at me, but I want to be a saint."

Imagine—a saint! Whatever his concept of sainthood, many in our secular society would view that ambition as eccentric. Yet if we are Christians, it ought to be the highest priority of our life. The essence of sainthood is simply to be like Jesus. Paul said that the overarching purpose of God the Father is to make us like His Son (Romans 8:29).

Of course, every believer is guaranteed perfect conformity to Christ in the world to come. But God does not want us to wait passively until we enter heaven for that supernatural transformation to take place (1 John 3:2). We are to be co-operating with the Holy Spirit to grow more and more like Christ "in this world" (4:17).

Yes, we are already saints by faith in Christ Jesus (Philippians 1:1). But each day we face the challenge of becoming what we are—Christlike in every area of our lives. — Vernon Grounds

*More like the Master I would live and grow,*
*More of His love to others I would show;*
*More self-denial, like His in Galilee,*
*More like the Master I long to ever be.* — Gabriel

---

**To belong to Christ is to be a saint;**
**to live like a saint is to be like Christ.**

# COME TO ME

READ:
John 6:30-40

I am the bread of life.
He who comes to Me
shall never hunger.
—John 6:35

THE BIBLE IN ONE YEAR:
■ Isaiah 30–31
■ Philippians 4

When Jesus lived on this earth, He invited people to come to Him, and He still does today (John 6:35). But what do He and His Father in heaven have that we need?

*Salvation.* Jesus is the only way to have forgiveness of sin and the promise of heaven. "Whoever believes in Him should not perish but have eternal life" (John 3:15).

*Purpose.* We are to give all of our heart, soul, mind, and strength to following Jesus. "Whoever desires to come after Me, let him deny himself, and take up his cross, and follow Me" (Mark 8:34).

*Comfort.* In trial or sorrow, the "God of all comfort . . . comforts us in all our tribulation" (2 Corinthians 1:3-4).

*Wisdom.* We need wisdom beyond our own for making decisions. "If any of you lacks wisdom, let him ask of God, . . . and it will be given to him" (James 1:5).

*Strength.* When we're weary, "the LORD will give strength to His people" (Psalm 29:11).

*Abundant Life.* The fullest life is found in a relationship with Jesus. "I have come that they may have life, and that they may have it more abundantly" (John 10:10).

Jesus said, "The one who comes to Me I will by no means cast out" (John 6:37). *Come!* — Anne Cetas

*Jesus is calling to those who are weary,*
*And He is calling the thirsty ones too;*
*If for the Bread of Life you now hunger,*
*Hear His sweet voice saying, "Come."* — Hess

**Jesus invites us to come to Him for life.**

# SINLESS ANGER

READ:
Proverbs 15:1-18

"Be angry, and do
not sin": Do not let
the sun go down on
your wrath.
—Ephesians 4:26

THE BIBLE IN ONE YEAR:
■ Isaiah 32–33
■ Colossians 1

When Supreme Court Justice Byron White was in Salt Lake City to give a speech, he was attacked by an angry man. The suspect said he assaulted the respected judge because of his High Court decisions. He said, "Justice White is causing four-letter words to come into my living room through the TV set." Rationalizing his attack, he continued, "The only way I know how to stop it is to go to the source."

That's where the man went wrong. Of course, he had a perfect right to voice his strong opinions. He was even justified in becoming angry if he believed a Court decision encouraged immorality. But the manner he chose to express his indignation was as bad as, if not worse than, a wrong court decision.

Today's Scripture text says, "Be angry, and do not sin" (Ephesians 4:26). What others say and do may arouse our anger and in some cases should make us angry. But we must be careful we don't overreact and lose control. The apostle Paul reminded us that "though we walk in the flesh, we do not war according to the flesh" (2 Corinthians 10:3-4).

Should Christians ever become angry? Certainly! But we should never allow our anger to erupt in a sinful response. Two wrongs don't make a right.  — Richard De Haan

*When anger stirs within our hearts*
*Because of wrongs we see,*
*We must with love address the fault*
*If helpful we would be.*  — Branon

**It's not a sin to get angry when you get angry at sin.**

# HAVE A WONDERFUL DAY

**READ:**
**Proverbs 11:24-31**

Let each one give as he
purposes in his heart,
not grudgingly or of
necessity; for God loves
a cheerful giver.
—2 Corinthians 9:7

THE BIBLE IN ONE YEAR:
■ Isaiah 34–36
■ Colossians 2

After admiring a painting in a woman's home, I was surprised by her generosity when she took it down and gave it to me.

I've seen many similar acts of kindness. For years, my mother-in-law hung on to her archaic-looking refrigerator so she could give more money to the Lord's work.

A Christian family I know had saved money to buy a new car. But when they heard of a desperate need on a mission field, they kept their old car and gave to missions instead.

I've also heard of a Christian businessman in Ohio who puts something in his pocket every morning to give away — a pen, a trinket, even a ten-dollar bill. As the day unfolds, he looks for someone who would be blessed by receiving a gift. "By constantly looking for an opportunity to give," he says, "I have a wonderful day."

The old saying "Takers eat well, but givers sleep well" is only partially true. According to Proverbs 11:25, givers also eat well: "The generous soul will be made rich, and he who waters will also be watered himself."

We must not give grudgingly or merely out of a sense of duty but from the heart. It's the generous, cheerful giver whom God loves (2 Corinthians 9:7). — Joanie Yoder

*Give as you would to the Master*
*If you met His searching look;*
*Give as you would of your substance*
*If His hand the offering took.* — Anon.

**Many people readily give God credit,**
**but few cheerfully give Him cash.**

# HYPOCRITICAL REQUEST

READ:
Matthew 16:1-4

A wicked and adulterous generation seeks after a sign, and no sign shall be given to it except the sign of the prophet Jonah.
—Matthew 16:4

THE BIBLE IN ONE YEAR:
■ Isaiah 37–38
■ Colossians 3

A group of religious leaders asked Jesus to give them a "sign from heaven" (Matthew 16:1). They had witnessed many of His miracles, but they had either minimized them or attributed them to Satan. The Pharisees were now demanding that Jesus perform another miracle—perhaps like Joshua who commanded the sun and moon to stand still (Joshua 10:12-14), or like Elijah who called down fire from heaven (1 Kings 18:30-40). They did this to test Jesus.

Seeing their hypocrisy, Jesus said that while they could make weather predictions by looking at the sky, they were unable to read the much clearer "signs of the times" revealed in His ministry of teaching and healing (v.3).

Some people have told me they would believe in Jesus if He showed them miracles like those in the Gospels. But what makes them think they would react any differently than the religious leaders of Jesus' day?

Anyone who sincerely seeks the truth has all the evidence necessary for faith. The resurrection of Jesus is a historically credible event. The power of the risen Christ can be seen in many of His followers. The New Testament speaks to the mind and heart of every sincere, seeking soul. To ask for more is a hypocritical request.  — Herb Vander Lugt

*Some say they want a miracle,*
*And then they will believe;*
*Yet God already sent His Son—*
*The One they must receive.  — Hess*

**Demanding a miracle to believe in Jesus**
**ignores the evidence of His resurrection.**

# HELP WANTED!

**READ:**
2 Timothy 2:1-13

If anyone desires to come after Me, let him deny himself, and take up his cross, and follow Me. —Matthew 16:24

THE BIBLE IN ONE YEAR:
■ Isaiah 39–40
■ Colossians 4

Perhaps the most effective advertisement ever written appeared in a London newspaper early in the 20th century: "Men wanted for hazardous journey. Small wages, bitter cold, long months of complete darkness, constant danger. Safe return doubtful." Those were the words written by Sir Ernest Shackleton, the famous South Pole explorer.

Commenting on the overwhelming response he received, Shackleton said, "It seemed as though all the men in Great Britain were determined to accompany us."

Shackleton's words remind me of Jesus' words in Matthew 16:24, "If anyone desires to come after Me, let him deny himself, and take up his cross, and follow Me." The Lord was calling people to go with Him on a hazardous journey—the way of the cross. He issued that call after telling His disciples that He was going to Jerusalem to suffer and be killed.

Through the centuries, thousands have responded to Jesus' words by forsaking all to follow Him. But unlike Shackleton's expedition that came to an end, the Lord's work goes on and volunteers are still needed. He continues to call for those who will serve Him regardless of the cost.

Have you answered His call? — Richard De Haan

*Never came the call more clear,*
*Midst the storms of hate and fear,*
*Jesus' love to show in this world of woe;*
*For His grace is ever near. — Loes*

---

**A faith that costs nothing and demands nothing is worth nothing.**

# WITNESS FROM A WHEELCHAIR

READ:
**Matthew 25:31-40**

_____

The Son of Man did not come to be served, but to serve.
—Matthew 20:28

_____

THE BIBLE IN ONE YEAR:
■ Isaiah 41–42
■ 1 Thessalonians 1

A woman named Nancy put this ad in her local newspaper: "If you are lonely or have a problem, call me. I am in a wheelchair and seldom get out. We can share our problems with each other. Just call. I'd love to talk." The response to that ad was surprising—30 calls or more every week.

What motivated this woman to reach out from her wheelchair to help others in need? Nancy explained that before her paralysis she had been perfectly healthy but in deep despair. She had tried to commit suicide by jumping from her apartment window, but her fall left her paralyzed from the waist down.

In the hospital, utterly frustrated, she sensed that Jesus said, "Nancy, you've had a healthy body but a crippled soul. From now on you will have a crippled body but a healthy soul." As a result of that experience, she surrendered her life to Christ. When she was finally allowed to go home, she prayed for a way to share God's grace with others, and the idea of the newspaper ad occurred to her.

Every believer can do something to help others. Limited as we may be by sickness, old age, or disability, we can still pray, call, or write. No matter what our condition, we can be effective witnesses for Jesus. — Vernon Grounds

_Lord, let me be a shining light_
_So others then may view_
_Your mercy and Your love displayed_
_In all I say and do._ — Sper

---

**Only after talking to God about people
are we ready to talk to people about God.**

# WHOLENESS OF LIFE

**READ:**
**Mark 2:1-12**

Son, your sins are
forgiven you. . . . Arise,
take up your bed, and
go to your house.
—Mark 2:5,11

THE BIBLE IN ONE YEAR:
■ Isaiah 43–44
■ 1 Thessalonians 2

A social worker told her colleagues about a young boy in an urban ghetto who appeared to be little more than a bit of twisted human flesh. He had been struck by a car several months before and had not received proper medical attention.

Although not part of her caseload, the social worker took the boy to an orthopedist, who performed surgery on his legs. Two years later the boy walked into her office without crutches. His recovery was complete. The two embraced. "If I accomplish nothing else in my life," said the social worker to herself, "I have made a real difference with at least this one!"

She paused, then said to her colleagues, "This was all several years ago now. Where do you think that boy is today?" Some suggested that he might be a school teacher, others a physician or a social worker. With deep emotion, the woman responded, "No, he's in the penitentiary for one of the foulest crimes a human can commit. I was instrumental in teaching him how to walk again, but there was no one to teach him where to walk."

We must point people to Jesus. Through Him, those with broken bodies, broken dreams, broken homes, and broken hearts receive wholeness of life. — Haddon Robinson

*Lord, help us to tell of Your love for mankind—*
*A love for the sin-sick, the broken, the blind;*
*And help them to see by the way that we live*
*A wholeness of being that You long to give.* — D. De Haan

**A person may go wrong in many different directions**
**but right in only one.**

# ORDINARY PEOPLE

READ:
Deuteronomy 4:5-14

---

Take heed to yourself,
. . . lest you forget the
things your eyes have
seen . . . . And teach
them to your children.
—Deuteronomy 4:9

---

THE BIBLE IN ONE YEAR:
■ Isaiah 45–46
■ 1 Thessalonians 3

David Isay, a radio producer, says that in a culture inundated with the stories of celebrities, we need to hear the recorded voices of ordinary people, because their lives and contributions are no less important. Isay is a driving force behind StoryCorps, "a national project to instruct and inspire people to record each other's stories in sound."

It's a great concept, especially for Christians. Think what it would mean for your great-great-grandchildren to hear and see you telling the story of your life—describing the people and events that shaped you and sharing what Christ means to you.

Just before God's people entered the Promised Land, Moses told them: "Only take heed to yourself, and diligently keep yourself, lest you forget the things your eyes have seen, and lest they depart from your heart all the days of your life. And teach them to your children and your grandchildren" (Deuteronomy 4:9).

That same responsibility of face-to-face communication is still ours. Yet we have the unusual opportunity of leaving a message for future generations. Begin recording your own uniquely important story. Or help a friend or relative record theirs. There is great value in the stories of ordinary people who know and love the Lord.  — David McCasland

Life's truest heroes never carve their name
On marble columns built for their acclaim;
They build instead a legacy that springs
From faithful service to the King of kings.  — Gustafson

---

**A life lived for God leaves a lasting legacy.**

# GLAD TO GET HOME!

**READ:**
Revelation 21:1-5

---

Here we have no continuing city, but we seek the one to come.
—Hebrews 13:14

---

THE BIBLE IN ONE YEAR:
■ Isaiah 47–49
■ 1 Thessalonians 4

In wintertime, a condition known as a "whiteout" sometimes occurs along the Lake Michigan shoreline. The air becomes so filled with powdery snow that you can't see more than a few feet ahead. You feel totally helpless, especially if you're driving, and that's what we were doing on a bitterly cold December day.

Our family had been invited to my sister's house for Christmas dinner. As we headed west toward Lake Michigan, the weather became treacherous, but we made it to our destination. Later, however, as we were driving home after dark, the situation grew even worse. The expressway was covered with ice, traffic slowed to a crawl, and several cars were in the ditch. Then all at once we were enveloped by a brief whiteout. Believe me, it was frightening. After a slow, tedious journey, we finally reached Grand Rapids and pulled into our driveway. I think every member of the family said, "I'm sure glad to get home!"

I wonder if we'll have a similar feeling when we enter heaven. The dangerous "whiteouts" of our earthly journey will be over. The temptations, stresses, and failures will all be in the past. Best of all, we'll be safe with our Savior.

Yes, we'll be so glad to get home! — Dave Egner

*When we all get to heaven,*
*What a day of rejoicing that will be!*
*When we all see Jesus,*
*We'll sing and shout the victory.* — Hewitt

---

**Heaven for the Christian is best spelled H-O-M-E.**

## ACTIVE WORSHIP

**READ:**
**Psalm 100**

___

Enter into His gates
with thanksgiving,
and into His courts
with praise.
—Psalm 100:4

___

THE BIBLE IN ONE YEAR:
■ Isaiah 50–52
■ 1 Thessalonians 5

In his book *Folk Psalms of Faith*, Pastor Ray Stedman says he wishes that all churchgoers could stand in the pulpit on a Sunday morning and watch the faces in the congregation during the sermon.

Although most people seem to give the minister their attention, many have their minds elsewhere. Stedman writes, "It would be fascinating at the end of a service to know where everybody had been!"

To receive the greatest benefit from a church service, we must prepare our hearts and become active participants. We must become wholeheartedly involved in singing the hymns, silently praying as the pastor leads the congregation in prayer, and worshiping from the heart as the choir sings.

Finally, we need to discipline ourselves to listen intently with a receptive heart to the teaching of God's Word. We must develop a hunger for truth that quiets our spirits, inspires worship, evokes praise to God, and moves us to serve Him.

It's easy to blame the pastor if we leave the service feeling empty and discouraged. But he's just one participant; we must do our part. Those who get the most out of worship are those who put the most into it. — Richard De Haan

*The house of God should be a place*
*For praise and reverent prayer,*
*Where holy thoughts our spirits fill*
*Each time we enter there.* — Bosch

___

**The heart of worship is worship from the heart.**

# FREE PRAYER

**READ:**
Ephesians 6:10-20

Praying always with all
prayer and supplication
in the Spirit, being
watchful to this end
with all perseverance.
—Ephesians 6:18

THE BIBLE IN ONE YEAR:
■ Isaiah 53–55
■ 2 Thessalonians 1

A pastor was asked to call on a woman in a psychiatric hospital and pray for her. After his visit, he thought how good it would be for somebody to go there regularly and pray for the residents. The "somebody" turned out to be him. On a table in one of the wards, he put up a sign saying "Free Prayer." Later he recalled, "Suddenly I had 15 people standing in line to get prayed for."

People often ask for our prayers, but do we faithfully pray for them? Many times we see others in great need but find it easier to discuss their plight with friends rather than to intercede for them. But people need and want our prayers.

Paul concluded his call to put on "the whole armor of God" (Ephesians 6:13-17) by writing, "Praying always with all prayer and supplication in the Spirit, being watchful to this end with all perseverance and supplication for all the saints" (v.18).

Oswald Chambers often referred to prayer as "the ministry of the interior" and said, "There is no snare, or any danger of infatuation or pride in intercession; it is a hidden ministry that brings forth fruit whereby the Father is glorified."

Faithful prayer—whether in public or private—is one of the greatest gifts we can give others. — David McCasland

*To give to others what they need,*
*We show no greater care*
*Than when we give them to the Lord,*
*Upholding them in prayer.* —D. De Haan

**Our intercession may be the key
to God's intervention.**

**October 19**

## A GOOD DAY TO DIE?

**READ:**
1 Kings 19:1-18

---

It is enough! Now, LORD, take my life!
—1 Kings 19:4

---

THE BIBLE IN ONE YEAR:
■ Isaiah 56–58
■ 2 Thessalonians 2

Hopelessness and anger combined to bring death to a young man in my neighborhood. Someone had beaten him up for something he said. To retaliate, he came back with a gun. The police were called. When they arrived he ran, shooting at them. To protect everyone, they shot him. He lost his life at age 21. Later it was reported that he had told a family member that morning: "Today would be a good day to die." I wonder what brought him to such despair.

There was a day when the prophet Elijah felt hopeless and wanted to die. He had just experienced a great victory over the prophets of Baal, but now his life was being threatened by the king's wife Jezebel. In fear, he ran into the wilderness (1 Kings 19:4). There he "prayed that he might die, and said, 'It is enough! Now, LORD, take my life!'"

We may think that Elijah was overreacting, but hopeless feelings are real. He wisely went to the right source for help—he cried out to God. The Lord knew Elijah needed restoration, so He provided for his needs (vv. 5-7). He revealed Himself to him (vv. 9-13) and renewed Elijah's sense of purpose by giving him work to do (vv. 15-17). God brought him hope by reminding him that he was not alone (v. 18).

Look to God. He is your source of hope.  — Anne Cetas

> Lord, give us grace to trust You when
> Life's burdens seem too much to bear;
> Dispel the darkness with new hope
> And help us rise above despair.  —Sper

---

**No one is hopeless whose hope is in God.**

# A GIFT OF GRACE

**READ:**
**2 Corinthians 8:7-15**

You know the grace
of our Lord Jesus
Christ, that though He
was rich, yet for your
sakes He became poor.
—2 Corinthians 8:9

THE BIBLE IN ONE YEAR:
■ Isaiah 59–61
■ 2 Thessalonians 3

In high schools in the US, being elected homecoming queen is a great honor for any young woman. But when a high school near Houston, Texas, crowned Shannon Jones, it was a special moment for her and for everyone in the community. Nineteen-year-old Shannon, who is an award-winning athlete and an active member of her church youth group, has Down syndrome.

Shannon knew this once-in-a-life-time experience was a gift from her younger sister Lindsey, who was the catalyst to elect her. Their dad said, "I'm so proud of Lindsey. Probably somewhere in the back of her mind, this is something she'd like to do." But she made it happen for Shannon.

The most inspiring acts of human love are only a shadow of the immeasurable gift our Savior has given us. Paul wrote, "You know the grace of our Lord Jesus Christ, that though He was rich, yet for your sakes He became poor, that you through His poverty might become rich" (2 Corinthians 8:9).

Christ left His glory in heaven and died on the cross for our sin so that we could be forgiven through faith in Him. His sacrifice was based on His love, not on our merit. All we are and all we have are the Savior's loving gifts of grace to us. —David McCasland

> *God gives His grace so rich, so free—*
> *No one will He deny;*
> *For He has promised in His Word*
> *An infinite supply.* —D. De Haan

**Grace is an unearned blessing to unworthy sinners.**

# NO UNKIND WORDS

**READ:**
Ephesians 4:29-32

Let no corrupt word proceed out of your mouth, but what is good for necessary edification.
—Ephesians 4:29

THE BIBLE IN ONE YEAR:
■ Isaiah 62-64
■ 1 Timothy 1

One of the greatest honors ever offered to me came during one of life's saddest times.

I was heartbroken last year when my good friend and co-worker Kurt De Haan died suddenly while out on his regular lunchtime run. Kurt was managing editor of *Our Daily Bread* from 1989 until the time of his death. Losing him was a huge blow to each of us at RBC Ministries, but his wife Mary and their four children were suffering the worst pain.

A couple of days before the funeral, I got a call from Mary, who asked if I would share a eulogy of Kurt. I was overwhelmed with this bittersweet privilege.

As I reflected on Kurt's life, one trait continued to surface. It was a remarkable characteristic, and it was something that I focused on in my eulogy. In the 22 years I had known him, worked with him, and talked with him, I never once heard Kurt say a negative word about any other person.

What a remarkable legacy of a true Christian heart! Kurt lived up to the standard of Ephesians 4:29-32. He sought to build up others, showing kindness and tenderheartedness instead of bitterness and malice.

Will others be able to say the same about us? —Dave Branon

*Instead of hurling angry words*
*That wound and stir up strife,*
*Use words of kindness, filled with love,*
*That heal and nourish life.* —Sper

---

**A kind word is the oil**
**that takes the friction out of life.**

# THE LEMON TREE

**READ:**
1 John 4:15-19

---

God is love, and he who abides in love abides in God, and God in him.
—1 John 4:16

---

THE BIBLE IN ONE YEAR:
■ Isaiah 65–66
■ 1 Timothy 2

People who have given up on love probably agree with the words to the song "Lemon Tree" by the folk group Peter, Paul, and Mary:

*"Don't put your faith in love,*
*my boy," my father said to me,*
*"I fear you'll find that love is like the*
*lovely lemon tree." Lemon tree very*
*pretty and the lemon flower is sweet*
*but the fruit of the poor lemon*
*is impossible to eat.*

Many people feel that way. "Love is bitter," they say, because they've been used or abused. But there is a love that is sweet: "God is love" (1 John 4:16).

The world wants to turn John's phrase around. "Love is God," they say, and seek love as the highest good. But John did not say that love is God. "God is love," he said. Author Frederick Buechner wrote, "To say that love is God is romantic idealism. To say that God is love is either the last straw or the ultimate truth."

The last straw? Yes, for some it is. They have looked for love in all the wrong places and have no other place to turn. But when they give themselves to God, as He is made real and personal in Jesus, they find the love they've been looking for all their lives.

God is not indifference, abandonment, and abuse, my friend. God is love. — David Roper

*Loved with everlasting love,*
*Led by grace that love to know—*
*Spirit, breathing from above,*
*Thou hast taught me it is so.* — Robinson

---

**God's love knows no limits.**

## ZEALOUS FOR GOD

READ:
2 Kings 13:14-19

Epaphras . . . greets you, always laboring fervently for you in prayers . . . . I bear him witness that he has a great zeal for you.
—Colossians 4:12-13

THE BIBLE IN ONE YEAR:
■ Jeremiah 1–2
■ 1 Timothy 3

We know little about Epaphras except that he was so concerned about the spiritual welfare of the people in Colosse that he is described as "laboring fervently . . . in prayers" for them (Colossians 4:12). When I was a pastor, I saw this kind of enthusiasm in the way new converts prayed and witnessed. But all too often, many of them gradually lost their zeal.

I believe it was King Joash's lack of enthusiasm that made Elisha so angry (2 Kings 13). The monarch had obeyed the dying prophet's command to shoot an arrow toward the east. He had heard Elisha's promise that God would bring his nation complete deliverance from Syria. Joash had obeyed the command to strike the ground with a bundle of arrows, which he did three times. So why did the prophet angrily tell him he should have struck the ground five or six times?

I believe it was because he felt Joash was following his instructions in a half-hearted manner. The king should have been far more enthusiastic in his response to God's wonderful message of victory over Israel's enemies.

The king's nonchalance cost him dearly. He won an incomplete victory. I wonder how many spiritual victories we forfeit because of our lack of zeal. — Herb Vander Lugt

*Let us serve the Lord with gladness*
*And enthusiastic praise,*
*Telling all who do not know Him*
*Of His great and wondrous ways.* — Sper

**Godly zeal is love on fire.**

# KING OF THE APES

**READ:**
2 Corinthians 10

---

He who glories, let him glory in the LORD.
—2 Corinthians 10:17

---

THE BIBLE IN ONE YEAR:
■ Jeremiah 3–5
■ 1 Timothy 4

Studies conducted by the National Geographic Society provide some fascinating insights into the behavior of chimpanzees. Observers noted how the leadership of a chimp community changed because of a dramatic bluff used by one of the lowliest members of the group.

Mike, as he was affectionately known, learned to dominate his chimp establishment with the aid of some empty kerosene cans and a heavy steel box. Hooting loudly, he would bang the metal objects together as he pushed them over the ground. This clamorous behavior frightened the apes so much that the leader surrendered his sovereignty to Mike.

Unfortunately, similar situations may be seen in the church. Those who generate the most activity often receive the greatest attention and honor. But a big program and a flashy personality are not necessarily evidence of divine blessing.

Paul warned against looking "at things according to the outward appearance" (2 Corinthians 10:7). The real measure of our labor is whether it is in keeping with God's Word and if it reflects His glory rather than our own.

Make sure that whatever you do, you do for the Lord. Then when you glory, it will be in Him! — Mart De Haan

*Help us not to cloud God's glory,*
*Nor with self His light to dim;*
*May each thought to Christ be captive,*
*Emptied to be filled with Him.* — Anon.

---

**You can't glorify yourself and Christ at the same time.**

# WHAT ARE YOU LIVING FOR?

READ:
2 Timothy 4:6-18

I have fought the good fight, I have finished the race, I have kept the faith.
—2 Timothy 4:7

THE BIBLE IN ONE YEAR:
■ Jeremiah 6–8
■ 1 Timothy 5

Many people living in their twilight years suddenly realize how empty and pointless their lives have been. They've made some successful business deals and had some fun, but in terms of satisfying friendships or lasting accomplishments, their lives have been zero. They have climbed the ladder of success, only to discover that all the while it had been leaning against the wrong wall.

As the apostle Paul looked back on his ministry, he saw that it had been rewarding but not easy. Measured by the world's yardstick of success, his life seems almost insignificant.

Paul wrote his second letter to Timothy while languishing in a cold, damp dungeon awaiting execution. In a matter of weeks, the apostle would stand before Nero, the half-insane emperor of Rome, and his life would end. But he knew that after his death he would receive the crown of life from the King of kings. And we now know that the influence of his life changed the course of history itself.

An ancient historian would have written volumes about the splendor of Nero and probably never even mentioned Paul. Yet today we name our dogs Nero and our sons Paul. I guess what we live for is pretty important after all.

By the way, what are you living for? — Haddon Robinson

*One life to live for Christ my Lord,*
*One life to do my part,*
*One life in which to give my all*
*With fervency of heart.* — Brandt

---

**There are no losers with Jesus and no winners with the devil.**

# LOST TREASURE

READ:
Mark 10:17-27

Sell whatever you have
and give to the poor,
and you will have
treasure in heaven.
—Mark 10:21

THE BIBLE IN ONE YEAR:
■ Jeremiah 9–11
■ 1 Timothy 6

Don takes walks on the city's railroad tracks and searches under freeway overpasses. He's not looking for lost treasure; he's looking for homeless people. Don met Jake, who lives in a makeshift underground shack and is mentally ill. He stops by to see Jake occasionally, making sure he's warm and has food. He tells Jake about Jesus because he wants him to find "treasure in heaven."

Jesus talked about this treasure with a rich young man who asked Him how to inherit eternal life. Jesus said, "Sell whatever you have and give to the poor, and you will have treasure in heaven; and come, take up the cross, and follow Me" (Mark 10:21).

Jesus wasn't teaching that we must give up our wealth to be acceptable to Him. We can never earn eternal life by our works. He was showing this man his spiritual bankruptcy. His heart was set on wealth, not Jesus.

That rich young man and our homeless friend have more in common than we might think. In the eyes of God, both are spiritually bankrupt. We all are, unless we have Jesus.

No good deed can earn eternal life—not helping the homeless or giving away all our money. Jesus wants us to give Him our heart. Then we'll have real treasure—treasure in heaven—and we'll seek to help others.  — Anne Cetas

*What shall I give Thee, Master?*
*Giver of gifts divine;*
*I will not hold time, talents, or gold—*
*For everything shall be Thine.*  — Grimes

**Salvation is given, not earned.**

# LETTERS TO GOD

**READ:**
**Psalm 65:1-8**

O You who hear prayer, to You all flesh will come. —Psalm 65:2

THE BIBLE IN ONE YEAR:
■ Jeremiah 12-14
■ 2 Timothy 1

Every year thousands of letters addressed to God find their way to a post office in Jerusalem. One letter, addressed to "God of Israel," requested assistance in getting a job as a bulldozer driver. Another said: "Please help me to be happy, to find a nice job and a good wife—soon." One man asked forgiveness for stealing money from a grocery store when he was a child.

But were those heartfelt requests heard by God? The psalmist said that God is the one who hears prayer (Psalm 65:2). Whether we say our prayers silently, voice them aloud, or write them on paper, they go directly to God. But He does not answer every request as we would wish. Our petitions may be self-serving (James 4:3), or sin may be blocking our fellowship with Him (Psalm 66:18).

More than giving us what we want, the Lord knows our deepest needs, and He wants us to discover the joy of His presence each day. Because of our faith in Christ, praying becomes our means of communion with God, not just a list of things we want from Him.

In His wisdom, God hears all our prayers. In His grace, He offers forgiveness for all our sins. In His love, He gives us eternal and abundant life through His Son. — David McCasland

*Teach me to pray, Lord, teach me to pray;*
*This is my heart-cry day unto day.*
*I long to know Thy will and Thy way;*
*Teach me to pray, Lord, teach me to pray.* —Reitz

**God hears more than our words—**
**He listens to our heart.**

# THE FROG'S "BLACKBOARD"

**READ:**
**Psalm 119:33-40**

---

Turn away my eyes
from looking at
worthless things, and
revive me in Your way.
—Psalm 119:37

---

THE BIBLE IN ONE YEAR:
■ Jeremiah 15–17
■ 2 Timothy 2

As a young boy, one of my favorite pastimes was hunting frogs along the banks of a pond near our home. I was unaware of their unique visual powers that enabled them to elude me so easily. Later I learned that the frog's optical field is like a blackboard wiped clean, and that the only images it receives are objects that directly concern him. These little amphibians are never distracted by unimportant things, but are aware only of essentials and whatever may be dangerous to them.

In the Christian life we frequently become preoccupied with the vain things of the world. We allow our lives to become so cluttered with materialistic and insignificant concerns that we lose perspective of the things that endure. In our text the psalmist asked God for help in fixing his attention on what is good and lasting (Psalm 119:37).

The words of the Lord should not depart from our eyes, but must be kept in our heart always (Proverbs 4:21). Then our field of vision will be wiped clean of unnecessary things, and we will see clearly what God wants us to do.

Have you become distracted by sin so that you can no longer discern what is really important? Then take a lesson from the frog's "blackboard" and center your gaze on Christ and His will for your life. — Mart De Haan

*O God, You know my wayward heart,*
*So prone to choose an earthly part;*
*From vain affections set me free,*
*That I may always look to Thee.* — Anon.

---

**The more attracted we are to Christ,**
**the less we'll be distracted by the world.**

# WORKING IN THE HARVEST

**READ:**
Matthew 9:35–10:4

Pray the Lord of the harvest to send out laborers into His harvest.
—Matthew 9:38

THE BIBLE IN ONE YEAR:
■ Jeremiah 18–19
■ 2 Timothy 3

While D. L. Moody was attending a convention in Indianapolis on mass evangelism, he did more than just talk about it. He asked a friend, who was a gifted musician, to meet him on a street corner at 6 o'clock one evening. The man stood on a box and sang a song. When a crowd gathered, Moody spoke briefly and then invited the people to follow him to the nearby convention hall.

Soon the auditorium was filled with spiritually hungry people, and he preached to them. When the convention attendees began to arrive, Moody stopped preaching and said, "Now we must close, as the brethren of the convention want to discuss the topic, 'How to reach the masses.'"

When Jesus saw the masses, He was "moved with compassion" for them (Matthew 9:36). He said to His disciples, "The harvest truly is plentiful . . . . Pray the Lord of the harvest to send out laborers" (vv.37-38). And He sent them out to preach the good news of His kingdom (10:1).

It is estimated that only 10 percent of the world's population of 6.3 billion are believers in Jesus Christ. And more than 25 percent have never heard of Jesus' love even once.

As His disciples today, let's not just talk about the need—let's pray and go. — Anne Cetas

*Far, far away, in heathen darkness dwelling,*
*Millions of souls forever may be lost;*
*Who, who will go, salvation's story telling,*
*Looking to Jesus, minding not the cost?* — McGranahan

**The next person you meet may be your mission field.**

# You Won't Get Away With It!

**READ:**
Galatians 6:1-9

Our transgressions are multiplied before You, and our sins testify against us.
—Isaiah 59:12

THE BIBLE IN ONE YEAR:
■ Jeremiah 20–21
■ 2 Timothy 4

A group of students at Renaissance High School in Detroit decided to cut classes to attend a rock concert in Hart Plaza. They felt they had gotten away with it, but the next day when *The Detroit News* appeared on the newsstand, it carried a color photo of the concert—right there on the front page. And who was in that picture? That's right—the delinquent students of Renaissance High, easily recognizable by anyone.

The Bible teaches that we cannot hide our iniquities. Oh, we may be able to cover them up for a while and even get away with them for an extended period of time. But the day will inevitably come when we must face up to them, either in this world or in the next. Paul told the Galatians, "Do not be deceived, God is not mocked; for whatever a man sows, that he will also reap" (Galatians 6:7).

Perhaps you have some secret sin that you are hiding. If so, I urge you to confess and forsake it. Or maybe you are gradually being drawn into a situation that you know is wrong and you're tempted to pursue it, thinking you won't get caught. Then I plead with you to go no further. Your picture may not appear on the front page of a newspaper, but the Bible says you won't get away with it! —Dave Egner

*The sinful things that we may do*
*Are often hid from human view,*
*But judgment day will bring to light*
*Those things that we have not made right.* —D. De Haan

**The seeds of wrongdoing may be sown in secret,
but the crop cannot be concealed.**

# HOW TO TREAT HALLOWEEN

**READ:**
**Hebrews 11:32–12:3**

The memory of the righteous is blessed, but the name of the wicked will rot.
—Proverbs 10:7

THE BIBLE IN ONE YEAR:
■ Jeremiah 22–23
■ Titus 1

The word *Halloween* comes from All Hallows' Eve, which was the evening before a religious holiday in Medieval England that became known as All Saints' Day. It was a time set aside by the church to commemorate its saints.

Today's celebration of Halloween, however, is more closely related to pagan customs that originated in ancient Europe. The Druids believed that the spirits of the dead returned to their former haunts during the night of October 31, so they lit torches and set out food for these unwelcome visitors. They did this out of fear, thinking they would be harmed if they didn't.

The Bible warns against all dabbling in the occult and preoccupation with witches and ghosts. What then can Christians do? One enterprising pastor had a special gathering in which he asked some of the church people to come dressed in the costumes of Bible heroes and the great saints of church history. In a dramatic way they were calling to mind the sufficiency of God's grace in the lives of His people.

Yes, the example set by that great "cloud of witnesses" in Hebrews 12:1 encourages our faith. Remembering them on Halloween can remind us of the triumph of trusting the Lord. — Herb Vander Lugt

*Faith of our fathers, living still*
*In spite of dungeon, fire, and sword—*
*O how our hearts beat high with joy*
*Whene'er we hear that glorious word!* — Faber

---

**The greatest gift anyone can give us is a godly example.**

# THE PINE LOOPER

READ:
Jeremiah 17:1-10

He shall be like a tree planted by the waters, which spreads out its roots by the river.
—Jeremiah 17:8

THE BIBLE IN ONE YEAR:
■ Jeremiah 24–26
■ Titus 2

In the summer of 1992, a fire blackened 4,500 acres of forest about 35 miles north of Atlantic City. One homeowner saw a fireball with 60-foot flames come roaring up across the street from his house, before veering away. The Associated Press quoted him as saying, "I've worked 25 years of my life here. The thought of having it gone in 10 minutes makes you want to stay for the last possible minute."

The fire was difficult to contain because of dry conditions. The forest was dry despite rainfall, partly because of an insect called the pine looper, which defoliates trees.

The dry-tree condition behind this New Jersey fire has a parallel in the history of Israel. Jeremiah said that his countrymen had become like dry shrubs in a desert rather than green trees by a river (17:6-8). Even more alarming, he said they had aroused the fire of God's anger (v.4) by trusting in man and departing from the Lord (v.5). For Christians today, it's life's fiery trials that threaten to scorch our souls if we're trusting in our own strength.

Father, forgive us for making ourselves dry and leafless. Without Your mercy, we would be consumed when the heat comes. Teach us to root ourselves in the river of Your sufficiency. — Mart De Haan

*The person who relies upon*
*The Lord's sufficiency*
*Is like a tree that's planted by*
*Deep waters flowing free.* —Sper

---

**The fires of life will not destroy you
if you're watered by the River of Life.**

# WIN OR LOSE, DO GOOD

**READ:**
Titus 3:1-8

---

Remind them to be subject to rulers and authorities, to obey, to be ready for every good work. —Titus 3:1

---

THE BIBLE IN ONE YEAR:
■ Jeremiah 27–29
■ Titus 3

When the results of today's presidential election are known, US citizens will either be glad or sad, depending on their political persuasion. Those who voted for the winner are likely to accept the authority of the government he establishes. Most others will submit, though grudgingly.

Christians are to go beyond mere submission to governing authorities and follow the guidelines given in the Bible. In writing to Titus, Paul said we should also be peaceable and considerate, and we should do good without slandering anyone (3:1-2).

Titus was working among believers in Crete, a place notorious for its unruly inhabitants. There were good reasons to say bad things about the people living and ruling there, but Paul warned Christians not to do it.

In fact, seven times in his short letter to Titus, Paul mentioned the importance of doing good: loving what is good (1:8), teaching what is good (2:3), doing what is good (2:7,14; 3:1-2,8,14).

Paul's letter is a timely reminder that as Christians we are to do what is good for people, regardless of whether we approve of their values and agree with their policies. It may not be easy, but it's the right thing to do. — Julie Link

*From the example of Jesus,*
*Who went about doing good,*
*We are to honor our Savior*
*By helping wherever He would.* — Hess

---

**Christians can be constructive**
**if they refuse to be destructive.**

## ANOTHER CHANCE

**READ:**
Luke 22:24-34

---

Do you love Me? . . .
Tend My sheep.
—John 21:16

---

THE BIBLE IN ONE YEAR:
■ Jeremiah 30–31
■ Philemon

Jesus promised Peter something every repentant believer craves — another chance (Luke 22:31-34). After telling him Satan would sift him as wheat, Jesus reassured Peter that He had prayed that his faith would not fail. Although Peter had insisted he would never forsake Him, Jesus said he would deny Him three times before dawn. In expectation of Peter's restoration, Jesus recommissioned him for future ministry: "When you have returned to Me, strengthen your brethren" (v.32).

Preacher George Duncan said, "I don't think many church-vacancy committees would have considered Peter a suitable candidate for a church!" Duncan pointed out that at Pentecost, however, God chose Peter to deliver the most vital sermon in church history. "It would seem," Duncan said, "that some Christians have a message of forgiveness for the unbeliever, but no message of forgiveness for the believer. I'm glad that God does!" Because of that forgiveness, a new day of service dawned for Peter.

Indeed, if you are a repentant believer like Peter, you too can trust the Lord to give you another chance. Confess your sin and experience His forgiveness, healing, and restoration (1 John 1:9). — Joanie Yoder

> *When we confess our sins to God,*
> *We're washed as white as snow;*
> *Then He will send us out again —*
> *His love and grace to show.* — Sper

---

**God's forgiveness always comes
with another chance.**

## "RETRONYMS"

READ:
John 3:1-17

Do not marvel that I said to you, "You must be born again."
—John 3:7

THE BIBLE IN ONE YEAR:
■ Jeremiah 32–33
■ Hebrews 1

What do regular coffee, acoustic guitars, and black-and-white television have in common? All are what journalist Frank Mankiewicz calls "retronyms" — words or phrases created because a familiar word needs to be distinguished from a term that refers to a new development or invention.

Once, all coffee was regular, all guitars were acoustic, and all TVs were black and white. Not so today, thus the need for a growing list of retronyms, including *decaf mocha java, electric guitar,* and *high-def television*.

It could be said that Jesus turned the phrase *physical birth* into a retronym when He told an inquiring man named Nicodemus, "Unless one is born again, he cannot see the kingdom of God" (John 3:3).

Nicodemus was a religious person who didn't grasp the idea of second birth. "How can a man be born when he is old?" he asked Jesus. "Can he enter a second time into his mother's womb and be born?" (v.4). Jesus further explained the difference between being born of the flesh and being born of the Spirit, then concluded, "Do not marvel that I said to you, 'You must be born again'" (v.7).

Our Christian life begins when we invite Jesus to live within us. It's a miracle! We're born again.  — David McCasland

*Rejoice, O soul, the debt is paid,*
*For all our sins on Christ were laid;*
*We've been redeemed, we're justified—*
*And all because the Savior died.*  — D. De Haan

---

**Natural life came by God's breath;**
**eternal life comes by Christ's death.**

# MARCHING OFF THE MAP

**READ:**
**Genesis 12:1-4**

Get out of your country, from your family and from your father's house, to a land that I will show you. —Genesis 12:1

THE BIBLE IN ONE YEAR:
■ Jeremiah 34–36
■ Hebrews 2

Life is what happens to us while we are making other plans. Our lives are subject to detours and corrections that we never expected or imagined.

Abraham and Sarah could testify to that. They were planning for retirement when life "happened" to them. God adjusted their agenda. He told Abraham, "Get out of your country, from your family and from your father's house, to a land that I will show you" (Genesis 12:1). So this old couple packed up the tent and headed out to only God knew where.

When Alexander the Great had completed his conquest of Persia, he headed east. Author Halford Luccock said the general "marched off his maps."

That happened to Sarah and Abraham. God gave them marching orders without a map. They needed only enough faith to begin the journey, and they headed out to unknown territories and unimagined adventures. God never told them He would turn them "every which way but loose" before fulfilling His promise of a son who would become a great nation.

Make your plans. But write them on paper, not in concrete. God and life have a way of intruding and leading you on a journey that you might not have anticipated in your wildest dreams. — Haddon Robinson

*Many things about tomorrow*
*I don't seem to understand;*
*But I know who holds tomorrow*
*And I know who holds my hand.* — Stanphill

---

**A man's heart plans his way,**
**but the LORD directs his steps.** —Proverbs 16:9

# THE GOOD ATHEIST

**READ:**
**Luke 10:25-37**

You shall love your neighbor as yourself.
—Romans 13:9

THE BIBLE IN ONE YEAR:
■ Jeremiah 37–39
■ Hebrews 3

When a man learned that an elderly woman could no longer buy her medicine and pay her rent, he came to her rescue. He took her into his home and treated her as if she were his mother. He gave her a bedroom, prepared the food for her meals, bought her medicine, and transported her whenever she needed medical attention. He continued to care for her when she could no longer do much for herself. I was amazed when I learned that this good man was a zealous atheist!

The Jews were shocked by Jesus' parable of the Good Samaritan, because He put him in a positive light. They despised the Samaritans the way I tend to look down on atheists.

A lawyer had tested Jesus by asking how he could inherit eternal life. Jesus asked him what the law said. The man answered that he must love the Lord with all his heart and his neighbor as himself (Luke 10:25-27). He asked Jesus, "Who is my neighbor?" (v.29). In Jesus' story, the Samaritan was the neighbor who showed kindness to the wounded man.

Jesus wanted this parable to challenge His listeners. The stories of the Good Samaritan and the good atheist remind us of this high standard of God's Word: "Love your neighbor as yourself" (Romans 13:9). — Herb Vander Lugt

*To love my neighbor as myself*
*Is not an easy task,*
*But God will show His love through me*
*If only I will ask. —Sper*

**Needy people need our helping hand.**

# THE WAR IS OVER!

**READ:**
Hebrews 4

---

[Jesus] came and preached peace to you who were afar off and to those who were near. —Ephesians 2:17

---

THE BIBLE IN ONE YEAR:
■ Jeremiah 40–42
■ Hebrews 4

The bitter conflict had finally ended between the North and the South. The soldiers of the US Civil War were free to return to their families. But a number of them remained hidden in the woods, living on berries. They either didn't hear or didn't believe that the war was over, so they continued enduring miserable conditions when they could have been back home.

It's something like that in the spiritual realm too. Christ made peace between God and man by dying in our place. He paid sin's penalty on the cross. Anyone who accepts His sacrifice will be forgiven by a holy God.

Sadly, many people refuse to believe the gospel and continue to live as spiritual fugitives. Sometimes even those who have placed their trust in Christ live on almost the same level. Either out of ignorance or unwillingness, they fail to claim the promises of God's Word. They do not experience the joy and assurance that should accompany salvation. They do not draw from their relationship with God the comfort and peace He intends for His children. They are the objects of His love, care, and provision but live as if they were orphans.

Have you been living apart from the comfort, love, and care of your heavenly Father? Come on home. The war is over! — Richard De Haan

*We fail, O Lord, to realize*
*The fullness of what You have done,*
*So help us trust Your saving work*
*And claim the triumph You have won.* — D. De Haan

---

**Christ's victory over death
means peace for His saints.**

# THE LITTLE EVANGELIST

READ:
Mark 12:28-34

Love the LORD your God with all your heart, with all your soul, with all your mind, and with all your strength. —Mark 12:30

THE BIBLE IN ONE YEAR:
■ Jeremiah 43–45
■ Hebrews 5

My 6-year-old neighbor Michael and I were talking in my front yard when two new neighbor kids stopped by. After I asked them their names, Michael's first question to them was: "Do you love God?" Sugar, a 5-year-old boy, quickly responded, "No!" Michael gave him a look of disapproval and concern. When 4-year-old Nana noticed he wasn't pleased with that answer, she said, "Yes!"

Michael's "witnessing strategy" may not be the most effective, but he does have an important question for the people he meets (and I've heard him ask it of several others as well).

Jesus was asked, "Which is the first commandment of all?" (Mark 12:28). He answered, "The LORD is one. 'And you shall love the LORD your God with all your heart, with all your soul, with all your mind, and with all your strength'" (vv.29-30).

Jesus was referring to Old Testament times, when God had told the Israelites to place Him as the one and only God in their lives and nation. The pagan nations around them had many gods they loved and worshiped, but God's people were to be different.

Loving God is to be our top priority too. So, Michael wants to know, "Do *you* love God?" — Anne Cetas

*FOR FURTHER THOUGHT*
*Have you trusted in Jesus as your Savior?*
*What evidence is there in your life that you love God?*
*How are you showing God's love to others?*

**If you truly love the Lord,
you'll want others to love Him too.**

# HOPE FOR WORRIERS

**READ:**
Psalm 23

---

The LORD is my shepherd; I shall not want. —Psalm 23:1

---

THE BIBLE IN ONE YEAR:
■ Jeremiah 46–47
■ Hebrews 6

E veryone worries occasionally, but I was once a "professional worrier." My daily preoccupation was mulling over my worries, one by one.

Then one day I had to face an uncomfortable medical test, and I was frantic with fear. Finally I decided that during the test I would focus on the first five words of Psalm 23, "The LORD is my shepherd." This exercise in meditation not only calmed me, but I gained several fresh insights. Later, as I slowly meditated through the entire psalm, the Lord gave me more insights. Eventually I was able to share at conferences what the Lord had taught me.

If you're a worrier, there's hope for you too! Rick Warren, author of *The Purpose-Driven Life,* wrote: "When you think about a problem over and over in your mind, that's called worry. When you think about God's Word over and over in your mind, that's meditation. If you know how to worry, you already know how to meditate!"

The more we meditate on God's Word, the less we need to worry. In Psalm 23, David meditated on his great Shepherd instead of worrying. Later, God chose him to be the shepherd of His people (Psalm 78:70-72). God uses those who can honestly say, "The Lord is my shepherd." — Joanie Yoder

> *When fear and worry test your faith*
> *And anxious thoughts assail,*
> *Remember God is in control*
> *And He will never fail.* — Sper

---

**The more we think about God's Word,
the less we'll think about our worries.**

# WALKING OUR FAITH

READ:
Romans 2:17-24

---

Do you see that faith was working together with his works, and by works faith was made perfect? —James 2:22

---

THE BIBLE IN ONE YEAR:
■ Jeremiah 48-49
■ Hebrews 7

Often we Christians are urged not just to "talk the talk" but to "walk the talk." The same advice may be expressed in these words: Don't let your behavior contradict your professed belief. At other times we are admonished to be sure that life and lip agree. If our conduct doesn't harmonize with our confession of faith, however, that discrepancy nullifies the testimony of the gospel which we proclaim.

As far as we can know, Mahatma Gandhi never became a Christian, but he made a statement that we who follow Jesus would do well to ponder. When asked to put his message into one short sentence, he replied, "My life is my message."

Certainly we should explain the gospel message as clearly as possible. Yet the clearest explanation isn't going to win hearts for our Lord unless His love is embodied in our lives. To quote the apostle Paul in 1 Corinthians 11:1, "Imitate me, just as I also imitate Christ." And holding himself up as a pattern, he wrote in Philippians 4:9, "The things which you learned and received and heard and saw in me, these do, and the God of peace will be with you."

Pray, then, that like Paul we may live out our saving faith before the watching world. —Vernon Grounds

*Let the beauty of Jesus be seen in me —*
*All His wonderful passion and purity!*
*O Thou Spirit divine, all my nature refine,*
*Till the beauty of Jesus be seen in me.* —Orsborn

---

**The world is watching us —
do they see Jesus?**

## THE AGONY OF THE CROSS

READ:
Isaiah 53

[Jesus] humbled Himself and became obedient to the point of death, even the death of the cross.
—Philippians 2:8

THE BIBLE IN ONE YEAR:
■ Jeremiah 50
■ Hebrews 8

As Christians, we understand the spiritual significance of Christ's sacrifice at Calvary, but it's easy to forget about the tremendous agony He endured there. The worst aspect was separation from the Father, but the physical suffering was also horrible beyond comprehension.

In his book *Dare To Believe,* Dan Baumann shares some thoughts that can deepen our gratitude for what the Savior did for us. He wrote, "We have perhaps unwisely and sometimes unconsciously glamorized the cross. Jewelry and steeples alike are often ornamental and attractive but carry nothing of the real story of crucifixion. It was the most painful method of public death in the first century. The victim was placed on a wooden cross. Nails . . . were driven into the hands and feet of the victim, and then the cross was lifted and jarred into the ground, tearing the flesh of the crucified and racking his body with excruciating pain. Historians remind us that even the soldiers could not get used to the horrible sight, and often took strong drink to numb their senses."

With a fresh awareness of our Savior's physical agony, let's thank Him anew for His sacrifice at Calvary. He loved us so much that He was willing to die for us — even the painful death of the cross. — Richard De Haan

*Was it for crimes that I have done*
*He groaned upon the tree?*
*Amazing pity! Grace unknown!*
*And love beyond degree!* — Watts

**We can never sacrifice enough**
**for the One who sacrificed His all for us.**

# GLOOM INDEX

**READ:**
Acts 16:16-31

---

At midnight Paul and Silas were praying and singing hymns to God.
—Acts 16:25

---

**THE BIBLE IN ONE YEAR:**
- Jeremiah 51–52
- Hebrews 9

Gray skies, blue mood. It's common enough to produce what some have called the "gloom index." That's a way of describing the amount of cloudy weather a region can expect during a winter season.

A related idea is called Seasonal Affective Disorder (SAD). The theory is that weather-sensitive people experience a certain amount of cloud-induced melancholy.

Other factors might be figured into a gloom index. Think about what Paul and Silas endured (Acts 16). Any one of their troubles was enough to ruin the sunniest day. Imagine the irritations of dealing with greedy profiteers who had turned a demon-possessed girl into a sideshow (vv.16-17). Think about the pain of confronting an angry mob and furious judges (v.22), of receiving a whipping and imprisonment (v.23), and of having your feet locked in stocks (v.24).

But Paul and Silas rose above it (v.25). How did they do that? They were filled with the Holy Spirit, and they had a sense of mission. They were motivated by a desire to obey God and spread the message of Christ.

Like them, we can rise above the mood swings prompted by our circumstances. By being strong in the Spirit, we can overcome the gloom index. — Mart De Haan

*God often sends me joy through pain,*
*Through bitter loss, divinest gain;*
*Yet through it all — dark days or bright —*
*I know my Father leads aright.* — Conklin

---

**God's Son can brighten our darkest days.**

# AIN'T IT AWFUL!

READ:
Lamentations 3:25-42

---

Let us search out and examine our ways, and turn back to the LORD.
—Lamentations 3:40

---

THE BIBLE IN ONE YEAR:
■ Lamentations 1–2
■ Hebrews 10:1-18

A friend told me about a man who shouted the same three words each day from his street-corner newsstand. "Ain't it awful!" he would say to passersby while extending a newspaper. People bought a paper because they just had to know what terrible thing had occurred.

Tragedy and dire predictions always make the front page, but if we become preoccupied with bad news, we will succumb to what my friend calls "awfulizing" — a pervasive pessimism that clouds every situation with gloom.

If anyone had a good reason for being despondent, it was the prophet Jeremiah. For 40 years, he declared God's judgment on the rebellious and unrepentant nation of Judah. Jeremiah suffered because of their disobedience, but he clung to his faith in God's goodness. Even after witnessing the destruction of Jerusalem and the captivity of his people, Jeremiah wrote: "The LORD will not cast off forever. Though He causes grief, yet He will show compassion according to the multitude of His mercies. Let us search out and examine our ways, and turn back to the LORD" (Lamentations 3:31-32,40).

Disobedience to God can cause great pain, but the doorway out of discouragement leads to the Lord, who "is good to those who wait for Him" (v.25). — David McCasland

*Turn not aside, discouraged one,*
*Stir up your gift, pursue your goal;*
*In God's own time you'll see Him work,*
*He'll give you hope and lift your soul.* —D. De Haan

---

**Awful circumstances cannot alter
the goodness of God.**

# MORE THAN SOCIALIZING

READ:
Hebrews 10:19-25

---

Be kindly affectionate to one another with brotherly love.
—Romans 12:10

---

THE BIBLE IN ONE YEAR:
■ Lamentations 3–5
■ Hebrews 10:19-39

Church can be a great place to get caught up on the latest football games, golf scores, family news, health concerns, or just to visit with friends. A cup of coffee together, a warm handshake, a friendly pat on the back are all part of the social interaction we need as human beings.

All of this is good, but New Testament fellowship goes much deeper than merely socializing when we get together at church. It takes place when we consider how we can lift up, build up, and brighten up our brothers and sisters in Christ.

The Bible clearly says that we are to "serve one another" (Galatians 5:13), forgive as we are forgiven (Ephesians 4:32), and "bear one another's burdens" (Galatians 6:2). From the first century, believers have gathered in Jesus' name to "consider one another in order to stir up love and good works" and to exhort one another (Hebrews 10:24-25).

Christian fellowship takes place when we offer encouragement to our friends, pray for them, and confess our sins and weaknesses to one another. These are the elements that make fellowship genuine.

What about your church? Are you merely socializing? Or are you practicing true Christian fellowship? — Dave Egner

*We Christians have a kinship with*
*All others who believe,*
*And from that bond of faith and love*
*A mutual strength receive.* — Hess

---

**Christian fellowship builds us up**
**and binds us together.**

# WHAT GOD HAS DONE

**READ:**
Acts 26:6-23

---

King Agrippa, I was
not disobedient to
the heavenly vision.
—Acts 26:19

---

THE BIBLE IN ONE YEAR:
■ Ezekiel 1–2
■ Hebrews 11:1-19

In a debate at Boston College, Christian scholar William Craig Lane convincingly set forth the historical arguments for believing in Jesus' resurrection, much as the apostle Paul did in Acts 26. Then Lane told the story of his conversion.

As a child he never went to church, but in his teens he began to be plagued by questions about death and the meaning of life. He started going to church, but the sermons didn't answer his questions. What he saw in his churchgoing classmates led him to conclude that most Christians were phonies. He became an angry loner. One day a girl who always seemed to be happy told him that her joy came from having Jesus in her life, and she assured him that Jesus wanted to live in him too.

Lane spent the next 6 months soul-searching and reading the New Testament. "I came to the end of my rope and cried out to God," he said. "I cried out all the bitterness and anger that was within me. And I felt this tremendous infusion of joy, and God became at that moment a living reality in my life — a reality that has never left me."

We tell others our logic for believing in Jesus, which is based on God's Word. But it's also important to tell them what He has done for us personally. — Herb Vander Lugt

> *You may be tempted to debate*
> *To change another's view,*
> *But nothing speaks with greater power*
> *Than what Christ does for you.* —Sper

---

**When telling others what Jesus can do for them,
tell them what He has done for you.**

## As Is

**READ:**
2 Corinthians 5:14-21

If anyone is in Christ, he is a new creation; old things have passed away; behold, all things have become new.
—2 Corinthians 5:17

THE BIBLE IN ONE YEAR:
■ Ezekiel 3–4
■ Hebrews 11:20-40

The beat-up old car sits on the used-car lot, rusty and forsaken. Years of abuse and hard driving have taken their toll on the formerly shiny automobile.

A man walks onto the lot and is attracted to this rust bucket. He plunks down cash and the salesperson hands over the keys while saying, "I'm selling you this car 'as is.'" The new owner just smiles; he knows his cars, and he's about to restore this castoff to its former beauty.

Across town, a troubled woman sits in forlorn sadness, contemplating where she went wrong. Years of abuse and hard living have taken their toll on what was once a vibrant young girl. She's been mistreated by others so many times that she feels she has little value anymore. And after making her own mistakes and living with her own bad choices, she's sure she will be left on life's junk heap forever.

But then someone tells her about Jesus. Someone mentions that Jesus specializes in castoffs, that He is waiting to transform anyone who trusts Him — even her. Someone tells her that Jesus will take her "as is." She believes. She trusts. And Jesus begins to restore another lost person to the abundant life He has promised. —Dave Branon

*The new life in Christ has begun—*
*The past with its darkness is gone;*
*Look closer to see what the Savior has done,*
*For change is beginning to dawn.* —Hess

**Salvation is not turning over a new leaf,**
**but receiving a new life.**

# PAIN IS NOT POINTLESS

**READ:**
Isaiah 28:23-29

This also comes from the LORD of hosts, who is wonderful in counsel and excellent in guidance.
—Isaiah 28:29

THE BIBLE IN ONE YEAR:
■ Ezekiel 5–7
■ Hebrews 12

During times of hardship, I often feel like whining, "Who needs this pain? I certainly don't!" But Isaiah 28 and my own experience tell me this is a shortsighted reaction. Not that we need hardship just for its own sake, but we do need to be changed and to mature. In God's hand, hardship can be an effective tool to bring about our much-needed growth.

In verses 23-28, we read the prophet's "poetic parable," written to help the people of Israel understand how God works and what He intended to accomplish in their lives through tough times. A farmer is portrayed skillfully plowing the ground, planting his crops, and threshing the harvest. If the soil could talk, it might have whined, "Who needs this painful plowing?" But the pain is not pointless. Isaiah said that the farmer is taught by God to work in measured and well-timed ways, handling delicate crops with care and others more vigorously, but always with a sure harvest in view.

Our reassurance during tough times is that the farmer's God is our God, "who is wonderful in counsel and excellent in guidance" (v.29). His dealings with us are always thoughtful and purposeful, producing in us "the peaceable fruit of righteousness" (Hebrews 12:11). — Joanie Yoder

> *God has a purpose in our heartaches —*
> *The Savior always knows what's best;*
> *We learn so many precious lessons*
> *In every sorrow, trial, and test.* — Jarvis

---

**When you trust in God,
pain is an opportunity for progress.**

# GOD'S ASTONISHING PROMISE

READ:
Hebrews 13:5-6

---

I will never leave you
nor forsake you.
—Hebrews 13:5

---

THE BIBLE IN ONE YEAR:
■ Ezekiel 8–10
■ Hebrews 13

The writer to the Hebrews quotes God as saying to His people, "I will never leave you nor forsake you" (Hebrews 13:5). How does that strike you? Is it just some pleasant piety that evokes a wide yawn?

This isn't like saying we have coffee with the President or a Supreme Court justice. Knowing people like that would say something significant about us. But to claim that God is with us every moment of every day, as close as our skin, in every turn of life, tear-stained or drenched in smiles — some would say that borders on insanity.

Yet throughout history men and women have staked their lives on that truth. Abraham, Moses, Rahab, Joshua, David, Esther, just to name a few. The promise was true for them, but how can we know it's true for us?

It is true for us because of Jesus. By His coming, He says, "I want to be with you; I gave Myself to you; I gave Myself for you. Do you really think I would ever forsake you?"

How do you respond to this astonishing promise? Say it's too good to be true. Say it sounds unbelievable. But don't ignore it. In your hurts, your fears, your struggles, your temptations, there is no more wonderful promise than this: "I will never leave you nor forsake you." — Haddon Robinson

*Though all around is darkness,*
*Earthly joys have flown;*
*My Savior whispers His promise*
*Never to leave me alone.* — Anon.

---

**No matter where you go, God goes with you.**

# JOYFUL TRIALS

**READ:**
**James 1:1-12**

---

Count it all joy when
you fall into various
trials. —James 1:2

---

**THE BIBLE IN ONE YEAR:**
■ Ezekiel 11–13
■ James 1

The Bible tells us to respond to difficult circumstances in a way that is directly opposed to our natural tendency. One of the most challenging of those commands is this: "Count it all joy when you fall into various trials" (James 1:2).

Other translations speak of viewing our difficulties with pure joy, considering ourselves happy — not resisting trials and temptations as intruders but welcoming them as friends. I don't know about you, but that's not the first thing that pops into my mind.

This outlook would seem absurd and unattainable if not for the reason behind it: "knowing that the testing of your faith produces patience" (v.3). An attitude of joy is not based on what we feel but on what we know of God and His work in our lives. Therefore, a painful process that yields a desired goal can be welcomed as a friend.

It's not the testing of our strength but the trying of our faith in Almighty God that develops our endurance. Through it all, the Lord promises wisdom for today (v.5) and a crown of life for those who persevere (v.12).

My natural response to difficult circumstances is "Oh, no!" The Lord wants me to see what He can accomplish through them and say, "Oh, yes!" — David McCasland

*The deeper meaning of my trials*
*O Lord, You've kept from me;*
*But some small part of Your great plan*
*I pray, Lord, help me see.* —D. De Haan

---

**Joy in trials comes from knowing**
**that the outcome will be good.**

November 20

# LET THE WHOLE WORLD HEAR

**READ:**
Acts 1:1-8

---

Go into all the world and preach the gospel to every creature.
—Mark 16:15

---

THE BIBLE IN ONE YEAR:
■ Ezekiel 14–15
■ James 2

Fritz Kreisler (1875-1962), the world-famous violinist, earned a fortune with his concerts and compositions, but he generously gave most of it away. So, when he discovered an exquisite violin on one of his trips, he lacked the money to buy it.

Later, having raised enough money to meet the asking price, he returned to the seller, hoping to purchase that beautiful instrument. But to his great dismay it had been sold to a collector. Kreisler made his way to the new owner's home and offered to buy the violin. The collector said it had become his prized possession and he would not sell it.

Disappointed, Kreisler was about to leave when he had an idea. "Could I play the instrument once more before it is consigned to silence?" he asked. Permission was granted, and the great virtuoso filled the room with such heart-moving music that the collector's emotions were deeply stirred. "I have no right to keep that to myself," he exclaimed. "It's yours, Mr. Kreisler. Take it into the world, and let people hear it."

To sinners saved by grace, the gospel is like the rapturous harmonies of heaven. We have no right to keep it to ourselves. Jesus tells us to take it into our world and let people hear it. — Vernon Grounds

> *I'll tell the world how Jesus saved me*
> *And how He gave me a life brand new;*
> *And I know that if you trust Him*
> *That all He gave me He'll give to you.* — Fox

---

**Someone told you about Jesus.
Have you told someone lately?**

# NOTHING HIDDEN

**READ:**
1 Timothy 5:24-25

---

All things are naked and open to the eyes of Him to whom we must give account.
—Hebrews 4:13

---

THE BIBLE IN ONE YEAR:
■ Ezekiel 16–17
■ James 3

A woman had been misrepresented and maligned by an envious co-worker. Her gentle attempts at a private confrontation had only made matters worse. She decided she would swallow her pride and let the matter ride. "I'm glad the Lord knows the true situation," she said.

That woman expressed a profound truth that both warns and comforts us. In 1 Timothy 5:24-25 the apostle Paul pointed out that nothing can be concealed forever. I thought of that when the news reported the arrest of a highly respected person for crimes he had been committing for years.

But some people cleverly cover up their sinful conduct and die without ever being found out. Others go through life without ever holding a position of honor. Yet, after they die, we learn that in their own quiet way they had touched many lives through their kind words and deeds.

Hebrews 4:13 warns us, "There is no creature hidden from His sight, but all things are naked and open to the eyes of Him to whom we must give account."

We can't hide our hypocrisy from God. That's a solemn warning. But the Lord also sees every encouraging smile, every kind word, and every loving deed done in the name of Jesus. That's a comforting assurance. — Herb Vander Lugt

*All wrongs will one day be set right*
*By God who sees both bad and good;*
*All motives and all deeds will then*
*Be fairly judged and understood.* — D. De Haan

---

**Christ's judgment will reveal, and reward.**

# CLOSET CHRISTIANS

**READ:**
**Matthew 5:13-16**

Let your light so shine before men, that they may see your good works and glorify your Father in heaven.
—Matthew 5:16

THE BIBLE IN ONE YEAR:
- Ezekiel 18–19
- James 4

A businessman gave his heart to Jesus as a result of a Billy Graham evangelistic event. When he told his co-workers, his Christian business partner was elated. But the new believer hadn't known about his faith, and said, "You know, you're one reason I resisted becoming a Christian for several years. I figured that if someone like you could live a good life and not be a Christian, there was no need for me to become one."

A friend of mine and I were doing business in a local bank. He needed to change a $100 bill. By mistake the teller counted out six $20 bills. When my friend discovered the error, he walked back into the bank and quietly told her what had happened. The teller said, "I can't thank you enough. I would have had to make up the difference. Obviously, you are an honest man." He replied, "The reason I am honest is that I'm a committed follower of Jesus Christ. Giving you back the money is something He would want me to do."

Christians should lead exemplary lives. But it's important that we reveal the Source of strength and life who enables us to be different. As Jesus said, "Let your light so shine before men, that they may see your good works and glorify your Father in heaven" (Matthew 5:16). — Haddon Robinson

*Like a brightly shining light*
*In the darkness of the night,*
*We will stand for truth and right—*
*Let the whole world know!* —Peterson

**It's the life behind the words**
**that makes your testimony effective.**

# "JUST AS I AM"

READ:
John 6:35-40

All that the Father gives Me will come to Me, and the one who comes to Me I will by no means cast out.
—John 6:37

THE BIBLE IN ONE YEAR:
■ Ezekiel 20–21
■ James 5

Charlotte Elliott learned an important lesson about Jesus one sleepless night in 1834. She was an invalid, so when her family held a bazaar in Brighton, England, to raise money to build a school, she could only watch from afar.

That night she was overwhelmed by her helplessness and could not sleep. But her sadness turned to joy when she realized that God accepted her just as she was.

Her experience inspired these well-loved words: "Just as I am, without one plea but that Thy blood was shed for me, and that Thou bidd'st me come to Thee, O Lamb of God, I come! I come!" When she published the poem in *The Invalid's Hymn Book,* she included with it John 6:37.

Jesus always accepts people as they are. In John 6, the people had come from miles around to hear Jesus. When the crowd became hungry, He miraculously fed them with a boy's unselfish gift of five loaves and two fish. Then the Lord offered Himself as "the bread of life," promising that He would not turn away anyone who came to Him.

It's still true today. No one who comes to Jesus will be turned away. Come to Him with all your sin. He'll accept you just as you are. — Dave Egner

*Just as I am, Thou wilt receive,*
*Wilt welcome, pardon, cleanse, relieve;*
*Because Thy promise I believe,*
*O Lamb of God, I come! I come!* — Elliott

**No one is too good or too bad to be saved.**

# GIVE THANKS AND REMEMBER

**READ:**
**Hebrews 13:1-16**

---

Do not forget to do good and to share, for with such sacrifices God is well pleased.
—Hebrews 13:16

---

THE BIBLE IN ONE YEAR:
■ Ezekiel 22–23
■ 1 Peter 1

One of today's most popular syndicated newspaper columns is "Dear Abby." Started in 1956 by Abigail Van Buren, the advice column is written today by her daughter Jeanne Phillips. In a recent edition, she included this Thanksgiving Prayer written many years before by her mother:

*O Heavenly Father:*
*We thank Thee for food*
*and remember the hungry.*
*We thank Thee for health*
*and remember the sick.*
*We thank Thee for friends*
*and remember the friendless.*
*We thank Thee for freedom*
*and remember the enslaved.*
*May these remembrances*
*stir us to service.*
*That Thy gifts to us may be used*
*for others. Amen.*

The words of this prayer echo the clear teaching of Scripture. Our thanksgiving to God should always be accompanied by thinking of those in need. "Therefore," said the writer to the Hebrews, "by [Jesus] let us continually offer the sacrifice of praise to God, that is, the fruit of our lips, giving thanks to His name" (Hebrews 13:15).

But there is more to it than thankfulness. We are to put actions behind our gratitude. "Do not forget to do good and to share, for with such sacrifices God is well pleased" (v.16).

Be thankful for God's many blessings, but be sure to remember those who have less. —David McCasland

---

**Serving others is a way of thanking God.**

# BE FILLED WITH THANKFULNESS

**READ:**
**Romans 1:18-22**

Let us continually offer
the sacrifice of praise
to God, that is, the
fruit of our lips, giving
thanks to His name.
—Hebrews 13:15

THE BIBLE IN ONE YEAR:
■ Ezekiel 24–26
■ 1 Peter 2

Throughout history, many cultures have set aside a time for expressing their thankfulness. In the US, Thanksgiving Day originated with the pilgrims. In the midst of extreme hardship, loss of loved ones, and meager supplies, they still believed they were blessed. They chose to celebrate God's blessings by sharing a meal with Native Americans who had helped them survive.

We know we've lost the spirit of that original celebration when we catch ourselves complaining that our Thanksgiving Day has been "spoiled" by bad weather, disappointing food, or a bad cold. It's we who are spoiled — spoiled by the very blessings that should make every day a day of thanksgiving, whatever our circumstances.

Billy Graham wrote, "Ingratitude is a sin, just as surely as is lying or stealing or immorality or any other sin condemned by the Bible." He then quoted Romans 1:21, one of the Bible's indictments against rebellious humanity. Then Dr. Graham added, "Nothing turns us into bitter, selfish, dissatisfied people more quickly than an ungrateful heart. And nothing will do more to restore contentment and the joy of our salvation than a true spirit of thankfulness."

Which condition describes you? — Joanie Yoder

*A grumbling mood of discontent*
*Gives way to thankfulness*
*When we consider all God's gifts*
*And all that we possess.* —Sper

---

**Gratitude is a God-honoring attitude.**

# WATCH YOUR EYES

READ:
## Matthew 6:19-23

The lamp of the body is the eye. If therefore your eye is good, your whole body will be full of light.
—Matthew 6:22

THE BIBLE IN ONE YEAR:
■ Ezekiel 27–29
■ 1 Peter 3

The ability to discern between good and evil is determined by the things on which we focus our spiritual eyes. If we set our eyes on money, for example, we may have the good life for a while, but our judgment will become clouded. We'll make choices that defy our own values—choices that may devastate our families and destroy us in the end.

The Bible warns, "Those who desire to be rich fall into temptation and a snare, and into many foolish and harmful lusts" (1 Timothy 6:9). If we love money we'll go to any extreme to get it. And then, "How great is that darkness" (Matthew 6:23).

In C. S. Lewis' *The Chronicles of Narnia*, Edmund's lust for sweets leads him to betray his beloved brother and sisters. Eustace's desire for the dragon's gold eventually turns him into a dragon. Greed overcomes Prince Caspian on Deathwater Island as he dreams of the power its magic water will bring him.

Food, money, power—wherever we focus our spiritual eyes determines what we desire, and whether our lives are filled with light or filled with darkness. Jesus said, "The lamp of the body is the eye. If therefore your eye is good, your whole body will be full of light" (Matthew 6:22).

Be careful where your eyes lead your desires. — David Roper

*No greater peace can flood our soul*
*Than when we choose a heavenly goal,*
*But when we covet worldly gain*
*We choose a path that brings us pain.* — D. De Haan

**Cure for covetousness: Think of something to give instead of something to get.**

# POINTING FINGERS

**READ:**
Psalm 14

---

There is none who does good, no, not one.
—Psalm 14:3

---

THE BIBLE IN ONE YEAR:
■ Ezekiel 30–32
■ 1 Peter 4

An employee in the bill-collection department of a large store gave me an insight into human nature. He told me that he repeatedly gets the following response from customers who are delinquent in paying their bills: "I know you must have others who owe a lot more than I do. Get off my back, will you!"

The employee then told me, "They miss the point entirely. Sure, there are a lot of others who owe more. But somehow I have to tell them in a nice way, 'Look, what somebody else owes isn't the issue. Our records say that *your* account is overdue!'"

The tendency of sinful man has always been to shift attention from himself by pointing the finger at others. Religious people excuse their inconsistencies by referring to the "pagans" around them. And the "pagans" try to sidestep the issue by talking about the hypocrisies of the religious. But God is not fooled by finger-pointers.

When someone else appears to be a greater sinner than we are, it's just an illusion. The sooner we realize that no one owes more to God than we do, the more likely we are to receive His free forgiveness. He extends His pardon only to those who humbly acknowledge that they are hopelessly in debt. — Mart De Haan

*My sin, O Lord, defies Your Word,*
*It scorns Your holy name;*
*I will not make excuse for wrong —*
*Christ's blood is what I claim.* — D. De Haan

---

**One sin rationalized becomes two.**

# WORTHY OF WORSHIP

READ:
Psalm 99

Exalt the LORD our God, and worship at His footstool—He is holy. —Psalm 99:5

THE BIBLE IN ONE YEAR:
■ Ezekiel 33–34
■ 1 Peter 5

As Moses was tending his father-in-law's sheep in the desert, his attention was drawn to a strange sight. A bush was burning without being consumed. When Moses turned to look more closely, God said to him, "Take your sandals off your feet, for the place where you stand is holy ground" (Exodus 3:5).

Joshua had a similar experience when he approached the captain of the host of the Lord. As Joshua drew nearer, he was given this command: "Take your sandal off your foot, for the place where you stand is holy" (Joshua 5:15).

The experiences of Moses and Joshua teach us that a holy God demands our reverence and respect. True, we are encouraged to "come boldly to the throne of grace" (Hebrews 4:16). We can enter the presence of God with confidence because Jesus has opened the way for us through His death on the cross. But never are we to approach God with disrespect. Never are we to profane His name.

Our heavenly Father is not "the man upstairs." He is God, the One who is high and lifted up. And because of His majesty and holiness, we are to exalt and worship Him. As the one true God, He is worthy of our adoration. Let's give Him our highest praise. — Richard De Haan

*You alone are worthy, Lord,*
*To be worshiped and adored;*
*We to You our tribute bring*
*As our hearts rejoice and sing.* — Hess

**True worship acknowledges**
**the true worthship of God.**

# HOW TO CLEAN ANYTHING

**READ:**
1 John 1:5-10

---

The blood of Jesus
Christ His Son cleanses
us from all sin.
—1 John 1:7

---

THE BIBLE IN ONE YEAR:
■ Ezekiel 35–36
■ 2 Peter 1

*C*onsumer *Reports* published a booklet with the intriguing title *How To Clean Practically Anything*. It offers advice on what solvent to use to remove a wide assortment of stains. Living as I do with drips and drops, that is my kind of book.

Did you know that glycerin will remove stains made by a ball-point pen? Boiling water can remove berry stains. Parents of small children should keep a gallon of vinegar handy to get rid of crayon marks. Bleach works well for mildew. Lemon juice performs minor miracles on rust stains.

I haven't tried them all, but I assume that scientists have put these common cleansing agents to the test.

What you will not find in this little book is how to deal with the most serious stain of all — the stain made on your life by sin. Deep, ugly stains made by hostile words and shame-filled actions. Tears won't touch them. Zeal can't erase them. At times we are convinced that we have gotten on with our lives and the sins are gone, but in an unguarded moment we notice the stain seeping through.

The Bible tells us just what we need: "The blood of Jesus Christ His Son cleanses us from all sin" (1 John 1:7). That's the only remedy that works. — Haddon Robinson

*Jesus paid it all,*
*All to Him I owe;*
*Sin had left a crimson stain —*
*He washed it white as snow.* — *Hall*

---

**We may whitewash sin,**
**but only Jesus' blood can truly wash it white.**

**November 30**

# SOUNDS OF SILENCE

READ:
Colossians 3:12-17

---

Let the word of Christ
dwell in you richly
in all wisdom.
—Colossians 3:16

---

THE BIBLE IN ONE YEAR:
■ Ezekiel 37–39
■ 2 Peter 2

During a Sunday morning worship service, I was intrigued to see the interpreter for the deaf continue to sign during an instrumental piano offertory. After the service I asked her what she was saying during that time when no words were being spoken or sung. She said that she had signed the words to the hymn being played, and also answered questions her "audience" asked about the pianist, her style, and her training.

"Instrumental music can be a blank place in worship for the deaf," she told me. Instead of taking a break or enjoying it alone, she thought of those who couldn't hear and kept the worship service unbroken for them.

That experience broadened my understanding of Colossians 3:16, "Let the word of Christ dwell in you richly in all wisdom, teaching and admonishing one another in psalms and hymns and spiritual songs." As we allow God's Word to fill our hearts and have free rein in our lives, we can share it with others through words of instruction, encouragement, and praise to the Lord. Imagine the impact it could have in our homes, in private conversations, and in worship together.

As you encourage others by sharing God's Word from your heart, it will be music to their ears. — David McCasland

*Sing praise to God who reigns above,*
*The God of all creation,*
*The God of power, the God of love,*
*The God of our salvation.* — Schutz

---

**Let God's Word fill your heart
and guide your words.**

# DEAD DUCKS DON'T FLUTTER

**READ:**
Romans 7:14-25

---

What I will to do, that I do not practice; but what I hate, that I do.
—Romans 7:15

---

THE BIBLE IN ONE YEAR:
■ Ezekiel 40–41
■ 2 Peter 3

Many years ago, a wealthy man went duck hunting with a hired hand named Sam. They took a horse and carriage, and along the way a rim came off one of the wheels. As Sam hammered it back on, he accidentally hit his finger. Instantly he let go with some bad words. He quickly fell to his knees, asking God's forgiveness. "Lord, it's so difficult at times to live the Christian life," he prayed.

"Sam," said the man, "I know you're a Christian, but tell me why you struggle so. I'm an atheist, and I don't have problems like that."

Sam didn't know what to say. Just then two ducks flew overhead. The man raised his gun and two shots rang out. "Leave the dead one and go after that wounded bird!" he shouted. Sam pointed at the duck that was fluttering desperately to escape and said, "I've got an answer for you now, Boss. You said that my Christianity isn't any good because I have to struggle so. Well, I'm the wounded duck, and I struggle to get away from the devil. But Boss, you're the dead duck!"

That insight fits Paul's description of his Christian experience in Romans 7:14-25. Struggle is one evidence of God's work in our lives. Forgiveness of sin is available, so don't despair. Remember, dead ducks don't flutter. — Dennis De Haan

*Struggle, yes, it's part of living,*
*Nothing's gained on beds of ease;*
*But when our heart is set on Jesus,*
*Struggle drives us to our knees.* — D. De Haan

---

**If Jesus lives within us,
sin need not overwhelm us.**

## RETURNING GOD'S LOVE

READ:
Malachi 3:16-18

---

"I have loved you,"
says the LORD.
—Malachi 1:2

---

THE BIBLE IN ONE YEAR:
■ Ezekiel 42–44
■ 1 John 1

The book of Malachi begins with this wholehearted word from the Lord to His halfhearted worshipers: "I have loved you" (1:2). Though Israel had long been the object of God's love, they no longer returned His love.

God listed the ways His people had offended His love through their disobedience. Israel's response was to question God. When He implored them, "Return to Me, and I will return to you," they questioned Him in their blindness, "In what way shall we return?" (3:7). With divine "tough love," the Lord exposed their many blind spots. He did this so that they might repent and accept His love, and return it with wholehearted obedience.

We too are often halfhearted in our faith, appearing to love and serve God but really loving and serving ourselves. Today, as in Malachi's time, God looks for people who reverence Him by maintaining two spiritual practices: speaking to each other about Him, and meditating on His wonderful attributes (v.16). The first is fellowship with God's people; the second is fellowship with God Himself. Not only are we to receive and share God's love, we are also to return it through glad obedience.

Such worshipers are God's "jewels" (v.17). Are you one of them? — Joanie Yoder

*"We love You, Lord Jesus," we often will say,*
*But are we as ready His will to obey?*
*Let's heed what God's Spirit would have us to do—*
*That's how we show Him a love that is true.* — D. De Haan

---

**To love God is to obey God.**

# LOOKING FOR GOD?

**READ:**
**Matthew 21:28-32**

---

Tax collectors and harlots enter the kingdom of God before you.
—Matthew 21:31

---

THE BIBLE IN ONE YEAR:
■ Ezekiel 45–46
■ 1 John 2

My wife and I were having dinner with another couple at a fishing lodge in Montana. It was interrupted when a fellow fisherman in a drunken rant began to regale us with tales of the houses of ill-repute he had visited.

Though his comments were crass and offensive, I caught a note of pathos in his voice and thought of something G. K. Chesterton had said: "Even when men knock on the door of a brothel they're looking for God."

Chesterton was right. Many desires are evidence of a deeper hunger for God. This man, who seemed so far from God, was closer than he realized.

Every man knows he was made for lofty pursuits, yet he easily wanders into paths that demean and debase him. He becomes less manly than he ought to be, and he knows it. There's a nagging feeling that he ought to be something more. Some cover it up with self-righteousness, as the Pharisees did, or else they ignore it. Others know they have lost their way. That elusive feeling, when followed up, may bring them to God.

"Tax collectors and harlots enter the kingdom of God before you," Jesus told the Pharisees (Matthew 21:31). That's why I think the drunken fisherman is much more likely to repent than the Pharisees were. — *David Roper*

*Our heart is made for God alone,*
*For only He can satisfy;*
*But oh how much we yearn for things*
*That in the end are but a lie.* — *D. DeHaan*

---

**Within each one of us there is a God-shaped vacuum that only God can fill.** —Pascal

# READ ALL OF IT

**READ:**
Psalm 119:97-112

All Scripture is given
by inspiration of God,
and is profitable for
doctrine, for reproof,
for correction,
for instruction in
righteousness.
—2 Timothy 3:16

THE BIBLE IN ONE YEAR:
■ Ezekiel 47–48
■ 1 John 3

Some Christian families follow the practice of reading through the whole Bible. After evening meals, they read a chapter or two. They read from Genesis to Revelation, skipping nothing. Even the genealogies with their hard-to-pronounce names are read aloud.

We might question the relevance of such a method for small children, but it does acquaint all the family members with the entirety of God's Word. It also exposes children to the sinful depths and spiritual heights of which we are capable, and it teaches them right and wrong.

If you've never done so, why not embark on your own program of reading the Bible straight through? Try doing it as a family or for your personal devotions.

There are two persuasive reasons for resolving to undertake such a program. One is Paul's declaration that all Scripture is God-breathed and profitable (2 Timothy 3:16). The other is the testimony of believers whose lives have been changed by following such a practice.

Read God's Word straight through and you'll begin to see the unfolding plan of God's redeeming grace, and that you were the object of His love even before you were born. Do it once, and you'll want to do it again. — Vernon Grounds

*Oh, may these heavenly pages be*
*My ever dear delight,*
*And still new beauties may I see,*
*And still increasing light.* —Steele

---

**Those who only sample the Bible
never acquire a taste for it.**

# NO ANSWERS

**READ:**
Job 42:1-6

Shall the one who
contends with the
Almighty correct
Him? —Job 40:2

THE BIBLE IN ONE YEAR:
■ Daniel 1–2
■ 1 John 4

Just before Christmas 2003, Lydia came home from work to the sight of flames shooting out of her house. She was devastated by more than the loss of her home — seven of her family members died in the flames. When news about the tragedy spread that morning, a deacon from her church rushed to comfort her. She had some deep questions for him, but he had no answers.

Lydia could relate to Job's story. He lost all 10 of his children (Job 1:18-19), yet he continued to worship God (v.21). Then his health was affected, and his wife urged him to curse God and die (2:9). Job's friends thought they had the answer — he must have sinned and deserved his troubles.

Job complained bitterly to the Lord and pleaded for an explanation and relief, but God didn't give him any answers. He didn't even tell him about Satan's request to test him (1:6-12; 2:1-6). Instead, He reminded Job that He was the all-wise God and that Job was not. Job was humbled, and he repented for having questioned God's authority (42:1-6).

This side of heaven, we may not find answers for our desperate questions of "Why did this happen?" and "Why me?" But we can rest in the truth that God is in control and that He loves us. — Anne Cetas

*Though darker, rougher, grows the way*
*And cares press harder day by day,*
*With patience in His love I'll rest,*
*And whisper that He knoweth best. — Pentecost*

---

**God does not have to answer our questions,
but He will always keep His promises.**

# It's The Knees

READ:
James 5:13-18

Continue earnestly
in prayer.
—Colossians 4:2

THE BIBLE IN ONE YEAR:
■ Daniel 3–4
■ 1 John 5

Both of my knees were hurting, and I could not figure out why. I hadn't done anything to damage them or put undo pressure on them.

Or had I? I recalled that over the previous few days I had been working on the walls in our house, scrubbing them and getting them ready for painting. And then I had painted them. All the while, as I stood on the short ladder to reach the top, I had been pressing my knees against the ladder for balance. I was, in effect, being supported by my knees.

Then a new thought came to mind: *When was the last time my knees hurt because I was on them praying?* It had been a while.

Although it's true that people pray all the time without kneeling, the question I asked myself is a convicting one. Whether we are on our knees, standing up, or seated, how often do we use prayer to support ourselves? We can find help from many sources — friends, counselors, books — but there's nothing better than the support and strength we get from God when we pray.

"The effective, fervent prayer of a righteous man avails much" (James 5:16). Prayer has power. We are to "continue earnestly in prayer, being vigilant" (Colossians 4:2).

How are your knees? — Dave Branon

*When I kneel before my Master,*
*I can feel His presence there,*
*And the load of care and sorrow*
*Seems much easier to bear.* — Anon.

---

**Prayer does not require eloquence but earnestness.**

# How To Be Unpopular

READ:
Jeremiah 23:16-23

Woe to the shepherds
who destroy and
scatter the sheep
of My pasture!
—Jeremiah 23:1

THE BIBLE IN ONE YEAR:
■ Daniel 5–7
■ 2 John

In 1517, Martin Luther nailed his Ninety-Five Theses to the door of the castle church in Wittenberg. Luther became known as a reformer, and we remember his bold stand as a turning point in church history.

The fiery priest demonstrated great courage in expressing outrage at the church's practice of selling forgiveness through indulgences, which allowed the people to sin intentionally in exchange for money.

Luther's passion to stop these practices did not make him popular with the religious authorities of his day. In fact, his efforts resulted in a series of attempts to silence him.

Long before Luther, the prophet Jeremiah felt the power of God's Word in his heart "like a burning fire shut up in my bones; I was weary of holding it back, and I could not" (Jeremiah 20:9). Jeremiah and Luther refused to allow God's truth to be compromised.

Living for God is about grace and forgiveness, but it's also about boldly standing for the truth. Having God's Word in our heart doesn't always result in warm, pleasant feelings. Sometimes His truth becomes a blazing fire that causes us to challenge corruption — even though we may be attacked for it. —Julie Link

> Sure I must fight if I would reign;
> Increase my courage, Lord.
> I'll bear the toil, endure the pain,
> Supported by Thy Word. —Watts

---

**It's better to declare the truth and be rejected
than to withhold it just to be accepted.**

# BAD NEWS?

READ:
Psalm 112:1-10

---

He will not be afraid of evil tidings; his heart is steadfast, trusting in the LORD.
—Psalm 112:7

---

THE BIBLE IN ONE YEAR:
■ Daniel 8–10
■ 3 John

Several years ago, before cell phones became common, a seminar leader asked the audience, "If someone came into this meeting, called your name, and said, 'You have a phone call,' would you assume that it was good news or bad news?" Most of us admitted we would think it was bad news, but we weren't sure why.

It points out a common burden many people carry — the fear of bad news. It may be a natural concern for the safety of those we love, but it can become an irrational dread of tragedy.

When we are most afraid, we most need confidence in God. Psalm 112 speaks of a person who fears the Lord, delights in His commandments, and is gracious to others (vv.1,4-5). But perhaps most striking is: "He will not be afraid of evil tidings; his heart is steadfast, trusting in the LORD" (v.7).

A hymn by Frances Havergal reminds us that a trusting heart is the answer for a worried mind: "Stayed upon Jehovah, hearts are fully blest; finding, as He promised, perfect peace and rest."

The Bible doesn't promise that we will never receive bad news. But it does assure us that we don't have to live each day in gnawing fear of what might happen. "His heart is established; he will not be afraid" (v.8). — David McCasland

> *Hidden in the hollow of His blessed hand,*
> *Never foe can follow, never traitor stand;*
> *Not a surge of worry, not a shade of care,*
> *Not a blast of hurry touch the Spirit there.* — Havergal

---

**Faith in the living God
can take the fear out of living.**

# AFRAID TO BE AFRAID

READ:
Psalm 56

> Whenever I am afraid,
> I will trust in You.
> —Psalm 56:3

THE BIBLE IN ONE YEAR:
■ Daniel 11–12
■ Jude

A young woman was waiting for a bus in a crime-ridden area when a rookie policeman approached her and asked, "Do you want me to wait with you?" "That's not necessary," she replied. "I'm not afraid." "Well, I am," he grinned. "Would you mind waiting with me?"

Like that policeman, we as Christians must be willing to admit that sometimes we become fearful — about dying, about getting cancer, about losing our mind, about losing our job, about our children getting in trouble, about getting old. We don't like to confess it, so we may ignore, deny, or repress those fears. But to overcome our fear, we must first acknowledge it.

The psalmist recognized his fears. "Whenever I am afraid," he said, "I will trust in You" (Psalm 56:3). This trust in the Lord gave him a growing confidence. "I will not fear," he said (v.4). And again, "I will not be afraid" (v.11). This was much more than self-talk. It was a conscious decision to trust in God: "I will."

We can conquer our fears. To admit that we are afraid is to admit that we are human. But to admit being afraid and then trusting the Lord and going forward will take the fear out of fear. — Dennis De Haan

> *I can walk with Christ in safety,*
> *Trusting Him, my faithful Guide;*
> *There's no reason to be fearful,*
> *Knowing He is by my side.* — Hess

**We have nothing to fear but fear itself.**

# DANGEROUS PROVERBS

**READ:**
**Ezekiel 18:1-9**

> If he has walked in My statutes and kept My judgments faithfully—he is just; he shall surely live!
> —Ezekiel 18:9

THE BIBLE IN ONE YEAR:
■ Hosea 1–4
■ Revelation 1

There is a hidden danger in any proverb. A proverb is a general principle — not an absolute truth — and it can be misused. "Like father, like son," we say, but it depends on who says it and why. There is truth in it, but when someone quotes it to justify the shambles he has made of life, the proverb serves as an excuse to play the victim.

The prophet Ezekiel wanted to get the Hebrew captives in Babylon to return not only to their homes but to their God. It was a tough sell. The people responded by taking refuge in a proverb: "The fathers have eaten sour grapes, and the children's teeth are set on edge" (Ezekiel 18:2).

This saying blamed their captivity on an earlier generation. "You can't be serious about asking us to repent," they protested. "It's our parents' fault. They ate the sour grapes and we have to bear the consequences."

So God declared through Ezekiel, "You shall no longer use this proverb in Israel" (v.3). Each person bore responsibility for his own actions. "The soul who sins shall die," God said (v.4). But "if he has walked in My statutes and kept My judgments faithfully — he is just; he shall surely live!" (v.9).

Proverbs are wonderful tools for guidance. They were never intended to excuse our bad behavior. — Haddon Robinson

*Don't hide your sin and cover up,*
*Pretending that there's nothing wrong;*
*Instead, confess it and repent,*
*And God will fill your heart with song.* — Sper

---

**A good test of character:**
**When we do wrong, whom do we blame?**

# A PLEASANT DIVERSION

READ:
Romans 11:33–12:2

---

Do not be conformed to this world, but be transformed by the renewing of your mind.
—Romans 12:2

---

THE BIBLE IN ONE YEAR:
■ Hosea 5–8
■ Revelation 2

A friend was looking for a church to join and told me she had found just what she was looking for: "I like this church because I don't have to change my lifestyle of partying. It doesn't make me feel guilty or require anything of me. I feel good about myself when I'm there."

Her story makes me wonder how many people are in that type of situation. Their "Christianity" is what author W. Waldo Beach calls "a pleasant weekend diversion."

But is that the kind of life Jesus calls us to? Beach says, "No amount of air-conditioning and pew-cushioning in the suburban church can cover over the hard truth that . . . discipleship is costly; that, for the faithful, there is always a cross to be carried. No one can understand Christianity to its depths who comes to it to enjoy it as a pleasant weekend diversion."

Being a Christian means that we know Jesus personally. We have received Him by faith as our Savior from sin, and we present ourselves to Him. We deny our will and choose His instead. He transforms our thinking, our values, and our priorities to reflect what is acceptable to God (Romans 12:1-2).

Is your religion just a pleasant weekend diversion? That's no substitute for a vital relationship with Jesus! — Anne Cetas

*"Take up your cross," the Savior said,*
*"If you would My disciple be;*
*Take up your cross with willing heart*
*And humbly follow after Me." —Everest*

---

**Discipleship demands discipline.**

December 12

# SERVING WITHOUT DISTRACTION

READ:
Luke 10:38-42

---

Martha was distracted
with much serving.
—Luke 10:40

---

THE BIBLE IN ONE YEAR:
■ Hosea 9–11
■ Revelation 3

While Martha served Jesus unsparingly, her sister Mary sat at His feet, listening and learning. Charles H. Spurgeon (1834–1892) believed that Martha's mistake wasn't her serving, but rather that she allowed it to distract her attention from Jesus. Spurgeon believed that we should be Martha and Mary in one. He wrote, "We should do much service, and have much communion at the same time. For this we need great grace. It is easier to serve than to commune."

I once met a young mother who found the grace to do both. She hungered after God and His Word but was unavoidably immersed in family life each day. Then an idea came to her. In each room she placed paper and a pencil on a high surface, away from tiny hands. As she served the Lord in household responsibilities, she also kept herself open to God. Whenever a Scripture came to mind, or something to confess, to correct, or to pray about, she jotted it on the nearest pad of paper. In the evening after the children were asleep, she gathered her pieces of paper and pondered them prayerfully over her open Bible.

This woman found a way to be Martha and Mary at the same time. May we too discover ways to serve God and to commune with Him. — Joanie Yoder

*Our service for the Lord each day*
*Can make us feel distressed,*
*But spending time each day with Christ*
*Can make our service blest.* — D. De Haan

---

**To keep your life in balance, lean on the Lord.**

# CAVE MAN

**READ:**
Psalm 142

---

Attend to my cry,
for I am brought very
low. —Psalm 142:6

---

THE BIBLE IN ONE YEAR:
■ Hosea 12–14
■ Revelation 4

David was stuck in a cave (Psalm 142). Some Bible commentators think this was when he was running from King Saul, who wanted to kill him (1 Samuel 22:1). Trouble and troublemakers hounded him. Hemmed in by his circumstances and smothered by danger, he turned to God for help.

- David was frightened, so he poured out his complaint to God (v.2).
- He felt alone and uncared for, so he cried out to God (vv.1,4-5).
- His situation was desperate, so he pleaded for rescue (v.6).
- David was trapped, so he begged for freedom (v.7).

What cave surrounds you today? A cave of despair brought on by grief or illness? A cave of difficulties caused by your own poor decisions? Are you stuck in a cave of questions or doubts that rob you of joy and confidence?

Here's what David did when he was trapped in his cave: He asked God for mercy, he sought refuge in Him, and he promised to use his eventual freedom as a way to praise God. In the end, he looked forward to the comfort of fellow believers.

Complaint followed by faith. Desperation followed by praise. Loneliness followed by fellowship. We can learn a lot from a cave man. — Dave Branon

*When we experience suffering,*
*God's comfort will abound;*
*For tribulations teach us where*
*True comfort can be found.* —Sper

---

**In every desert of calamity,**
**God has an oasis of comfort.**

# BELIEVING IS TRUSTING

READ:
**Romans 5:1-11**

I am not ashamed
of the gospel of Christ,
for it is the power of
God to salvation for
everyone who believes.
—Romans 1:16

THE BIBLE IN ONE YEAR:
■ Joel
■ Revelation 5

Occasionally I meet people who know they have a spiritual need but are reluctant to make a personal commitment to Christ. Although they have seen what faith in Christ has done for others, they are confused by the advice they get from some good churchgoing people.

One man told me he had been advised to join a certain church to be saved. He was told by someone else that he had to be baptized in a particular church. Still others spoke vaguely about trying to obey the Sermon on the Mount. And one of his friends said he needed to go through a period of intense sorrow for sin before he could expect God to save him.

Frankly, I don't blame that confused man for saying to me, "I don't want to read any pamphlets or tracts. Show me right from the Bible how I can be saved." So we started reading passages in Romans and discussing them. By the time we reached the fifth chapter, he said, "It's clear to me now. All I need to do is place my trust in Jesus Christ." He did, and he found peace.

We have saving faith when we believe what the Bible says about us and about Jesus Christ, and when we act upon that truth by placing our trust in Him.

If you have not done so, trust Jesus now.  — Herb Vander Lugt

> *God sent His Son to die for us —*
> *No other life would do;*
> *So why not trust in Christ today,*
> *Accept His gift to you.*  — Branon

---

**We are saved not by what we do
but by trusting what Christ has done.**

# PERFECT PEACE IS POSSIBLE

**READ:**
Isaiah 26:1-9

---

You will keep him in perfect peace, whose mind is stayed on You, because he trusts in You. —Isaiah 26:3

---

THE BIBLE IN ONE YEAR:
■ Amos 1–3
■ Revelation 6

Few things (if anything at all) in this fallen world can be called perfect. But God promises to keep us in "perfect peace" if we keep our minds focused on Him and continue trusting Him (Isaiah 26:3).

So why do we find it so difficult to trust Him? Often, it's because we're afraid that things won't go as we want them to unless we control them ourselves. The less we are in control, the more anxious and worried we become.

Author Hannah Whitall Smith wrote, "It is not hard, you find, to trust the management of the universe, and of all the outward creation, to the Lord. Can your case then be so much more complex and difficult than these, that you need to be anxious or troubled about His management of you?"

Yet we often think our situation is too difficult for God. If we can't solve things ourselves, we doubt that He can. We have our Christian beliefs, yes — but that isn't the same as believing God. Believing God is a personal response that grows out of our Christian faith and is expressed by our increasing trust in Him and His promises.

As our mind remains on Him, He keeps us in perfect peace. This has been the experience of countless believers, and you can experience it too. — Joanie Yoder

*If God's creation helps us see*
*What wonders He can do,*
*Then we can trust His promises*
*For they are always true.* — D. De Haan

---

**God can be trusted in the dark
as well as in the light.**

# THE GIFT OF FAMILY

READ:
Exodus 20:1-20

Honor your father
and your mother.
—Exodus 20:12

THE BIBLE IN ONE YEAR:
■ Amos 4–6
■ Revelation 7

Through her books and lectures, Edith Schaeffer has become much appreciated for her insights into the value of life's ordinary days. When she and her husband Francis were first married, both sets of parents lived nearby. The newlyweds divided each Sunday afternoon and evening between the Schaeffers and the Sevilles.

After a few years, Edith and Francis moved to Switzerland, where they could talk with their parents only once a year in a brief phone conversation.

Looking back half a century later, Edith wrote of being glad for the way they had used those Sunday afternoons. She noted that "proximity of loved ones is not an endless situation." She concluded that a package labeled "time to care for parents and exhibit love" doesn't just arrive someday. We must show love while we can.

The fifth of the Ten Commandments says: "Honor your father and your mother, that your days may be long upon the land which the LORD your God is giving you" (Exodus 20:12). The command to love and respect our parents applies equally to children living at home, newly independent young couples, and empty-nesters.

Seize each moment you have to love and honor your family. The opportunity won't last forever. — David McCasland

*PUTTING IT INTO ACTION*

• *Plan a regular time to call a family member.*
• *Help an aged relative with a project or housework.*
• *Write a letter to someone you love but cannot visit.*

---

**Time is one of the greatest gifts
we can give each other.**

# EARTH WALK

**READ:**
John 1:11-18

---

The Word became flesh and dwelt among us, and we beheld His glory. —John 1:14

---

THE BIBLE IN ONE YEAR:
■ Amos 7–9
■ Revelation 8

After the *Apollo XV* mission, Colonel James Irwin related some of the high points of his experience. He told of their weightless bodies floating free in the space capsule, the rising crescent of the earth as seen from the moon, and the triumphal splashdown before a watching world.

Irwin also spoke of the impact the experience had on his spiritual life. He said that from the lunar surface he sensed both the glory of God and the plight of earthbound man. As he came back to earth, he realized he couldn't content himself with being merely a celebrity. He would have to be a servant, telling his fellowman of a better way to live. Irwin concluded by saying that if we think it a great event to go to the moon, how much greater is the wonder that God came to earth in the person of Jesus Christ!

Because man walked on the moon, science and technology have made tremendous advances. But because God walked on earth, we know both our origin and our destiny. We can know our Creator personally (John 1:1,14,18), and we can live in His light (v.9). Through Jesus' sinless life and sacrificial death, we can know the joy of having our sins forgiven and experience the fullness of an abundant life — all because God walked on the earth. — Mart De Haan

> *Down from His glory, ever-living story,*
> *My God and Savior came, and Jesus was His name.*
> *Born in a manger, to His own a stranger,*
> *A Man of sorrows, tears, and agony.* —Booth-Clibborn

---

**God made His home with us
so that we might make our home with God.**

# CARETAKERS, NOT OWNERS

**READ:**
Psalm 95

---

All things come from
You, and of Your own
we have given You.
—1 Chronicles 29:14

---

THE BIBLE IN ONE YEAR:
■ Obadiah
■ Revelation 9

John Hauberg and his wife live in a stunning home in Seattle. It is built mostly of glass inside and out. Hundreds of glass artifacts decorate the light-flooded rooms, and even the sinks, shelves, and mantelpieces are made of glass. You might think that the Haubergs would be in constant fear that something would break. On the contrary, they invite visitors to roam freely throughout their entire home.

John is also a connoisseur of Native American crafts, but he has donated his entire collection to the Seattle Art Museum. His motive is not to hoard but to share. "I'm not an owner," he says. "I am a caretaker."

John Hauberg's comment expresses a basic biblical principle that applies to all our possessions: We aren't owners; we are caretakers. Legally, of course, we own our possessions. But as Christians, we gladly acknowledge with David that "the earth is the LORD's, and all its fullness, the world and those who dwell therein" (Psalm 24:1).

By right of creation, God holds the deed to all that exists, including what we possess. He allows us to use the resources of His world for a time. But in the end it all reverts to Him.

Are we being wise and generous caretakers of what belongs to God? — Vernon Grounds

*Naught that I have my own I call,*
*I hold it for the Giver;*
*My heart, my strength, my life, my all*
*Are His, and His forever.* — Small

---

**All we own is on loan from God.**

# Isn't He Beautiful!

**READ:**
Isaiah 9:1-7

---

Unto us a Child is
born, unto us a Son
is given.
—Isaiah 9:6

---

THE BIBLE IN ONE YEAR:
■ Jonah
■ Revelation 10

A group of children from our city were in a worship service, and we started to sing. Ariel, age 7, leaned close to me and softly said, "I love this song; it makes me cry."

The music and words about Jesus, her Savior, touched her heart: "Isn't He beautiful? Beautiful, isn't He? Prince of peace, Son of God, isn't He?"

Yes, the Lord Jesus is beautiful. We don't find a specific reference in the Bible describing Him that way, but His personal character is strong yet gentle, holy yet forgiving, majestic yet humble — all combined. Simply beautiful!

In his prophecy, Isaiah described Jesus and His coming in this way: "Unto us a Child is born, unto us a Son is given; and the government will be upon His shoulder. And His name will be called Wonderful Counselor, Mighty God, Everlasting Father, Prince of Peace" (Isaiah 9:6).

Jesus is the Wonderful Counselor — giving us comfort and wisdom. The Mighty God — acting with power and authority. The Everlasting Father — providing for all our needs and protecting us. And the Prince of Peace — offering reconciliation with God and others.

Isn't Jesus beautiful! Worship Him.  — Anne Cetas

*Beautiful Savior! Lord of the nations!*
*Son of God and Son of Man!*
*Glory and honor, praise, adoration*
*Now and forevermore be Thine!* — Seiss

---

**Jesus is the image of the invisible God.**
—Colossians 1:15

# TRIED BY FIRE

READ:
Psalm 66:1-12

You, O God, have
tested us; You have
refined us as silver
is refined.
—Psalm 66:10

THE BIBLE IN ONE YEAR:
■ Micah 1–3
■ Revelation 11

"The main end of life is not to do but to become," F. B. Meyer said. And for this we are being prepared every day. As silver is refined by fire, the heart is often refined in the furnace of sadness. The psalmist said in his sorrow, "We went through fire" (Psalm 66:12).

The refining process may be very painful, but it will not destroy us, for the Refiner sits by the furnace tending the flame. He will not allow us to be tried beyond our endurance; it is for our good.

We may not understand why we have to endure such misery year after year. The ordeal seems endless and pointless. Our days are wasted, or so it appears. We feel as if we are doing nothing of lasting significance.

But God is doing what matters — we are being refined. He is placing us into a crucible in which we acquire patience, meekness, humility, compassion, and the other "quiet" virtues our souls naturally lack.

So don't be afraid and don't fret. Your present trial, as painful as it may be, has been screened through God's wisdom and love. The Refiner sits beside the crucible tempering the flames, monitoring the process, waiting patiently until His face is mirrored in the surface. — David Roper

*"As thy day thy strength shall be!"*
*This should be enough for thee;*
*He who knows thy frame will spare*
*Burdens more than thou canst bear.* — Havergal

---

**The fires of testing can produce a shining testimony.**

## ROAD BUILDERS

**READ:**
Hebrews 12:12-24

---

Make straight paths
for your feet, so that
what is lame may not
be dislocated, but
rather be healed.
—Hebrews 12:13

---

THE BIBLE IN ONE YEAR:
■ Micah 4–5
■ Revelation 12

The cover of a recent *Our Daily Bread* pictures a leaf-strewn road through the mountains of Vermont. Those who use the road can enjoy a smooth and beautiful ride over difficult terrain. To make this possible, others had to work hard to chart the route, clear the trees, and level the rough spots.

In a way, all Christians are road builders. We are paving the way of faith for the next generation. The faithfulness of our lives may determine how difficult their journey will be. Will they have to repair the damage we have done to the road? Will they be able to build new roads for others to find the way to God?

To be good road builders, we must heed the advice found in God's Word. The author of Hebrews instructed us to live in peace and be holy (12:14), to make sure no one misses the grace of God, and not to permit a root of bitterness to grow and cause trouble (v.15).

Those of us who have come to Jesus owe gratitude to those who have made "straight paths" for our walk of faith (v.13). In turn, we must remember those who will follow us and make straight paths for them. Let's practice our faith in a way that makes it easy for others to come to Jesus and to follow Him. What kind of road builder are you? —Julie Link

*Oh, may all who come behind us find us faithful;*
*May the fire of our devotion light their way;*
*May the footprints that we leave lead them to believe,*
*And the lives we live inspire them to obey.* — Mohr

---

**A life lived for God leaves a lasting legacy.**

# SMALL SPARK, BIG FIRE

READ:
James 3

The tongue is a little member and boasts great things. See how great a forest a little fire kindles!
—James 3:5

THE BIBLE IN ONE YEAR:
■ Micah 6–7
■ Revelation 13

In June 2002, the Hayman fire destroyed more than 137,000 acres of beautiful mountain forest in Colorado. Smoke darkened the skies, choking residents of cities 40 miles away. Thousands of people evacuated their homes, and millions of dollars were spent fighting a blaze that began with a single match.

Small spark, big fire. That's the way James described the damage done by our reckless and careless words. "See how great a forest a little fire kindles! And the tongue is a fire, a world of iniquity. . . . It defiles the whole body, and sets on fire the course of nature; and it is set on fire by hell" (3:5-6).

The Bible urges us not to underestimate the destructive potential of what we say. One incendiary remark can kindle an inferno of emotional harm. The best way to avert the flames of anger is to keep from striking that first match. We must let the wisdom of God check our thoughts before they leave our tongues. "The wisdom that is from above is first pure, then peaceable, gentle, willing to yield, full of mercy and good fruits, without partiality and without hypocrisy" (v.17).

As we draw on God's wisdom through His Word, we can smother the sparks of dissension and instead speak words of peace. — David McCasland

*One careless word can be a spark*
*Igniting anger into flame;*
*It can destroy relationships*
*And bring reproach to Jesus' name.* — Sper

---

**Words can't break bones,
but they can break hearts.**

# CELEBRATE THE BABY

**READ:**
Luke 2:8-14

---

There is born to you this day in the city of David a Savior, who is Christ the Lord.
—Luke 2:11

---

THE BIBLE IN ONE YEAR:
■ Nahum
■ Revelation 14

Why do we celebrate Jesus' birthday so differently from other birthdays? When it's time to honor historical figures who have a day set aside for them, we don't think about them as babies. We don't have pictures of cute little Abe Lincoln in his log cabin in Kentucky. No, we remember him for his contributions as an adult.

It is proper, though, that we celebrate Jesus as a child. Think about it. When He was born, shepherds came to honor Him (Luke 2:15-16). Later, wise men from the East brought Him gifts (Matthew 2:8-12). These people had no idea what Christ would eventually accomplish as an adult. But they were right in doing what they did, because Jesus' birth was the most remarkable event in human history.

How amazing! God in human form. The Creator of the universe visiting this planet. Let's never hesitate to celebrate this baby at Christmas. Marvel at His incarnation. Stand in awe of the tiny baby who had created His worshipers. Then step back in wonder, for the story gets even better. This baby grew into manhood, lived a perfect life, and willingly died for your sins and mine.

Celebrate the baby and trust the Savior. That's how to make Christmas complete. — Dave Branon

*How wonderful that we on Christmas morn,*
*Though centuries have passed since Christ was born,*
*May worship still the Living Lord of men,*
*Our Savior, Jesus, Babe of Bethlehem.* — Hutchings

---

**Wise men today worship not only the Child of Bethlehem, but also the Man of Calvary.**

# BORN TO DIE

READ:
Matthew 1:18-25

The Son of Man did not come to be served, but to serve, and to give His life a ransom for many.
—Matthew 20:28

THE BIBLE IN ONE YEAR:
■ Habakkuk
■ Revelation 15

Although millions celebrate Jesus' birthday, few seem to be aware of its real significance.

We recognize that His birth was unusual because He was born of a virgin. His life was unique too, for He was the only one who lived without sinning. His death was also unusual. Jesus was not a martyr. He was not the victim of unfortunate circumstances, dying for a worthy cause. Nor did He lay down His life just to set a good example. There's much more to it than that. The Lord Jesus came into this world to be our Savior!

Jesus Himself said that He came "to seek and to save that which was lost" (Luke 19:10). Who are the lost? The Bible tells us that "all have sinned" and that "the wages of sin is death" (Romans 3:23; 6:23). In order to save the world, Jesus had to die for it. He came and lived the perfect life and then died the death we should have died. The true meaning of Christmas is that Jesus was born to die. Because He was crucified and then rose from the dead, forgiveness of sin and assurance of heaven is now offered to all who believe (John 1:12).

Have you accepted God's gift of salvation? If not, do so today, and this will be your most meaningful Christmas ever. — Richard De Haan

*God offers new life;*
*Yea, what more could He give?*
*For He sent the Redeemer*
*That sinners might live!* —Morgan

**Unless we see the cross overshadowing the cradle,**
**we have lost the real meaning of Christ's birth.**

# HIDING IN PLAIN SIGHT

READ:
Luke 1:26-35

---

You will conceive in
your womb and bring
forth a Son, and shall
call His name JESUS.
—Luke 1:31

---

THE BIBLE IN ONE YEAR:
■ Zephaniah
■ Revelation 16

A Baltimore congregation found the answer to their financial troubles on the wall of their church. And it had been "hiding" there for more than 25 years! Someone finally recognized a piece of art hanging in the chapel — it was a valuable woodblock print by Albrecht Dürer, dated 1493. The work shows the angel telling Mary she would give birth to God's Son.

Some members just could not believe they had been unaware of the value of the old masterpiece, saying in effect, "If it were real, why would it be here?"

What about us? Are we overlooking the value of the event depicted on that woodblock print?

Jesus isn't hiding. The truth that God came to earth in human form is plainly announced in His Word. It is reflected in our art and in our hymnbooks. But the significance of Christ's birth is still neglected. We get so wrapped up in activities and programs that we miss the immeasurable worth of knowing who that Baby was.

What's missing is our worship. Think about the meaning of His birth. Jesus is God! He came to save us from our sins (Matthew 1:21) and give us eternal life (John 3:14-18).

This Christmas, join with the wisemen and shepherds and give praise to Jesus — God who became Man.  — Mart De Haan

> He left His Father's throne above,
> So free, so infinite His grace!
> Emptied Himself of all but love,
> And bled for Adam's helpless race.  — Wesley

---

**Christ's birth brought the infinite God to finite man.**

# LETDOWN

READ:
Luke 2:8-20

---

Mary kept all these
things and pondered
them in her heart. Then
the shepherds returned,
glorifying and praising
God. —Luke 2:19-20

---

THE BIBLE IN ONE YEAR:
■ Haggai
■ Revelation 17

The night of Jesus' birth was exciting for Mary and Joseph. There before their eyes was the miracle Baby whose coming into the world had been announced by an angel. The shepherds too were excited when they saw and heard "a multitude of the heavenly host praising God" and heralding His birth (Luke 2:13).

But it wouldn't be long before Mary and Joseph would face the ordinary tasks of caring for a new baby and all the accompanying responsibilities. The shepherds would be back on the hillside tending their sheep. All the elements were in place for an emotional letdown, which often follows an emotional high.

I don't believe they experienced any "after-Christmas blues," however. Mary didn't quickly forget all that had happened, and the shepherds couldn't easily forget what they had heard and seen (vv.19-20). The angelic message had proven true, and their lives were filled with new hope and anticipation.

There's no reason for an after-Christmas letdown. We have the full story. Jesus came to die for our sins, then conquered death for us by rising from the grave. We have more truth to ponder and more reason to glorify God than Mary and the shepherds did. — Herb Vander Lugt

*Life's ebb and flow that moves our hearts*
*From heights of joy to feelings low*
*Cannot exhaust God's matchless grace*
*Nor stem that never-ending flow.* —D. De Haan

---

**Feeling let down today?**
**Try looking up.**

# THE PLACE OF GOING FORTH

**READ:**
Micah 5:1-4

---

Bethlehem . . . , out
of you shall come forth
to Me the One to be
Ruler in Israel.
—Micah 5:2

---

THE BIBLE IN ONE YEAR:
■ Zechariah 1–4
■ Revelation 18

A lot of attention was suddenly focused on the small town of Bethlehem. Jews from many parts of the world came to be counted in a census. Mary and Joseph traveled there from Nazareth. Shepherds came from the fields to see the Baby lying in a manger (Luke 2:15-16) after a multitude of angels had come to announce, "Glory to God in the highest, and on earth peace, goodwill toward men!" (vv.13-14).

Every Christmas, in our imagination, we go to Bethlehem to celebrate Jesus' birth. But we cannot stay there; we must leave. The angels returned to heaven. Mary and Joseph went to Jerusalem, then sought safety in Egypt.

The shepherds' exit gives a clear message to us. They left the stable and told everyone about the holy Child. "And all those who heard it marveled at those things which were told them by the shepherds" (v.18).

It's appropriate for us to do the same. Micah prophesied that from Bethlehem would go forth a Ruler of Israel, the eternal Maker of the world, who had come to save mankind from sin (Micah 5:2). This season, let's join those who have gone forth from their visits to Bethlehem to proclaim the good news of Christ, who came to save us.  — Dave Egner

> *Go tell it on the mountain,*
> *Over the hills and everywhere —*
> *Go tell it on the mountain*
> *That Jesus Christ is born!*  — Traditional

---

**The gospel is one gift you can keep
and still pass on to others.**

# WHEN GOD THUNDERS

READ:
Psalm 81:6-10

---

You called in trouble,
and I delivered you;
I answered you in the
secret place of thunder.
—Psalm 81:7

---

THE BIBLE IN ONE YEAR:
■ Zechariah 5–8
■ Revelation 19

Thunder rolls across the Sawtooth Mountains, crashing and echoing through the peaks and canyons, shaking the ground with celestial sonic booms. My old dog cuts and runs. I stand amazed and delighted.

The storm reminds me of the "secret place of thunder" from which God answered His people (Psalm 81:7). Israel cried out from the straw pits and brick kilns of Egypt. In time, God's salvation rolled over the land in peals of thunder (Exodus 9:13-34).

Another psalm speaks of the storm that overshadowed Israel as they passed through the Red Sea (Psalm 77:16-20). Its thunder spelled doom for the Egyptians but deliverance to God's people. Each resounding clap was the comforting voice of a Father speaking to His children.

When Jesus foretold His death in John 12:28-29, He called on His Father to glorify His name. A voice answered from heaven saying, "I have both glorified it and will glorify it again." To the crowd, it sounded like thunder.

Are you in trouble? Cry out to God in your sorrow and distress. You may not hear the thunder roll, but it will reverberate through the heavens once again as He answers you "in the secret place of thunder." God will speak comfort to your heart and deliver you from your fears. — David Roper

*The lightning of a mighty storm,*
*Its thunder from on high,*
*Reminds us that our powerful God*
*Will answer when we cry.* — D. De Haan

---

**Those who trust in God find comfort in His power.**

# INCOMPATIBLE?

**READ:**
**1 Peter 3:8-17**

---

All of you be of one mind, having compassion for one another; love as brothers, be tenderhearted, be courteous.
—1 Peter 3:8

---

THE BIBLE IN ONE YEAR:
■ Zechariah 9–12
■ Revelation 20

A quote in *Sports Illustrated* magazine expresses a truth that we as people of faith sometimes neglect: "What counts most in creating a successful team is not how compatible its players are, but how they deal with incompatibility." When we don't get along with others, we are tempted to ignore them and shove them aside.

God calls us to take a different approach: "All of you be of one mind, having compassion for one another; love as brothers, be tenderhearted, be courteous; not returning evil for evil or reviling for reviling, but on the contrary blessing, knowing that you were called to this" (1 Peter 3:8-9).

Oswald Chambers reminds us in *My Utmost For His Highest:* "In the spiritual life, beware of walking according to natural affinities. Everyone has natural affinities; some people we like and others we do not like. We must never let those likes and dislikes rule in our Christian life. If we 'walk in the light,' as God is in the light, God will give us communion with people for whom we have no natural affinity."

It is natural to have likes and dislikes. But when we seek to honor the Lord in our relationships, compassion, love, humility, and kindness are the God-ordered, supernatural steps in dealing with incompatibility. — David McCasland

*We have a common enemy*
*Who would destroy the life*
*Of Jesus' precious bride, the church,*
*Through worldliness and strife.* —Sper

---

**The way to preserve the peace of the church**
**is to promote the unity of it.**

# DO ANGELS SLEEP?

READ:
Deut. 30:11-14

---

The word is very near you, in your mouth and in your heart, that you may do it.
—Deuteronomy 30:14

---

THE BIBLE IN ONE YEAR:
■ Zechariah 13–14
■ Revelation 21

A friend of mine has a 5-year-old daughter who is on her way to becoming a theologian. One day she asked her father, "Do angels sleep?" After pondering the theological dimensions of her question, he answered, "Yes, I think they might." His daughter moved in with a follow-up question, "Well, then, how do they get their pajamas on over their wings?"

We may be more like that little girl than we think. We never seem to outgrow asking interesting questions that do not need to be answered. It's healthy to be inquisitive, but it isn't healthy to obsess over matters that don't really matter. Such questions may sidetrack us from our faith.

What we need to know about God and His will for us is clearly spelled out in Scripture. The words He spoke through Moses to His people are true for us today. "For this commandment which I command you today is not too mysterious for you, nor is it far off. . . . But the word is very near you, in your mouth and in your heart, that you may do it" (Deuteronomy 30:11,14).

The Bible isn't a riddle; it's a revelation. It tells us all we need to know to be all that God wants us to be in every situation in life. — Haddon Robinson

> *God's Word reveals what we should know*
> *To live for Him each day;*
> *His principles we must commit*
> *To study and obey.* — Sper

---

**The Bible is as wise in what it leaves unsaid
as in what it says.**

# PAST, PRESENT, & FUTURE

**READ:**
Philippians 3:15-21

---

I press toward the goal . . . . Brethren, join in following my example.
—Philippians 3:14,17

---

THE BIBLE IN ONE YEAR:
■ Malachi
■ Revelation 22

In his painting "An Allegory of Prudence," 16th-century Venetian artist Titian portrayed Prudence as a man with three heads. One head was of a youth facing the future, another was of a mature man eyeing the present, and the third was of a wise old man gazing at the past. Over their heads Titian wrote a Latin phrase that means, "From the example of the past, the man of the present acts prudently so as not to imperil the future."

We need that kind of wisdom to overcome the anxiety created by our past failures and the fear of repeating them in the future — an anxiety that keeps us from living to the fullest now.

Paul was able to "forget" his past and anticipate his future (Philippians 3:13-14). This doesn't mean his memory was erased; it means that Paul was free of any guilt or pride he may have felt from his past actions, because God had forgiven him. This attitude enabled him to live in the present and "press toward the goal for the prize of the upward call of God in Christ Jesus" (v.14). So he had one driving passion — to know Christ better.

As we close the chapter of 2004, let's rededicate ourselves to Christ. Jesus will enable us to live fully in the present as we gain wisdom from the past and face the future with courage. — Dennis De Haan

*Standing at the portal*
*Of the opening year,*
*Words of comfort meet us,*
*Hushing every fear.* —Havergal

---

**Never let a bleak past overshadow a bright future.**

# Where To Find It In The Bible

The Bible is God's Word—His message to us. It contains His answers to the problems, questions, and dilemmas that are common to us all. But it's a big book—and to many people it is very confusing. This keeps them from getting the help they need from the Word. So if you need spiritual help, or if you don't know where to look for familiar passages of Scripture, here is some assistance.

## DIFFICULT SITUATIONS

**In danger:** Psalm 91; Luke 8:22-25

**Depressed:** Psalm 34; 139; Romans 8

**Worried:** Matthew 6:25-34; Philippians 4:6-9

**In doubt:** John 20:24-31; Hebrews 11

**Facing a crisis:** Deuteronomy 33:27; Psalm 121;
   Hebrews 4:16

**Discouraged:** Psalm 23; 42; Isaiah 40; Matthew 5:1-12

**Afraid:** Hebrews 12:1-2; Matthew 10:16-31;
   Deuteronomy 31:6

**Tempted:** Psalm 1; 1 Corinthians 10:12-13; James 4:7

**Lonely:** Psalm 27; Hebrews 13:5; 1 John 1:7

**Lack assurance of salvation:** Romans 8:16,38-39;
   1 John 5:10-13; John 10:27-30

**Want Forgiveness:** Psalm 51; 130:3-4; Acts 13:38-39;
   1 John 1:9

**Desire comfort in troubling circumstances:** John 16:33;
   2 Corinthians 1:3-4; 12:9

**Need courage to assume responsibility:** Joshua 1

**Facing death:** John 14; 1 Corinthians 15:51-58;
   2 Corinthians 5;1-8; Philippians 1:21-23

**Wondering if God's Word is true:** 2 Timothy 3:15-17;
   2 Peter 1:19-21

## KEY EVENTS AND TEACHINGS

**The Sermon on the Mount:** Matthew 5–7
**The Ten Commandments:** Exodus 20
**The Beatitudes of Jesus:** Matthew 5:3-12
**The account of creation:** Genesis 1–2
**The record of Jesus' birth:** Luke 2
**The crucifixion and resurrection:** Matthew 27–28
**The Lord's Prayer:** Matthew 6:9-13
**The faith hall of fame:** Hebrews 11
**The founding of the New Testament church:** Acts 2
**The tabernacle in the wilderness:** Exodus 25–30
**The love chapter:** 1 Corinthians 13
**The prophecy of Jesus the suffering Servant:** Isaiah 53

## GOD'S PLAN OF SALVATION

**Admit that you have sinned:** Romans 3:10,23
**Realize that sin brings spiritual death:** Romans 6:23
**Acknowledge that you can't save yourself:** Ephesians 2:8-9
**Recognize Jesus as the Savior you need:** John 20:31;
    Acts 4:12; Romans 5:8
**Come to Jesus and personally trust Him as your Savior:**
    Matthew 11:28; John 1:12-13; 6:37; Romans 10:9-10

## GUIDELINES FOR CHRISTIAN LIVING

**Read God's Word:** 2 Timothy 3:14-17; 1 Peter 2:1
**Pray:** Matthew 6:6-13; 1 John 5:14-15
**Guard your thoughts and actions:** Philippians 4:8-9
**Relate properly to others:** Romans 12:9-21
**Help those around you:** Galatians 6:10

# TOPIC INDEX

| TOPIC | DATE |
|---|---|
| Aging | Feb. 3; June 16; Aug. 16 |
| Anger | Jan. 29; Mar. 29 |
| | May 13; Oct. 9 |
| Attitude | Jan. 6 |
| Bible | Jan. 15,18; Mar. 16 |
| | May 15; July 4,7,14,15,21 |
| | Aug. 9,14; Sep. 30; Oct. 2 |
| | Nov. 9; Dec. 4,30 |
| Character | Mar. 22; Apr. 19 |
| | July 8; Dec. 7 |
| Children | May 16 |
| Christlikeness | July 23; Aug. 11 |
| | Sep. 7; Oct. 3 |
| Church | June 13; Oct. 17,24 |
| | Nov. 14; Dec. 11 |
| Commitment | Jan. 12,31; Mar. 9 |
| Compassion | Feb. 27; Mar. 18 |
| | Sep. 22 |
| Complaining | May 25 |
| Confession | June 18; Sep. 10 |
| | Nov. 29 |
| Conscience | May 8; Sep. 20 |
| Consecration | Aug. 15 |
| Contentment | July 12 |
| Criticism | Feb. 16 |
| Cross | July 11 |
| Death | Jan. 8; Feb. 7,21 |
| | Mar. 28; Apr. 6,28; May 23 |
| | June 3,14,30; Aug. 27,28 |
| | Sep. 13,25; Dec. 5 |
| Dependence On God | Mar. 1 |
| Depression | Oct. 19; Nov. 12 |
| Discipline | June 5,24 |
| Discouragement | Nov. 13 |
| Doubt | Sep. 2,8 |

| TOPIC | DATE |
|---|---|
| Encouragement | May 12 |
| | Aug. 2; Nov. 30 |
| Enthusiasm | Oct. 23 |
| Evangelism | Jan. 5,22; Mar. 6,13 |
| | Apr. 4,30; May 17; Aug. 7 |
| | Oct. 29; Nov. 20 |
| Faith | Mar. 12,20; May 8 |
| Faithfulness | Apr. 14; May 18 |
| | June 30; Aug. 8,23; Oct. 18 |
| Family | Dec. 16 |
| Fathers | June 20 |
| Fear | July 5; Aug. 4,6; Dec. 8,9 |
| Fear Of God | Mar. 23; May 14 |
| Fellowship | July 19; Aug. 18 |
| | Sep. 28; Nov. 14 |
| Fellowship With God | Jan. 21 |
| | June 9,23 |
| Forgiveness | Jan. 1,13; Feb. 2,13 |
| | Apr. 10; June 28; July 24 |
| | Oct. 1; Nov. 3,27,29; Dec. 1 |
| Friendship | May 3; Aug. 26 |
| | Sep. 1,3,16 |
| Future | Jan. 13; July 5 |
| Giving | Jan. 2; Feb. 28; Oct. 10 |
| God As Creator | Aug. 10 |
| God's Care | July 9 |
| God's Family | July 19 |
| God's Glory | Sep. 7 |
| God's Goodness | May 10; |
| | July 26; Aug. 21 |
| God's Grace | Jan. 20; June 10 |
| | Aug. 19; Oct. 20; Dec. 1 |
| God's Guidance | Sep. 9,15,24,30; |
| | Apr. 20; Nov. 5 |

# TOPIC INDEX

| TOPIC | DATE |
|---|---|
| God's Help | Feb. 10,18; Mar. 10,11 |
| | Apr. 5,25; May 24; Dec. 28 |
| God's Judgment | Apr. 23 |
| | Aug. 27; Nov. 21; Dec. 10 |
| God's Love | Feb. 4,5,13,24 |
| | May 11; June 24; July 2,13,20 |
| Sep. 11,23,27; Oct. 22; Dec. 2,5,20 | |
| God's Power | Feb. 20; Mar. 7 |
| | Apr. 3,22; July 8,29; Dec. 28 |
| God's Presence | Aug. 24 |
| | Sep. 17; Oct. 6; Nov. 18 |
| God's Protection | Mar. 10 |
| | June 19 |
| God's Provision | Aug. 29 |
| God's Sovereignty | July 25 |
| Sep. 17,19,24; Oct. 6; Nov. 5,17 | |
| God's Will | Oct. 28 |
| Gospel | July 31 |
| Greed | July 12; Nov. 26 |
| Grief | Mar. 28; Aug. 28 |
| | Sep. 2,25,27 |
| Growth | Jan. 6; Feb. 22 |
| | Mar. 15,17,26; May 28 |
| June 5,6,16,24; Sep. 4; Oct. 3 | |
| | Dec. 31 |
| Guilt | Oct. 1 |
| Happiness | July 26 |
| Heaven | Jan. 8; Feb. 7 |
| Apr. 18,27; May 23; July 1, 10,27 | |
| | Sep. 25; Oct. 16 |
| Holy Spirit | Mar. 19; May 30 |
| | July 22,29; Sep. 15 |
| Honesty | Jan. 16; Feb. 17 |
| Hope | Jan. 1; July 1,31 |
| | Oct. 19; Nov. 12; Dec. 26 |

| TOPIC | DATE |
|---|---|
| Humility | July 23; Sep. 21 |
| Hypocrisy | Oct. 11; Nov. 21 |
| Idolatry | Feb. 26 |
| Jesus as Savior | July 14; Oct. 11 |
| | Nov. 23; Dec. 24 |
| Jesus' Birth | Dec. 17,19,23,25,27 |
| Jesus' Character | Aug. 22 |
| Jesus' Death | Mar. 25; Apr. 8,9 |
| | May 31; Nov. 11 |
| Jesus' Example | Nov. 10 |
| Jesus' Resurrection | Mar. 27 |
| | Apr. 11 |
| Jesus' Return | May 20; June 3 |
| | Oct. 7 |
| Joy | Jan. 7; Apr. 1; July 3 |
| | Aug. 21,31 |
| Judging Others | Jan. 9; Nov. 27 |
| Kindness | Mar. 3; Aug. 2,20 |
| | Sep. 16; Oct. 10,13; Nov. 2 |
| Knowing God | Apr. 13 |
| Leadership | Feb. 23 |
| Life's Purpose | Mar. 6,17; July 25 |
| | Oct. 25 |
| Loneliness | Aug. 24; Dec. 13 |
| Love | Jun. 2; Aug. 5,12,13; Dec.29 |
| Love For God | Feb. 14; June 21 |
| | Nov. 8 |
| Love For Others | Sep. 12,29 |
| | Oct. 21; Nov. 2,6 |
| Miracles | Oct. 11 |
| Money | Mar. 9; July 6 |
| Mothers | May 9 |
| Nation | July 4 |
| Nature | Feb. 12; Aug. 10 |

# TOPIC INDEX

| TOPIC | DATE |
|---|---|
| Obedience | Jan. 15,23,26 |
| | Feb. 1; Mar. 14,19 |
| | Apr. 24; June 7,11,22; July 7 |
| | Aug. 9; Nov. 13; Dec. 2 |
| Occult | Oct. 31 |
| Peace | Jan. 19; May 1; June 8 |
| | Sep. 14 |
| Persecution | Feb. 10 |
| Perseverance | June 25,30; |
| | July 30; Aug. 23; Dec. 20 |
| Possessions | Jan. 25; Feb. 25 |
| Praise | Feb. 12; June 27 |
| | Aug. 1; Sep. 26 |
| Prayer | Jan. 14,28; Feb. 11 |
| | Mar. 5; Apr. 7; May 5,6 |
| | June 15,27; Aug. 4; Oct. 18,27 |
| | Dec. 6 |
| Prejudice | Nov. 6 |
| Pride | Feb. 8; May 7; |
| | July 20; Aug. 18 |
| Quiet Time | Jan. 14; Mar. 2 |
| Repentance | Mar. 30; May 27 |
| | Nov. 3; Dec. 3,10 |
| Salvation | Jan. 3,30 |
| | Feb. 5,7,15,20,24; Mar. 31 |
| | Apr. 10; May 2,22,31; June 12,26; |
| | Sep. 5; Oct. 20,26 |
| | Nov. 4,7,11,16,23; Dec. 14,17,23 |
| Satan | Apr. 2,16 |
| Service | Feb. 19,23,29 |
| | Mar. 2,8,24; Apr. 21,29 |
| | May 12,29; June 10,17,25 |
| | July 7,27,30; Aug. 8; |
| | Oct. 12,24; Dec. 12 |

| TOPIC | DATE |
|---|---|
| Sin | Jan. 1,13,18; Feb. 6 |
| | Apr. 24; June 4,18,28,29 |
| | July 17,24,28; Aug. 25; Sep. 10,18 |
| | Oct. 9,28,30; Dec. 1,10 |
| Speech | Apr. 15; Aug. 20; Dec. 22 |
| Spiritual Warfare | Feb. 11 |
| Stewardship | Dec. 18 |
| Submission | Sep. 21 |
| Temptation | Feb. 6; June 1 |
| | Sep. 18 |
| Testimony | Jan. 10,22; Aug. 11 |
| | Sep. 20; Oct. 15,31; |
| | Nov. 8,10,22; Dec. 21 |
| Thankfulness | Jan. 7; Mar. 21 |
| | May 26; Nov. 24,25 |
| Time | Jan. 31; Mar. 9 |
| Trials | Jan. 4,20,24,27; Feb. 10,18; |
| | Mar. 4,11; Apr. 3,5,12,25,26 |
| | May 4,11,21,24; June 6 |
| | July 1,9; Aug. 3,4,17,30,31 |
| | Sep. 8; Oct. 4; Nov. 17,19 |
| | Dec. 5,13,20,28 |
| Trust | Oct. 4 |
| Truth | Jan. 16; Mar. 16 |
| | Jul. 14,15,21; Aug. 14,17; Dec. 7,30 |
| Unity | Aug. 18; Sep. 28 |
| Wisdom | June 7,11 |
| Witnessing | July 16; |
| | Sep. 1,5; Oct. 5,7,13,14,29 |
| | Nov. 15,20,22; Dec. 27 |
| Work | Feb. 9; Sep. 6 |
| Worry | June 23; Nov. 9 |
| Worship | Jan. 11,17; May 19 |
| | July 18; Sep. 26; Oct. 17; |
| | Nov. 28,30 |

# You Were On His Mind

If you do not know Jesus Christ as your Savior and Lord, I challenge you to look at life first as it is lived according to the mindset of the world. See it in all its selfishness, pride, and destruction. Now, imagine living with the attitude of Christ. There is an undeniable difference in these two mindsets.

Carefully consider that all Jesus did—His selflessness, sacrifice, servanthood, humility, and patience—was out of love for you and concern for your eternal destination. He was obedient to the point of dying on the cross so that you could experience eternal life. Someone expressed the heart of Christ this way: "When He was on the cross, you were on His mind."

The Old Testament described this passion in the mind of our God: "'I know the thoughts that I think toward you,' says the LORD, 'thoughts of peace and not of evil, to give you a future and a hope'" (Jeremiah 29:11).

> By this we know love, because He laid down His life for us. —1 John 3:16

Will you turn to this Savior who loves you and accept by faith this wonderful gift? The Bible tells us, "The wages of sin is death, but the gift of God is eternal life in Christ Jesus our Lord" (Romans 6:23).

It's true—Jesus Christ loves you! That love in your life can make all the difference in the world.

Excerpted from the booklet *The Mind Of Christ*, © 2002 RBC Ministries.
Read it on the Web at **www.discoveryseries.org/q0209**